BUREAUCRATIC ENCOUNTERS

A Pilot Study
in the Evaluation of Government Services

BUREAUCRATIC ENCOUNTERS

A Pilot Study
n the Evaluation of Government Services

DANIEL KATZ · BARBARA A. GUTEK
ROBERT L. KAHN · EUGENIA BARTON

Survey Research Center • Institute for Social Research
The University of Michigan
Ann Arbor, Michigan

ISR Code No. 4003

Library of Congress Catalog Card No. 74-620202
ISBN 0-87944-172-0 paperbound
ISBN 0-87944-173-9 clothbound

Published by the Institute for Social Research
The University of Michigan, Ann Arbor, Michigan 48106

Table of Contents

BUREAUCRATIC ENCOUNTERS

List of Tables

ix

BUREAUCRATIC ENCOUNTERS

Preface

This monograph reports the results of a pilot study in the delivery of government services. As such, we hope that it will lead to more comprehensive evaluation of agency performance and thereby to improvement in the quality of service and the satisfaction of human needs. The research presented here can be viewed in several contexts: It is a continuation of a long-established program of work on organizational behavior and effectiveness. It is an effort to contribute to the emerging area of evaluative research. And it represents one aspect of the broad research development having to do with social indicators as measures of system support and the quality of life.

In the last of these contexts, this research should be seen as one of a set of related activities at the Institute for Social Research, supported by the National Science Foundation through its RANN division. The freedom and flexibility of that support have contributed a great deal to what merit the work possesses.

The work on social indicators proceeds at many universities and research organizations. At the Institute for Social Research it is the major theme in a substantial number of research projects and a secondary theme in many others. Our project, like the others, has benefited from the interest and ideas of Angus Campbell. Indeed, his paper, "Social Accounting in the 1970's" (*Michigan Business Review*, 1971, *23*, 2-7) can be read as a call for research on bureaucratic encounters.

A monograph does not appear merely through the good intentions of its authors. The production side of the enterprise was carried out by the many supportive units of the Institute for Social Research: the Sampling, Interviewing, Coding, and Computing sections, and the Omnibus office. Jamal Rassoul was especially helpful with problems of data analysis. Above all we are indebted to a magnificent secretary, a tireless worker and a dedicated colleague in the single person of Grace L. Stribley.

Daniel Katz
Barbara A. Gutek
Robert L. Kahn
Eugenia Barton

Chapter 1

INTRODUCTION

The objective of this study was threefold: (1) to obtain information about the utilization and underutilization of major government services among various sectors of the population; (2) to find out how people evaluate government offices which have dealt with their problems; and (3) to see how their own experiences with public bureaucracy are related to their more general attitudes toward government; i.e., how the various dimensions of support for the political system are interrelated. The three chapters which follow deal respectively with these three issues.

The impetus for this investigation came from two sets of interests. The first is a concern about public accountability and feedback, specifically the use of the experiences of people with government agencies as relevant information to improve agency functioning. The second interest is broader in scope and is related to current research on social indicators as reflections of the quality of life of the individual, and as measures of commitment or support for the social system. Satisfactions with public services can well be regarded as an indicator of social well-being in both senses.

Most discussion about improving the functioning of public agencies comes from policy makers concerned with broad strategies of governmental programs, from administrators who face practical problems in their own agencies, or from specialists who talk in terms of increasing the technology of delivery systems. There is a vast and profound neglect of the perceptions, experiences, and reactions of the people who themselves are supposedly being served. There is lip service to the notion of public accountability as feedback, but the feedback comes more often from a technician concerned with some measure of his own, than from any genuine digging into the basic materials of client experience.

Government agencies in particular have long been criticized for setting up informational feedback systems so limited that they

1

safeguard agencies from criticism and isolate them from adequate and valid information on matters of major relevance. Top officials often have to struggle to avoid becoming captives of closed informational systems. An example of the pseudo-feedback generated by such systems is the body count used by the military during the Vietnam war.

The perceptions, attitudes, and experiential reports of people about specific government offices and procedures constitute only one source of information about the functioning of public bureaucracy. It is, however, a relevant source, and its neglect in a pragmatic society is difficult to justify when many programs and agencies are in need of data to replace guesses and hunches. In private enterprise under competitive conditions, there is some direct feedback from the appropriate public when people exercise their discretionary power as consumers to purchase from one or another competing source. In private monopolies and public agencies, there is no such direct check on products or services. In such cases the need for systematic feedback from the people being served is all the more necessary.

Using the reactions of the clientele of an agency to help in the assessment of its functioning is of great practical importance, but there are broader issues involved. May not people's satisfaction or dissatisfaction with public agencies which directly affect their lives define a dimension of support (or lack of support) for the political system itself? For example, is it possible that what helps to keep the system going is not trust in national leadership, but the confidence people have in the public offices which touch their daily lives? If they feel they can rely upon the social security office for their monthly benefits, or upon the unemployment office to provide compensation, or upon some local leader to make a government agency responsive, they can accept a good deal of failure at the top levels in Washington without becoming alienated from the system. The experiential level of encounters with government agencies should not be neglected in any consideration of the problem of what ties people into the national political structure.

In general the problem of the integration of individuals into the political system has been approached from a negative viewpoint. There have been accounts oɩ increasing apathy, of anomie, and of alienation in the American population, especially among certain groups. These characteristics have been urged as indicative of societal malfunctioning. But such accounts rarely spell out their implicit assumption that positive commitment is necessary for societal well-being. If political apathy is considered a bad thing, what level of interest is good? And what forms of active interest and involvement in political affairs are assumed to constitute commitment mechanisms? If anomie is an indicator of social decline, then what kinds of shared national norms and values are indicators of social progress? In other words, to look at the negative side of attachment to the system is too fragmented an approach. The matter should be looked at from the point of view of the positive mechanisms of commitment to community and society. What are the levels and dimensions of system support? If these can be specified, then there can be more meaningful dialogue about apathy and alienation. It is a question of both what people are alienated from and what they are apathetic about. Some individuals may be alienated from the regime in power but not alienated from basic political institutions. Others may be alienated from conventional procedures for handling inequities in the system but not from democratic values.

The systematic investigation of various types of commitment and alienation and their interrelationships would require a large program of research. In this study of bureaucratic encounters we attempted to deal only with (1) trust in national political leadership, (2) confidence in the administrative machinery of government, (3) symbolic patriotism or attachment to national symbols, and (4) trust in one's fellows. Our interest here was threefold: (1) how are people's own experiences with public bureaucracy related to the way in which they support the system; (2) how are the support measures interrelated; i.e., are they mutually reinforcing or substitutable (does trust in one's fellows take the place of confidence in national leadership); and (3) are any groups in American society strongly disaffected on one or more dimensions of commitment?

METHODOLOGY

To obtain adequate information on the three objectives (of utilization of services, evaluation of specific agencies, and discovery of relationship of bureaucratic encounters to more general attitudes) ideally would require a series of studies of two types: special organizational investigations and national sample surveys.

The first type calls for samples of the personnel of given agencies and samples of their clients. Its objective would be the discovery of relationships of organizational characteristics to the functioning of the agency. To get at the specifics of how and why an agency functions as it does and how effective it is requires detailed study of particular agencies, including both members of their staffs at various hierarchical levels and members of the particular publics they service. A national sample cannot match agency personnel with agency clientele. Nor can it readily cumulate enough cases for given agencies to provide adequate samples of their specific publics. Nor can public responses be related to the realities of the programs being administered; such relationships require detailed knowledge of the programs.

The depth studies of specific agencies need to be complemented by national surveys which focus on the extent to which the public avails itself of public services and the extent of favorable and unfavorable experiences with public agencies in the nation as a whole.

It is important, moreover, to know the climate of opinion in which agencies function, to ascertain the support they receive from various segments of the public, to discover the general directions in which people want governmental agencies to move, and to see how these reactions to public agencies are related to general orientations of support for the political system at different system levels. For these purposes national surveys are the best strategy, and many of these measures for the nation as a whole comprise important social indicators which need to be repeated in trend studies.

One could justify starting a program of research with either type of study. This research follows the national survey pattern because it was possible to include it in the semi-annual omnibus investigation of the Institute for Social Research in the spring of 1973. For Omnibus surveys, a sample of 1500 adults, age 18 or over, is employed. The Spring 1973 Omnibus survey yielded 1,431 completed and usable interviews; the survey was in the field during April and May 1973. In general, our sample compares favorably with data collected in the 1970 census except for sex. Males account for about 47 percent of the population nationally; they account for only 43 percent of the sample. On the other hand, non-whites account for 12.5 percent of the census data and 12.8 percent of the respondents in the sample. The census data also show that about 23 percent of the adult population is age 60 or over, and in these data, 22 percent of respondents are age 60 or over.* As a national survey it did not attempt to relate the specific programs and procedures of given agencies in detailed fashion to the responses of the appropriate clientele. Rather it started with the individual's possible problems with respect to employment, job training, compensation for sickness, accident and unemployment, medical and health difficulties, dependency, and retirement. Respondents with such problems were asked if they had gone to a government agency for help, and were also asked to select the most important of their experiences with an agency and describe the episode in some detail. To supplement these open inquiries, people were also asked specific

---

*See Appendix A for a description of the general sampling procedure; see Appendix B for the interview schedule.

questions about various aspects of their agency experiences; e.g., how fairly were they treated, how efficient was the office, how much effort did the agency personnel make to help them, was it possible to appeal a past decision made about a problem, what were the agency personnel like?

People's encounters with public bureaucracy are not limited, however, to service agencies. They not only seek the help of government offices which do things for them, but they react to the offices which do things to them. Accordingly, people were asked about their experiences with four types of problems with control or constraint agencies, namely police interference with their rights, difficulties with income tax offices, problems about traffic regulation, and about vehicular licenses. The questions about experiences with control agencies closely paralleled the questions about service agencies.

In addition, more general questions of two types were asked of the sample. The first kind of inquiry concerned an evaluation of government administrative offices in general. Here questions were directed at common beliefs about public bureaucracy. Respondents were also asked to compare private enterprise and public offices on a number of specific criteria. The second type of inquiry concerned other possible dimensions of support for the political system and included items used by the Center for Political Studies, Institute for Social Research in earlier surveys which dealt with confidence in national leadership and interpersonal trust. Finally some questions were added to get at the nature of symbolic nationalism.

Thus the project, though national in scope, can be regarded as a pilot study. It attempted to get at some information of relevance to both the approach to organizational studies and to trend studies of the broader public. Though limited in the detail it could furnish on specific agencies on the one hand, and restricted in fully exploring the relationship of dimensions of system support on the other hand, it could still provide suggestive evidence about people's reactions to major agencies and about how specific experiences were related to more general evaluation and reactions to public office and political system.

THE GOVERNMENT SERVICES SELECTED FOR STUDY

Government agencies intrude on many aspects of a person's life, whether to regulate and control it or to provide support and service. Since the mid-1930's the service undertakings of government have grown tremendously. Among the programs available in the early 1970's are the Job Corps, Cooperative Extension Service, Minority

Business Enterprise, Medicare, WIN (Work Incentive Program), Public Housing, FHA, National School Lunch Program, Social Security, Food Stamps, Appalachian Regional Development, Weather Forecasts and Warnings, Model Cities, Unemployment Insurance, and various veteran's benefits. There are few areas of human functioning that are not touched by government bureaucracy.

Paralleling the expansion of governmental service programs has been the growth of government regulatory and control functions. The present study is concerned with both service and control responsibilities of the government. Seven service areas and four control functions were chosen for examination. The seven service areas chosen were selected because of their universality and significance to the individual. Retirement and medical and hospital problems sooner or later involve an overwhelming majority of the population. Getting a job, getting job training, getting unemployment compensation, getting workmen's compensation, and obtaining public assistance affect fewer people, but these economic issues take priority when they do strike.

The control areas were chosen to represent types of constraints placed on the individual by the government, namely taxes, driver and vehicular licensing,* traffic violations, and police interference. We were interested not in contact with a control agency as such, ut in difficulties or problems with the agency. The probabilities of finding such encounters were greater with the areas selected since the great majority of Americans do have contacts with income tax offices and driver and vehicular licensing bureaus. Police interference with one's rights is a less frequent occurrence, but by definition is in the problem category. Traffic violations do occur frequently and have a fair prospect of ending up as problems. Major emphasis in this report, however, is on service agencies since there appears to be less knowledge about the functioning of service than constraint agencies. In addition, emphasis is given to positive aspects of support for the political system rather than to alienation, anomie, or other negative concerns; therefore, more attention is appropriately awarded service agencies of the government.

Types of services, such as job training or retirement benefits, rather than specific agencies were selected as units of analysis since some duplication of specific services exists among agencies. Many different agencies are equipped to handle particular client groups such as veterans or persons whose income is below the poverty level. Thus

---

*In the following pages we will use *driver licensing* to refer to both *vehicular and driver licensing*.

a disabled person may receive job training through the state vocational rehabilitation agency, whereas someone else may receive job training through the state employment service. Likewise a veteran may receive disability benefits from the Veteran's Administration, but a non-veteran would receive disability from the Social Security Administration. We were more interested in the types of services offered than in specific agencies, and therefore principally used types of service in the analysis of data.

There are fewer overlapping roles of agencies with control functions. However, law enforcement agencies operate at several governmental levels such as city, county, and state, and while everyone is subject to federal income tax, some citizens also pay state and/or local income taxes.

Agencies for the Seven Service Areas

The agencies mainly responsible for the seven areas of service selected for this investigation are briefly as follows:*

1) The government agency utilized by most people when they are trying to find a job is the state employment service. Other agencies which may find jobs for people include the Veteran's Administration, vocational rehabilitation agencies, and some welfare offices.

2) Most job training is administered through state employment services and includes programs such as Job Corps, JOBS-NAM, Neighborhood Youth Corps, and Concentrated Employment Program (CEP). Juveniles who have had police contact sometimes receive job training through agencies associated with the juvenile court.

3) & 4) Workmen's compensation and unemployment compensation are administered through state agencies. Separate agencies providing these services for special interest groups do not exist.

5) Welfare services, however, are based on a categorical structure. There are separate sets of rules and regulations for the blind, the disabled, the elderly poor, and those poor families with dependent children. A general fund may cover individuals who do not fall into these categories.

6) Hospital and medical benefits come principally through Medicare and Medicaid. People 65 and over who receive social security retirement benefits are eligible for Medicare; the poor are eligible for Medicaid.

---

*See Appendix C for additional information about these programs and other legislation relevant to the areas of inquiry.

7) Retirement benefits are usually received from the Social Security Administration, although the Veteran's Administration also provides retirement benefits for some classes of veterans; and state and local government employees have their own pension funds.

The administration of Medicare benefits is not handled in its entirety by the federal Social Security offices even for non-veterans. In many states the Social Security Administration has contracts with insurance carriers, such as Blue Cross and Blue Shield, to process claims.

RELATED RESEARCH

Though the concept of evaluation research has had wide acceptance, there is little systematic knowledge available to the student, the practitioner, or the citizen about the effectiveness of given public policies and practices. The reason lies only partly in the relative dearth of research studies. In fact federal agencies have funded a fair number of projects. A number of these investigations, however, suffer from poor planning and inadequate implementation. For the greater part they consist of monitoring techniques, cost-benefit analyses, case studies, secondary analyses of data gathered for other purposes, *ex post facto* measurements of the effectiveness of a single program, and non-systematic assessments by so-called experts. Generally the reactions of the recipients of a service program are neglected in evaluating the functioning of public agencies.

Hyman and Wright (1967) suggest that methodological accompaniment to planned social change could provide unusual research opportunities. The researcher, they urge, can replace "the little experiments of his own making by the great experiments in social change that are underway. He must appreciate the opportunity and grab it. By his own inventiveness he must graft onto the ongoing activity the appropriate and feasible experimental design that rigorously tests the effectiveness of the program" (p. 743). Nevertheless, this advice has not been avidly seized upon, and evaluation research still lags far behind its potential in its piecemeal and scattered character. Even the good evaluation studies tend to be buried in the files of a single office and have not become a part of a scientific literature in professional journals and books, nor part of the operational programs of agencies.

No attempt will be made to review the research literature in the field though it would be a worthwhile undertaking to bring together what is known about effective agency functioning in relation to given social objectives. Instead, a few different types of studies will be reviewed which are informative about the major problems and suggestive for future research.

Effects of Welfare and Unemployment

The Department of Health, Education and Welfare in 1969 funded a study of the consequences of welfare policies for the AFDC recipient population (Meyers and McIntyre, 1969). The survey was conducted in 35 counties—10 urban and 25 rural—in 10 states. Structured personal interviews were conducted with 5,377 current AFDC recipients, 2,911 former recipients, 2,389 applicants who had been judged ineligible, and 955 participants in the Work Experience and Training Program, for a total of 11,632 respondents. In addition, questionnaires were filled out by 1,069 AFDC caseworkers in the selected locales. The principal finding of the study is "that material deprivation is more severe in states which afford smaller AFDC allowances . . ." (Meyers and McIntyre, 1969 p. xiv). More relevant to the present study was the attempt to see how policy decisions affect psychological characteristics of the respondents. Five indices were constructed to measure self-esteem, political participation, employment potential, powerlessness, and alienation. The alienation index measured a generalized disposition, whereas the powerlessness index had specific referents, namely the welfare department and medical care. Meyers and McIntyre found low correlations between the five indices and state policies involving (1) maximum amount payable, (2) eligibility restrictiveness, and (3) number of services. The highest correlation was attained for the powerlessness scale and maximum amount payable (-.26). It is interesting that agency practices do not have a greater effect on non-material aspects of respondents' lives. In fact further analysis utilizing 20 independent variables accounted for only 15 percent of the variance in self-esteem and 8 percent of the variance in alienation.

Respondents were also asked whether their family life had improved or worsened from an earlier situation. Among these AFDC families, economic factors rather than interpersonal matters were cited as the main reasons for either the improvement or deterioration in quality of family life.

The study also looked at welfare caseworkers' attitudes. The caseworkers were nearly unanimous in the belief that the community held negative stereotypes about AFDC recipients. The caseworkers themselves, however, viewed welfare recipients in a more favorable light.

One section of the HEW report is devoted to employment and self-image. The majority of respondents had been employed at some time but, in general, employment had been sporadic. Work and welfare were mutual supplements for many respondents. Younger respondents were more likely to have worked "in spurts." Older respondents were more likely to have worked all the time or not worked at all. Black respondents were more likely to have work experience than white or other minority respondents. At the time of the interview, 30 percent of respondents including 22 percent of active AFDC recipients were working. The data show a positive relationship between self-esteem and number of months of employment. The magnitude of the relationship is low, but is is consistent across states and ethnic groups. Since higher education is associated with more employment, education was partialed out, but the relationship between employment and self-esteem remained. Women who had been only employed and those who had been employed, but had also received welfare, both showed increasing self-esteem scores over a 37 month period, although esteem scores were slightly higher for the employment-only group. Welfare recipients who had not been employed at all over a 37 month period, moreover, showed decreasing self-esteem scores over the period. "Recipients of public assistance have never been held in high popular regard, and it may be supposed that they themselves tend to internalize the dis-esteem of the larger community. Lately, however, it has become fashionable to observe that AFDC recipients in particular do not find their dependence on public largesse objectionable and that, on the contrary, they take their legal rights seriously and indeed much prefer this mode of existence to working careers; moreover, their sense of self-esteem suffers no damage as a consequence." (Meyers and McIntyre, 1969, p. 136). The authors cite ample evidence showing that this popular stereotype is not true. Dependence on welfare over time results in lowered self-esteem.

Levens (1968) investigated powerlessness among black and Puerto Rican AFDC recipients via three aspects: fatalism, sense of control, and political activism. She noted that lower scores on powerlessness were found for those who had work experience and for those who had been on welfare for less than three years. Leven's main thesis, however, is that organizational affiliation reduces feelings of powerlessness, and in support of her position she found that AFDC recipients who belonged to welfare rights organizations also showed lower scores on the powerlessness index even when moderating variables such as work experience were controlled.

Another indication of the lowered self-esteem of welfare recipients may be inferred from Briar's study involving intensive interviews with 46 AFDC-U couples drawn from a California county welfare agency.

> . . .the stance these recipients adopt toward the welfare agency is not that of a rights-bearing citizen claiming benefits to which he is entitled by law but that of a suppliant seeking in the words of a number of recipients, 'a little help to tide us over until we can get back on our feet again' (Briar, 1966, p.53).

Briar found that 66 percent of respondents believed that the caseworker should know how welfare money is spent, and 60 percent indicated that they did not know of their right to appeal. Furthermore 30 percent of those interviewed (the modal response) answered "don't know" to a question asking to whom they should appeal.

The AFDC-U recipients' attempts to preserve self-esteem is described by Briar as follows:

> Our respondents almost never (and most respondents never) referred to welfare recipients as 'we' but as 'they'. This characteristic estrangement—also manifest in a tendency to view oneself as an atypical recipient, a self-conception which seemed to be held by nearly all the recipients interviewed—reflects the desire of these recipients to dissociate themselves from the image they have of other recipients. (Briar, 1966, p. 51).

While most people believe that the poor are unemployed (Ogren, 1973), this is not the case. The majority of heads of poor families work at least part-time. Mildred Rein (1972) examined the work-welfare choice among AFDC mothers in an integrative review of statistical surveys and empirical studies. Is welfare seen as a "last resort," or do people make a choice among welfare, work, or a combination of the two? First of all, most welfare mothers have had work experience. Rein cites studies showing that up to 80 percent of AFDC recipients have had work experience. She found that many women combine work and welfare, with welfare supplementing low-paying jobs, which concurs with the findings of Meyers and McIntyre (1969). Furthermore, Rein's data indicate that it is not so much a lack of education (although specific skills may be missing) as it is a case of lack of availability of jobs. She notes that, in a 1967 survey of AFDC mothers, 32.5 percent of high school graduates have worked as domestics, and some 28 percent of persons with some college education report domestic work as their usual occupation. "Although more educated women are more likely to work, more likely to work full-time, and more likely to work more, higher education does not necessarily determine the occupational bracket. As a group, working mothers had more education than AFDC mothers as a whole, but nevertheless they were more likely to consider themselves domestic workers" (Rein, 1972, p. 543). Rein concludes that with rising welfare payments more people become eligible for AFDC and that the trend will be toward an increasing number of recipients who use welfare to supplement low wages. Rein believes that an increase in a work-welfare situation is facilitated by attitudes within the community supportive of welfare as a means of livelihood. The fact that there may be less of a stigma in receiving welfare in a ghetto community, as opposed to the general population, may be the result of closer personal contact with welfare. Rein cites studies showing that from 15 percent to 43 percent of AFDC recipients were reared in families which received welfare at some point in time. The author concludes that work requirements will not succeed in reducing welfare roles and feels that giving mothers a choice of work, or welfare, or both, is a viable alternative.

Schiller (1973), in a survey of 52 empirical studies about welfare, found evidence to disprove five common assumptions about welfare reform measures based on data concerning recipients. The first assumption is that there is a qualitative difference between the working poor and the non-working poor. Schiller notes, along with Rein (1972) and Meyers and McIntyre (1969), that work and welfare often supplement each other. The second assumption is that welfare recipients need a special stimulus to seek employment, and the third assumption is that lack of child-care facilities is keeping large numbers of AFDC mothers from the work force. Schiller pointed out that the work ethic is evident in welfare recipients, that lack of jobs or family responsibilities, rather than lack of motivation, keeps welfare recipients from working. He also argues that instituting child-care facilities is no guarantee that substantial numbers of mothers will enter the labor force since many mothers perceive child-care facilities to be less adequate than home care. This is associated with the fourth assumption, that jobs are available. Schiller notes that "empirical studies suggest that there is a tremendous gap between public expectations and labor market realities" (Schiller, 1973). The fifth assumption is that welfare dependency is harmful to recipients and their families. Schiller provides some evidence supporting the contention that poverty rather than dependency is deleterious to welfare recipients and their families. Meyers and McIntryre's data (1969), however, suggest an effect of dependency on self-esteem over and above the effect of poverty. Schiller concludes that there are significant gaps in information about welfare and the relationship of welfare to work.

Public Attitudes Toward Government and Government Services

A less direct approach to the problem of evaluating service programs lies in studies of the beliefs and attitudes of the public about the merits of these services. Kallen and Miller (1971) believe for example that "...attitudes (toward welfare) have been little studied, despite their vast social importance and the implications an understanding of them may have for social policy."

Schiltz (1970) and other investigators of public opinion report two trends in attitudes toward government help over the past forty years:

1) There has been an increasing recognition of the necessary role of the government in service programs. For example, in 1939 only 16 percent of the people felt that the government should help to provide jobs for the unemployed. During World War II the percentage increased to over 70 percent, but after the war support declined to 57 percent in 1957 and 60 percent in 1960. In spite of some decline from the high point of World War II, the long term shift is marked. A similar trend in attitudes toward benefits for the unemployed can also be found over the past few decades.

2) Though accepting the appropriateness of the role of government in providing services, people have become more aware of the difficulties and potential abuses of public programs; and the worthiness of the recipients of public assistance is questioned. By the middle sixties there was little opposition to the government providing for the needy, but the question had become whether the "needy" were in fact in need. For example, Adams (1971) in his review of studies of attitudes toward unemployment insurance reports critical attitudes toward the need for unemployment compensation. Thus the Gallup poll in 1965 found that 75 percent of a national sample felt that people collecting unemployment compensation could be working. And 69 percent favored making the unemployment insurance laws more strict.

The facts do not necessarily support many public beliefs of this sort. But even popular misconceptions need to be taken into account because they can affect the support and cooperation which public agencies depend upon.

Perhaps the most comprehensive study of attitudes concerning public policy and government services was the nationwide survey conducted by Louis Harris and Associates for the Committee on Government Operations of the U. S. Senate in September of 1973. The major portion of the investigation dealt with general questions about (1) the relevant levels and agencies of government for handling different types of problems, (2) the appropriate role of the government in intervening in private and public matters, and (3) the many dimensions of system support, including confidence in the various branches of government and the extent of civic participation, political cynicism, and alienation.* In addition to the national study, a separate sample of 68 state leaders and 206 local officials was given parallel questions—the state leaders through an interview; the local officials through a written questionnaire.

In keeping with earlier findings the results of the Harris survey indicate the American public does accept the role of government in the lives of people, with 56 percent rejecting and 32 percent accepting the proposition that "the best government is the government that governs least." The leader group was more conservative with 48 percent of their number rejecting this notion and 41 percent accepting it. Moreover, some 89 percent of the public as against 62 percent of the leaders felt that "the federal government has a deep responsibility for seeing to it that the poor are taken care of, that no one goes hungry, and that every person achieves a minimum standard of living." But the majority of the people did oppose governmental intervention on such private matters as home inspection by officials to prevent wastage of fuel, car inspection every three months, and keeping one's gun at the local police station. In general, the image of elected federal officials is on the negative side, with unfavorable characteristics being mentioned more often than favorable traits. State and local elected officers fare somewhat better, and career officials have a positive image.

The Harris study, with its broad coverage of people's perceptions of government, had little time for their actual encounters with government offices and so offers little data on the utilization of service agencies and people's evaluation of their services. Respondents were merely asked: "Leaving aside paying taxes and filling out forms for licenses or Social Security, have you ever gone to your local government to get them to do something, or has that not happened to

---

*Reference is made to the Harris findings on the various aspects of system support in Chapter 4.

you?"* Those answering in the affirmative were then asked whether the people at the local government offices were helpful and whether they came away from the experience satisfied. The same three questions were also posed for the state and federal levels. Sixty-four percent of the sample reported that the personnel at the local office were helpful; 66 percent said the same for the state office; and 73 percent for the federal office. The figures on satisfaction are less favorable but are difficult to interpret. Respondents were given only four alternatives: "Highly satisfied, only somewhat satisfied, not satisfied at all, and not sure." This is basically a three point scale with the middle position poorly described—with no statement for the satisfied person, not enthusiastic about his experience, to endorse. Hence the percentages are only meaningful on a comparative basis for various types of services and various agencies. All that is learned here is that there is a slight tendency for the federal office to achieve a higher rating than the state or local office save that it is not known whether people are accurately referring to these levels.

An early study concerned with the public image of administrative agencies (Janowitz, Wright, and Delany, 1958), though limited to a single metropolitan community, did explore in some depth a number of basic perspectives toward administrative authority. The investigators were concerned with (1) generalized knowledge about the overall working of a system of administration, (2) instrumental knowledge about the individual's rights and obligations concerning a specific agency, (3) confidence in the bureaucracy to meet the client's interests, and (4) beliefs in the equitable operation of public agencies. The level of instrumental knowledge was found to be higher than the level of generalized knowledge with expected differences for social classes, save that the gap between classes was somewhat larger for instrumental than for generalized knowledge. The great majority of respondents had confidence that their own interests were being served by government agencies. A pervasive and deep-seated antagonism against organs of government was found among only a small minority, 10 to 15 percent. Nevertheless many people thought that the costs of government service were too high "considering what they get from government." People were also less supportive of administrative authority in that sizable numbers accepted stereotypes about the inequity of government operations.

---

*It is not clear why Social Security forms were included in this wording. Social Security is not administered through local government offices. It is true that people do not differentiate accurately between levels of government, but since the investigators were concerned with differences in attitudes for the various levels, it is curious that they should have added to the confusion of their respondents in this fashion.

Eldersveld (1967) replicated the Janowitz-Wright-Delany study in the Delhi area of India and found similar levels of knowledge, but much greater utilization of government services in India than in the U.S., though the samples are not necessarily representative of either country. He concluded that the upper classes were somewhat more alienated than the lower classes in India and that the alienation in his sample was greater than in the Janowitz investigation.

Effectiveness of A Single Program: Head Start

The ideal form of evaluation research would be a continuing research feedback built into both operational and staff functions. In practice, however, social scientists have only reached the stage of occasional studies of single programs. One of the few planned research efforts to evaluate a remedial program was the much debated investigation of the effects of pre-school training for deprived youngsters upon their subsequent cognitive and personal development. The Westinghouse Corporation and Ohio University conducted a study of the impact of Head Start for the Office of Economic Opportunity (Cicirelli, 1969). The investigators addressed themselves to the question of the extent to which children presently in the first, second, and third grades who had attended Head Start programs differed in their intellectual and social-personal characteristics from comparable children who did not attend. A sample of 104 Head Start centers across the country was chosen, and from these centers a sample of children found in local area schools was selected for testing. A matched sample of children from the same grades and the same schools who had not attended Head Start formed the control group. Both groups were given a series of tests covering various aspects of cognitive and affective development. The design was thus *ex post facto* but at least there was some research design to the study.

The findings were clear about the effects of *summer* Head Start centers. Students in the summer programs were no different from the control children on a battery of tests of cognitive ability and motivation. But the results for the *full-year* programs were more ambiguous. While there were no consistent improvement patterns over the range of tests for the national sample in the full-year program in comparison to the control group, there were some slightly, but significantly, higher scores on some of the sub-tests for the full-year program. Moreover, for some segments in the sample reflecting the most underprivileged groups, the gains were more consistent. Finally, apart from comparison with control groups, the Head Start children were still below the national norms of standardized tests in the second and third grades.

These findings were interpreted by many as not justifying the funds for continuing Head Start and in fact had something to do with its demise. The study does illustrate some of the problems of evaluation research.

In the first place, when research is to be used to guide policy decisions, it is tragic to employ weak research design. The *ex post facto* paradigm employed was not necessary for a new and continuing program, and reflects the lack of research understanding and commitment of top policy makers. The OEO did not establish a separate Evaluation Division until the autumn of 1967. Since the program was already in its third year, the Evaluation Division settled for an *ex post facto* design even though it was not too late to attempt a longitudinal study in addition.

In the second place, evaluation research should not be a single shot study of the overall outcome of a large program. It should be built into the many pieces of the major effort on a continuing basis. There were indications that some aspects of Head Start were effective for some groups. It would be important to know what specific processes were at work in these cases. In other words, within a nationwide program of remedial training, there should be room for experimentation with different procedures and practices.

In the third place, evaluation research requires that we distinguish between programs for disbursing benefits and programs for changing people, or to use Williams and Evans' terminology (1972) between maintenance and opportunity programs. The distribution of money or food is easier to set up on a large scale basis and easier to evaluate with respect to the limited objective of efficient and equitable disbursement. A nationwide effort to impart new skills to large groups of workers, or to develop safer driving habits, runs into difficulties of inadequate knowledge for achieving the desired results and, on the evaluation side, a lack of specification of significant variables to be measured. When the objective is to change people, experimentation is needed to provide clear models for both manipulation and for measurement (Williams and Evans, 1972).

*   *   *   *

The present study departs from much of the research tradition in the field in concentrating upon the experiences of people in their encounters with government agencies as one source for the evaluation of administrative effectiveness. Thus it stands between the more direct attempts to measure the outcomes of a program as in the Head Start investigation and the indirect approach of public opinion surveys concerned with the beliefs and attitudes of the general public toward government programs. One reason for looking at the specifics of people's interactions with given agencies as proposed in the present study is that it can fill in some of the meaningful processes intervening between the program as designed and the overall outcome.

Chapter 2

UTILIZATION AND UNDERUTILIZATION

This chapter is concerned with the utilization of government agencies and the contacts people have with government offices, that is, their experiences with both service agencies and with constraint or control agencies. The former, like the Social Security Administration, do things for people; the latter, like the Internal Revenue Service, do things to them. A central question has to do with what kinds of people utilize government services and what kinds of people have encounters with control agencies. A corollary question centers on underutilization. To what extent do people who need help fail to go to appropriate public offices? Who are these people and why do they not seek an available public service? Stereotypes exist about the kinds of people who have experiences with government agencies: senior citizens receive social security; welfare recipients are mainly black mothers with numerous children; seasonal workers receive unemployment compensation; young people are a problem group for police; income tax is a middle class headache, etc. This chapter will focus on characteristics such as age, sex, income, and education in an attempt to verify or disprove some of these common conceptions.

In the present study, seven service functions of government are specifically examined: job finding, job training, workmen's compensation, unemployment compensation, public assistance, hospital and medical care, and retirement benefits. In addition, difficulties or problems experienced by respondents in four areas of government control are examined: vehicular licenses, traffic violations, tax regulations, and police interference with individual rights.

19

UTILIZATION OF SERVICE AND CONSTRAINT AGENCIES

Respondents were asked if they had ever sought the help of an agency on problems for which the government provides services and if they had ever had difficulties with officials or offices in constraint agencies. They were also asked to give the approximate date of any service experience mentioned as well as the date for the most important service contact. For constraint experiences the date was ascertained only for the most important set of contacts. It should be kept in mind, then, that although the questions were concerned with any encounters the respondent had had, he was most likely to recall recent experiences.

Table 2.1 shows the percentage of contacts with service agencies of all respondents. Approximately 58 percent of persons in the sample have utilized at least one of the specified government services. Of the 58 percent who have contacted a government office, about half have done so for only one type of problem. Some 11 percent are heavy users, turning to public agencies for three or more kinds of problems.

Table 2.1

Number of Different Service Agency Contacts
of All Respondents

Number of Contacts with Different Agencies	Percent of Samples
None	42.2%
One	29.0
Two	17.7
Three or more	10.8
N.A.	0.3
Total	100.0%
N	(1,431)

Unemployment compensation was the most frequently sought service with one-quarter of the people reporting this use of government agencies (Table 2.2). It was followed closely by the use of public employment offices. (In order to receive unemployment compensation, a person must register with the employment service. While this requirement may often be fulfilled rather perfunctorily as in the case of workers who are only temporarily laid off, it may nevertheless serve to boost the number of reported contacts with the employment service.) In all, some 18.6 percent of our sample was either retired or receiving retirement benefits or both. According to U. S. Census estimates, the percentage of adults in the U.S. 62 and over in 1972 was 18.7. Though most people do not retire before 65, they can receive social security benefits at age 62 and in special cases before that, as in the case of a wife of a retiree with dependent children. Hence our 18.6 percentage is probably very close to the proportion in the total population eligible for social security benefits. It is worthy of note that, of the seven problem areas, finding a job, getting job training, and getting unemployment compensation affect more people than do the other four.

Table 2.2

Incidence of Problems and of Utilization
of Service Agencies

Problem	Percent of Total Sample Having Problem	Percent of Total Sample Utilizing Agency
Finding a job	33.1%	23.8%
Job training	30.3	8.9
Workmen's compensation	12.9	7.6
Unemployment compensation	27.2	25.6
Public assistance	12.2	11.9
Hospital/medical care	7.5	5.9
Retirement benefits	18.6	14.5
N	(1,431)	(1,431)

Respondents were given the opportunity of mentioning other problems they have had for which government services might be provided. Some 8 percent of respondents mentioned other service areas. Seventeen percent of those who mentioned an additional problem specified housing problems; 14 percent mentioned other job related problems; 14 percent mentioned issues in the area of education; and 13 percent listed legal assistance needs. The other responses fell into a broad range of problem areas from small business loans to emergency relief.

A considerable minority of the population does not utilize government services even when they have problems appropriate for consideration by an agency (Table 2.2). The largest gap is between the felt need for job training and the use of public agencies to get such training, with 30 percent of the people reporting the need, and only 9 percent going to a government office about it. Workmen's compensation, though not looming large as a common problem, did have a relatively high discrepancy between need and use, since four out of ten who do have the problem have not made contact with that service. At the other end of the ladder, almost everyone needing public assistance or unemployment compensation had been in touch with a government agency. Finding a job, getting hospital and medical care, or obtaining retirement benefits are intermediate in degree of utilization. Approximately one out of four persons with these difficulties did not avail himself of the services of a public office. We shall inquire into the reasons for the underutilization of some agencies when we turn to the correlations of factors with agency usage later in this chapter.

The experiences of respondents covered a wide time range, some apparently occurring over 30 years ago. The majority of incidents reported are of much more recent vintage, however. Forty-three percent of the most important service experiences and 81 percent of the most important constraint experiences did not occur prior to 1970 according to respondents (Table 2.3). It is not clear why difficulties

Table 2.3

Contacts from 1970 through May, 1973 as a Percentage
of Total Contacts

Type of Contact	Contacts 1970-1973	Total Contacts
Service contacts	45%	1,348
Finding a job	44	338
Job training	54	131
Workmen's compensation	38	97
Unemployment compensation	35	350
Public assistance	65	166
Hospital/medical care	70	80
Retirement benefits	39	186
Service contacts (most important contact)	43	680
Constraint encounters (most important)*	81	198

*Dates for constraint experiences were obtained only for the most important constraint encounter rather than for all constraint problems.

with control agencies are reported as occurring within the past three years so much more often than service problems. Fewer people report problems with control agencies than with service agencies, and it could be that older experiences of a disagreeable character are no longer salient in memory. Since people were having these experiences as well as more satisfying encounters in the years before 1970, it is interesting that they are not attributed to the earlier period. It can be that the people with unpleasant experiences keep having more of the same, and since they were asked about the most recent encounter, we are dealing with veridical reports.

There are inherent difficulties in asking parallel questions for constraint and service agencies. Whereas contacts are relevant for service agencies, problems or difficulties are relevant for control agencies. Almost everyone has had contact with some constraint agency, either in the form of filing an income tax return or getting a driver's license. Therefore the questions pertaining to constraint encounters were worded as follows: "Have you had or are you having any *difficulties* or *problems* with government offices or officials about any of the following matters?" Table 2.4 shows the percentage of people having difficulties with control agencies. Constraint experiences of the four types examined are more infrequent than service contacts. There is less variability in the percentages of constraint than

Table 2.4

Problems with Control Agencies

A. Type of Problem	Percent of Sample Reporting Difficulty
Driver's license	4.1%
Traffic violation	3.1
Income tax	6.4
Police interference	3.9
N	(1,431)

B. Total Number of Problems	Percent of Sample Reporting Difficulty
None	85.3%
One	11.2
Two or more	3.6
N	(1,431)

service experiences; income tax is the most commonly reported problem. About 85 percent of the sample has had no difficulties with the law, or its administrative agencies, according to their own account. In general, although a relatively small percentage of people report problems with constraint agencies, it should be remembered that 15 percent of the adult population is equivalent to some 17 million people. And 17 million people encountering difficulties with control agencies suggests a problem of considerable proportions.

BACKGROUND CHARACTERISTICS AND SERVICE AGENCY CONTACTS

While there are proportionately almost twice as many females as males receiving public assistance, males predominate in finding a job, job training, workmen's compensation and unemployment compensation—all work-related services (Table 2.5). It is to be expected that males would be heavier utilizers of work-related services since fewer females are in the labor force. However, even if the subset of the sample who are presently working is examined, it can be seen that working males utilize their agencies more than working females (Table 2.6). It is not readily apparent why the discrepancy exists. It is possible that women do not take advantage of the services to the same extent as males. In the case of job training, it is possible that such programs predominate in traditional masculine occupations or that males are given first priority. Men may also be more likely to be in hazardous occupations which may eventually result in workmen's compensation benefits. And a larger proportion of women than men may be part-time workers and hence not so fully eligible for all services.

Table 2.5

Relation of Sex to Utilization of Service Agencies

Problem	Sex	
	Male	Female
Finding a job	28.8%	20.1%
Job training	12.9	6.0
Workmen's compensation	12.3	4.2
Unemployment compensation	34.9	18.7
Public assistance	7.7	15.1
Hospital/medical care	6.1	5.9
Retirement benefits	13.4	15.4
N	(611)	(820)

Table 2.6

Percentage of Presently Working Males and Females
Seeking Help for Four Work-Related Services

Problem	Sex	
	Male	Female
Finding a job	30%	26%
Job training	14	8
Workmen's compensation	11	5
Unemployment compensation	35	22
N	(480)	(359)
Percent working	79%	44%
Total N	(611)	(820)

Slightly more women receive retirement benefits than men. This might be expected, as there are more elderly women than men (9 percent as compared to 6 percent in the 65 and over category). And despite the fact that more women than men receive retirement benefits, Blackwell and Ferguson (1973) report that women over 65 are the single poorest segment of the peopulation.

Table 2.7 reports the percentage of blacks and whites utilizing the seven government services. Perhaps the most interesting finding is

Table 2.7

Relation of Race to Utilization of Service Agencies

Problem	Race	
	White	Black
Finding a job	21.6%	46.8%
Job training	8.3	15.1
Workmen's compensation	8.0	5.6
Unemployment compensation	25.4	24.6
Public assistance	9.6	34.1
Hospital/medical care	5.0	13.5
Retirement benefits	15.6	5.6
N	(1,246)	(126)

the underutilization of retirement benefit programs by blacks. While today almost all employment is covered by the Social Security Act, it would appear that the types of employment held by blacks in the past were not covered by the social security program. It is also true that there are relatively fewer blacks than whites over 65. An additional explanation is that blacks are not collecting the social security to which they are entitled. It is also true that some part-time workers and domestics do not make their employment known to avoid income tax on present earnings as well as social security deductions. Hence they themselves are not eligible for retirement benefits. A larger proportion of blacks than whites do receive public assistance. For some blacks, receiving public assistance may be a result of not receiving social security.

A popular notion is that the needy among some minority groups would rather not work and hence do not take advantage of available agencies to find jobs and get job training. Our findings just do not support this belief. More than twice the proportion of blacks as whites utilize public employment agencies (47 percent as against 22 percent), and twice the proportion seek job training (15 percent as against 8 percent). These differences do not disappear even if income is controlled (Table 2.8). Relatively more blacks than whites in low

Table 2.8

Relation of Race and Income to Finding a Job

Race	Never a Problem	A Problem and Government Office Contacted	A Problem but No Government Office Contacted	N
		Income under $5,000		
White	73.3%	18.4%	8.3%	(266)
Black	48.8	46.5	4.7	(43)
		Income $5,000 to $9,999		
White	65.5	26.4	8.1	(296)
Black	42.3	40.4	17.3	(52)
		Income $10,000 to $14,999		
White	65.9	23.6	10.6	(331)
Black	37.5	62.5	0.0	(16)
		Income $15,000 and over		
White	70.2	18.1	11.7	(299)
Black	38.5	53.8	7.7	(13)

income groups seek jobs and job training. Moreover, in the lowest income category (under $5,000 family income), nine out of ten unemployed blacks did go to a government agency to find a job, but only six out of ten whites sought the help of a public agency. In seeking job training the pattern is less clear, but the ratio of utilization for blacks is about the same as for whites in the lowest income grouping, less in the two middle income categories, and higher in the top income bracket.

The fairly intensive effort by the government under the Manpower Development and Training Act, the Job Corps, JOBS-NAM, and related programs has been successful in producing heavy utilization of services of job training and job seeking by blacks. It has not been as successful in increasing the number of jobs available. This is reflected in the smaller proportion of blacks applying for workmen's compensation. It is also reflected in their relative equality with whites in applying for unemployment compensation even though they have a much higher percentage of unemployed. Only the previously employed are entitled to workmen's compensation and unemployment compensation. The problem, then, is not so much a matter of inadequate unemployment agencies or inadequate training facilities as a lack of jobs. This is essentially the thesis of Leonard Goodwin in *Do the Poor Want to Work?* Goodwin compared 2,000 poor (more than half of whom are welfare recipients) with 2,000 people having steady employment. He found that the poor and the welfare recipients had much the same work ethic and life aspirations as did middle class people. He does add, however, that a critical variable in keeping people off welfare rolls is a chance to experience success in jobs that pay enough to support them.

Age is a major determinant of the type of problem for which people seek help from a government agency. Both finding a job and receiving job training are highest among people 25 to 29 although the incidence of these needs continues through the thirties with little change (Table 2.9). It is only after 40 that there is a drop in the utilization of government services in employment and training. It is interesting, moreover, to find that 6 percent of the people over 70 are turning to public agencies for help in getting a job. When it comes to retirement benefits the older age groups, with a few exceptions, are the only people eligible; yet only 45 percent of the 60 to 69 age group and only 70 percent of those over 70 say they have gone to a government office about such benefits. Some 22 percent of those who are retired or are getting retirement benefits report that they have not tried to get help from a government office. This sizable total is due to to the ineligibility of some respondents, the routine nature of the service which led to its underreporting in other cases, or the fact that retirees do not know where to go. Age does not predict to the use of workmen's compensation, nor to public assistance. There is some indication of greater seeking of hospital and medical care in the group 70 and older, as would be expected, but curiously there is no significant increase in the age groups between 20 and 69 years. However, since older people have more lengthy and expensive illnesses, it is possible that more money is involved in their medical and hospital care than in the case of younger persons. That is the case with Medicaid. For example, in August, 1969, ADC recipients comprised 51 percent of the persons receiving Medicaid assistance, whereas the largest share of the money, 40 percent, was spent on OAA clients (H.E.W., 1972).

Table 2.9

Relation of Age to Utilization of Service Agencies

| | Age Group | | | | | | |
Problem	18-24	25-29	30-39	40-49	50-59	60-69	70+
Finding a job	33.5%	38.3%	31.7%	20.9%	17.8%	12.1%	5.9%
Job training	12.3	15.6	14.2	9.1	4.7	2.0	1.5
Workmen's compensation	7.4	7.8	6.3	8.7	9.3	7.0	7.4
Unemployment compensation	16.7	22.8	33.2	30.9	25.7	27.1	16.3
Public assistance	10.8	13.3	15.7	11.3	8.4	11.1	12.6
Hospital/medical care	7.4	5.6	6.3	3.9	6.1	3.0	11.1
Retirement benefits	0.5	0.0	1.1	2.6	6.5	44.7	70.4
N	(203)	(180)	(268)	(230)	(214)	(199)	(135)

Public assistance, hospital and medical care, and retirement benefits have higher rates of utilization among those respondents lacking a high school diploma (Table 2.10). It is not surprising that the less educated receive more welfare services. The fact that the poorly educated are more likely to be receiving retirement benefits is due in part to the historical increase in the median level of the nation's population. Thus the elderly are going to be more heavily represented in the lower education bracket than are the younger age cohorts. The

1970 U. S. census reports that in 1910, 19 percent of 18 and 19 year olds were enrolled in school; whereas in 1970, 57 percent of that age group were attending school (Department of Commerce, 1972). The U. S. census also reports that the median education level in 1970 was 12.2 years (Department of Commerce, 1972). It is the high school graduate who is most likely to receive unemployment compensation and job training according to the findings.

Table 2.10

Relation of Education to Utilization of Service Agencies

Problem	Years of Education		
	Fewer than 12	High school graduate	At least some college
Finding a job	17%	26%	29%
Job training	7	11	9
Workmen's compensation	8	8	6
Unemployment compensation	25	30	21
Public assistance	19	10	5
Hospital/medical care	9	6	2
Retirement benefits	27	8	7
N	(511)	(489)	(424)

Occupation is related to the differential use of public services, but the differences are not between the two white collar groups of professional-managerial and clerical-sales people. For both these categories, finding a job heads the list with similar percentages, and unemployment compensation is next. In the latter, the contacts with government offices are slightly higher for the clerical-sales people (Table 2.11). The white collar occupational roles thus seem similar in spite of differences in status and income; i.e., lower level people working in offices are very much like the managerial and professional groups. When we look at blue collar workers, however, we find some striking differences not only in comparison with white collar people, but also among the skilled, the semi-skilled, and the unskilled. Skilled and semi-skilled workers utilize employment services at rates which approximate utilization by white collar workers; only the unskilled differ from the white collar groups with increased frequency of contact with government agencies in finding a job. Logically, too, these untrained people are highest in their use of public assistance. The percentage of those seeking such assistance doubles from white collar occupations to the skilled and semi-skilled, and quadruples for the unskilled. The skilled category is the highest of all occupational groupings in utilizing public agencies for job training. The semi-skilled differ from the skilled in reporting relatively more use of unemployment compensation, and they outrank the laborers in this respect. As semi-skilled workers, they probably have less job security than the skilled and more unemployment insurance than the totally untrained. The lack of coverage of laborers is also manifest in the low use of workmen's compensation by these people compared to other blue collar groups.

Table 2.11

Relation of Occupation to Utilization
of Service Agencies

	Occupation					
Problem	Professional & Managerial	Clerical & Sales	Skilled	Semi-skilled	Laborers	Farmers
Finding a job	23.7%	25.7%	29.5%	27.5%	34.9%	0.0%
Job training	7.8	8.5	19.5	9.3	11.8	0.0
Workmen's compensation	6.9	6.7	14.1	13.4	8.6	3.6
Unemployment compensation	17.2	21.8	39.6	50.2	29.5	0.0
Public assistance	5.6	7.0	13.4	13.0	25.3	10.7
Hospital/ medical care	3.0	4.2	8.1	7.3	11.8	3.6
Retirement benefits	10.3	13.4	13.4	17.1	13.9	50.0
N	(232)	(284)	(149)	(193)	(186)	(28)

Service experiences are differentiated by income categories in Table 2.12. The largest proportion of contacts with respect to public assistance, hospital and medical care, and retirement benefits are by those persons in the lowest income category, under $5,000. This would suggest that a sizable number of persons with a yearly income of less than $5,000 are retirees. By contrast, the rest of the services are most heavily utilized by people in the $5,000 to $10,000 per year range, although people from families earning from $10,000 to $15,000 per year are only slightly less likely to have these work-related service contacts with government agencies. It is interesting to note that about 20 percent of individuals whose family incomes are in excess of $15,000 per year have received unemployment compensation and have utilized government job-finding services. It is possible, of course, that many of these individuals are youths whose parents earn over $15,000 per year, or that the service contact occurred a number of years previously when the person was less prosperous.*

Table 2.12

Relation of Income to Utilization of Service Agencies

	Income Group			
Problem	0-$4,999	$5,000-9,999	$10,000-14,999	$15,000+
Finding a job	22.6%	28.3%	24.9%	19.8%
Job training	6.7	11.3	10.9	7.1
Workmen's compensation	7.6	9.3	7.2	6.8
Unemployment compensation	22.3	30.2	27.9	20.7
Public assistance	26.3	14.3	5.3	2.5
Hospital/medical care	11.9	6.0	4.7	1.9
Retirement benefits	37.0	12.1	4.2	4.3
N	(327)	(364)	(358)	(323)

Since so many government services are work-related—i.e., concerned with finding a job or protecting the individual from the threat of unemployment by providing additional skills or paying him compensation if he is laid off or disabled—work status is an important variable in the present study. It is important to determine which of these work-related services are, in fact, helping those who need employment services. The working category includes those people who are temporarily laid off, on strike, on sick leave, etc. The unemployed category includes those people who are looking for work; the retired and permanently disabled are included in another group; and "other" is principally composed of housewives and students. In comparison to the other categories, a larger percentage of

---

*We found that, in general, the higher the income, the earlier the year of the government encounter for employment service and job training, but not for other service areas. It is possible, then, that employment service and job training were utilized in a less prosperous period and that, in fact, a higher income is at least partially a result of either of these government services.

the unemployed group has been the recipient of job finding, job training, public assistance, and hospital and medical care (Table 2.13). A much larger percentage of retired and disabled persons is receiving retirement benefits although almost 30 percent of this group is not receiving social security or other such benefits. More retired and disabled persons are also receiving workmen's compensation in comparison to the other three groups.

Table 2.13

Relation of Work Category to
Utilization of Service Agencies

	Work Status			
Problem	Working	Unemployed	Retired/ Permanently Disabled	Other
Finding a job	28.2%	50.0%	15.1%	12.8%
Job training	11.3	23.4	1.6	4.3
Workmen's compensation	8.7	9.3	11.4	2.9
Unemployment compensation	29.6	26.6	28.6	14.0
Public assistance	9.1	40.6	15.1	12.0
Hospital/medical care	4.6	18.8	9.7	4.7
Retirement benefits	2.7	1.6	70.8	15.5
N	(839)	(64)	(185)	(343)

Table 2.14 differentiates service agencies by four geographic regions of the country. In general little variability is attributable to geographic region. The South has a lower rate of utilization of workmen's compensation and unemployment compensation than the other regions. Rates of contact with hospital and medical care services are higher in the West and Northeast than in the north central area or the South. It might be pointed out again that rates of contact are not the same as money allocated. For example, the north central area shows the lowest rate of utilization of public assistance; yet many of the states in the area (e.g., Michigan, Ohio, Illinois) have high rates of public assistance in relation to budget need (H.E.W., 1973).

Table 2.14

Relation of Geographic Regions to Utilization of Service Agencies

	Geographic Region			
Problem	West	North Central	Northeast	South
Finding a job	24.7%	22.2%	24.0%	24.6%
Job training	8.6	8.9	8.3	9.6
Workmen's compensation	11.8	7.8	9.5	3.9
Unemployment compensation	30.9	23.2	34.0	18.7
Public assistance	12.5	9.9	14.3	11.9
Hospital/medical care	8.2	4.3	7.9	4.8
Retirement benefits	10.5	18.9	11.4	14.8
N	(255)	(423)	(315)	(438)

Background Characteristics and Level of Government Contact

It is also instructive to look at background characteristics as they relate to level of government service. In other words, does the federal government assist the same kinds of individuals as the state or local government? We can answer this question only with respect to what people consider their most important encounter with a public service agency rather than for all their experiences, a limitation set by a fairly brief interview schedule.

Table 2.15 compares the percentage of people utilizing different public services with the percentage of people naming the most important service in their experience. About half of the people who have utilized these seven government services had only one contact which is, of course, also the most important contact. For the rest of the respondents, however, there is room for discretion in the selection of the most important service received. There are some discrepancies between most important services and total utilization. Whereas most pensioners listed retirement benefits as the most important service, working age respondents did not single out any one of the work-related services, such as the heavily utilized job finding and unemployment compensation areas, as most important. Possible explanations for the singular importance of retirement benefits are that they serve a continuing need and that retirees typically have only one government agency contact; whereas working age people receive a variety of services. This is true to some extent with unemployment compensation in that recipients must register with the employment service in order to collect benefits.

Table 2.15

A Comparison of Percentages of Utilization and Most Important Experience for Seven Service Contacts

Problem	Utilization	
	Most Important Experience	Total Experiences
Finding a job	11.9%	23.8%
Job training	3.7	8.9
Workmen's compensation	2.8	7.6
Unemployment compensation	11.3	25.6
Public assistance	7.2	11.9
Hospital/medical care	3.1	5.9
Retirement benefits	12.1	14.5
N	(1,431)	(1,431)

Tables 2.16 through 2.19 represent a shift in frame of reference from total utilization to most important experience with a government agency. This reference point should be kept in mind.

Table 2.16

Utilization of Local, County, State, and Federal Levels of Government Services by Geographic Region for the Most Important Problem Area

Level of Government	Geographic Region				
	West	North Central	Northeast	South	Total
Local	9.0%	8.5%	24.2%	14.2%	13.8%
County	12.3	13.8	9.1	9.6	11.2
State	41.3	42.5	37.1	33.1	38.3
Federal	26.4	27.1	23.1	33.4	27.9
D.K. & N.A.	11.0	8.1	6.5	9.6	8.7
Total	100%	100%	100%	100%	100%
N	(155)	(247)	(186)	(239)	(827)

Note: Level of government reflects the respondent's perception of the level of government providing the needed service.

Table 2.17

Utilization of Local, County, State, and Federal Levels
of Government Services by Working Status for the Most
Important Problem Area

| Level of Government | Work Status | | | | |
	Working	Unemployed	Retired/ Permanently Disabled	Other	Total
Local	13.3%	19.6%	10.7%	16.5%	13.8%
County	10.9	25.5	7.5	11.3	11.2
State	48.7	25.5	18.2	31.8	38.3
Federal	20.3	15.7	51.5	30.5	27.9
D.K. & N.A.	6.7	13.7	11.9	9.9	8.7
Total	100%	100%	100%	100%	100%
N	(466)	(51)	(159)	(151)	(827)

Note: Level of government reflects the respondent's perception of the level of
government providing the needed service.

It is difficult for respondents to specify the level of government
for services received since many agencies obtain funding from several

Table 2.18

Utilization of Local, County, State, and Federal Levels
of Government Services by Race for the Most Important
Problem Area

| Level of Government | Race | | | |
	White	Black	Other	Total
Local	12.4%	25.3%	11.1%	13.8%
County	10.1	17.5	16.7	11.2
State	39.9	28.6	30.0	38.3
Federal	29.4	15.4	30.6	27.9
D.K. & N.A.	8.1	13.2	8.3	8.7
Total	100%	100%	100%	100%
N	(700)	(91)	(36)	(827)

Note: Level of government reflects the respondent's perception of the level of
government providing the needed service.

Table 2.19

Utilization of Local, County, State, and Federal Levels
of Government Services by Income for the Most
Important Problem Area

Level of Government	Income Group				
	0-$4,999	$5,000-9,999	$10,000-14,999	$15,000+	Total
Local	12.6%	16.0%	15.3%	8.5%	14.4%
County	15.7	13.3	7.6	5.4	11.5
State	20.5	40.0	54.1	50.0	38.6
Federal	39.0	23.6	17.5	29.2	28.0
D.K. & N.A.	12.2	7.1	5.5	6.9	9.1
Total	100%	100%	100%	100%	100%
N	(254)	(225)	(183)	(130)	(792)

Note: Level of government reflects the respondent's perception of the level of government providing the needed service.

levels of government. For example, public assistance money comes from federal and state sources on a matching basis. In addition, county and local levels may also provide money for clients who are ineligible for public assistance according to federal or state guidelines. However, each agency from which service is received is administered at only one level. For example, job training programs may be funded by the Department of Labor as authorized by the Manpower Development and Training Act, but the job training programs may be administered only through the state employment agency. Level of government was assessed subjectively and therefore reflects people's beliefs about which level of government is providing service. Some respondents may thus be characterizing the level of an agency on the basis of the source of support for the service. Others may be using administration as the basis for describing level. More government services are administered by state governments than by the federal government. In general, over the past 30 years, state governments have retained administrative control over service agencies while relying more and more heavily on the federal government for funds.

Table 2.16 shows that local government provides more services in the Northeast than in any other region, and people in the South receive less state aid, but more federal aid. These are differences, not in total frequency, but in frequency of *most important* experiences with a public agency.

When speaking of their most important experience, people in various working categories also show differences in level of government contacted (Table 2.17). A larger proportion of people in the working category report that they turn to the state government for job training, unemployment compensation, and workmen's compensation than do people in the non-working categories. The unemployed, who make up 11 percent of the sample, receive 45 percent of their important services from local and county agencies. Over half of the services received by the retired and permanently disabled come from the federal government, primarily through social security.

When reporting on their most important experience with a service agency, a larger share of whites than blacks are talking of federal offices (Table 2.18). This reflects the fact that relatively fewer blacks than whites are receiving social security. The situation is reversed for contacts with local agencies, with relatively more blacks having contact at the town or city level. It is also interesting that the data for other non-whites resembles the distribution for whites more than it does for blacks, although the numbers involved are very small (N=36).

Table 2.19 shows important service contacts by level of government and income. There are interesting differences in the locus of service for the various income groupings. For example, individuals in the $10,000 and above brackets turn frequently to state offices. The county directs its aid toward lower income persons, as does the federal government. The proportion of federal contacts, however, goes up for those persons with a family income of more than $20,000.

In general, the state government, in which unemployment compensation is the largest service, in fact helps middle class individuals. The federal government helps all retired individuals through social security and thus helps lower income individuals since retirees generally have minimal incomes.

An intriguing hypothesis is that the deprived groups in society turn more to the local level of government for help while those better off have recourse more to the higher level in the system. The facts, however, suggest some modifications in this theory. It is true that state governments do help middle class people through unemployment compensation, but many lower income people receive aid from social security at the federal level. As noted in chapter one, Steiner (1971) writes that "Social security provides more cash assistance to poor people than does public assistance." The support for services at the local or county level, while smaller in scope than at state and federal levels, may in fact consist largely of state or federal monies.

Collective Importance of Demographic Characteristics in Service Contacts

Finally, an overall assessment of the importance of the background characteristics was made by means of a Multiple Classification Analysis. The dependent variable was the number of service contacts (0, 1, 2, 3 or more), and the independent variables were the eight characteristics already mentioned, plus political party preference (Republican, Democrat, Independent, and other).

The Eta statistic is the zero order correlation (non-parametric), that is, the correlation between the particular independent variable or predictor and the dependent variable. Eta² is the amount of variance accounted for by the predictor. The Beta statistic is the partial correlation, or the relationship of the predictor to the dependent variable, with all other predictors held constant. Beta² is the amount of variance which the partial correlation takes into account. Both zero order correlations and partial correlations are low and account for very little of the variance associated with frequency of agency utilization (Table 2.20). Even the multiple correlation of all nine predictors accounts for only 20.5 percent of the variance (R = .45). *Income* and *working status* head the list but it is surprising that they do not yield higher correlations. Being poor and unemployed predicts very weakly to total utilization of government services. The poor may seek public assistance more than the affluent, and the unemployed may turn more to employment agencies than the employed but the use of public offices for many services is widely distributed throughout the population. Governmental services in job-related matters, health and medicine, in dependency and poverty, and in retirement do not comprise a welfare state for the deprived and needy; they are the way of life for the whole nation.

The bureaucracy serves different groups for different purposes. Thus blacks utilize employment agencies proportionately more than whites. Whites utilize unemployment compensation and retirement benefits proportionately more than blacks. But the government serves all segments of the population. It is sometimes assumed that, beginning with social welfare legislation for the poverty-stricken, society has moved toward a welfare state offering cradle-to-grave security for all citizens, based upon a reallocation of resources according to socialist principles. This is a distortion of social reality. Governmental intervention has worked not so much to shift resources as to perpetu-

Table 2.20

Demographic Determinants of Agency Utilization; First
Order and Partial Correlations

Predictor	Eta	Eta^2	Beta	Beta^2
Region	.108	.012	.137	.019
Sex	.079	.006	.132	.017
Age	.158	.025	.173	.030
Working status	.231	.053	.222	.049
Race	.117	.012	.063	.004
Education	.189	.036	.119	.014
Occupation	.241	.058	.175	.031
Income	.271	.074	.211	.045
Political party	.090	.008	.061	.004

Multiple R = .45 (population estimate = .41)
Variance explained (R^2) = 20.5% (population estimate = 17%)

ate the existing reward structure. Instead of showing significant changes in government services to redress inequities, we find that people in upper income groups utilize public agencies for finding a job, getting job retraining, getting workmen's compensation, and drawing unemployment insurance—just as much as people in the lower income groups. The affluent do not avail themselves of public assistance and retirement benefits in proportion to their number, but they do utilize effectively public resources in graduate and professional training of their children. Moreover, the growth of public bureaucracy increases the employment opportunities for the trained rather than for the uneducated. The disbursement of public funds within the nation is not so much a benefaction from the wealthy taxpayers to the poor, as a distribution of resources according to different types of needs and knowledgeability of groups about available services. These findings were anticipated in a study conducted in 1954 in the Detroit area by Janowitz, Wright, and Delany on the basis of which the authors conclude, "All the various strata, not just the lower social groups in the metropolitan community, have developed a stake in and a reliance on these new functions of government" (1958, p. 102).

BACKGROUND CHARACTERISTICS AND CONSTRAINT AGENCY CONTACTS

Table 2.21 shows the percentage of males and females having problems with different constraint agencies. A greater proportion of males than females report problems, a finding which is not very surprising. Males pay higher car insurance premiums because of their higher accident and traffic violation rates, and at all age levels more males than females are in prisons and jails.

Table 2.21

Relation of Sex to Problems
with Four Constraint Agencies

	Sex	
Problem	Male	Female
Driver's license	7%	2%
Traffic violation	5	1
Income tax	8	5
Police interference	7	2
N	(610)	(817)

The conventional belief that blacks have proportionately more encounters with control agencies than whites is not correct if the context is one of perceived problems in dealing with such offices. The percentages of both groups reporting difficulties with four different constraint agencies are almost identical (Table 2.22).

Table 2.22

Relation of Race to Problems
with Four Constraint Agencies

	Race	
Problem	White	Black
Driver's license	4%	4%
Traffic violation	3	3
Income tax	6	6
Police interference	4	3
N	(1,243)	(126)

Table 2.23 shows the distribution of problems by two age categories. Problems with constraint agencies are more prevalent among the
younger members of the population. There is a relatively low incidence of reported problems for individuals over age 30. The under 30
group, on the other hand, reports relatively more problems even with
income tax than the older group, though the difference here is not
significant.

Table 2.23

Relation of Age Group to Problems
with Four Constraint Agencies

	Age Group	
Problem	18-29	30+
Driver's license	8%	3%
Traffic violation	6	2
Income tax	9	7
Police interference	7	3
N	(383)	(1,042)

Table 2.24 presents some unanticipated results in that the college
educated group reports the greatest relative incidence of problems
with different constraint agencies. This is largely a matter of the
complexity of income tax requirements for higher income groups.

Table 2.24

Relation of Education to Problems
with Four Constraint Agencies

	Years of Education		
Problem	Fewer than 12	High school diploma	Some college
Driver's license	4%	4%	6%
Traffic violation	3	3	4
Income tax	3	6	12
Police interference	4	4	4
N	(509)	(487)	(423)

Table 2.25 shows the same tendency with respect to income tax problems in that white collar workers have proportionately more difficulties than blue collar workers. Blue collar workers, on the other hand, report more encounters with police over matters of individual rights.

Table 2.25

Relation of Occupation to Problems
with Four Constraint Agencies

Problem	Occupation	
	White Collar	Blue Collar
Driver's license	4%	5%
Traffic violation	3	3
Income tax	9	4
Police interference	3	7
N	(515)	(554)

Income categories (Table 2.26) provide mixed results with the under $5,000 group reporting proportionately more traffic violation problems and fewer driver's license problems. The over $10,000 group reports slightly more tax problems. There are no differences among income groups in frequency of difficulties with police.

Table 2.26

Relation of Income to Problems
with Four Constraint Agencies

Problem	Income Group		
	Under $5,000	$5,000-9,999	Over $10,000
Driver's license	3%	5%	5%
Traffic violation	5	4	2
Income tax	6	6	8
Police interference	4	4	4
N	(325)	(364)	(680)

Table 2.27 shows the distribution of respondents in four work categories. The unemployed report relatively more trouble with police than do people in other working categories. Table 2.28 provides evidence that proportionately more problems with constraint agencies are perceived in the West and the least in the South.

Table 2.27

Relation of Working Status to Problems
with Four Constraint Agencies

	Work Status			
Problem	Working	Unemployed	Retired/ Permanently Disabled	Other
Driver's license	5%	6%	2%	4%
Traffic violation	4	5	1	2
Income tax	7	6	9	6
Police interference	5	9	2	1
N	(836)	(64)	(185)	(342)

Table 2.28

Relation of Geographic Region to Problems
with Four Constraint Agencies

	Geographic Region			
Problem	West	North Central	Northeast	South
Driver's license	6%	4%	5%	3%
Traffic violation	4	2	5	3
Income tax	11	7	5	4
Police interference	8	2	4	3
N	(255)	(421)	(315)	(438)

There are a number of speculations that can be made about the data on constraint agency contacts. In general, the results do not support the notion that out-groups (poor, blacks, uneducated, young, etc.) have more problems with constraint agencies. It should be noted, however, that the definition of "problem" is very subjective in the present analysis. The question asked of respondents was: "Have you had or are you having any *difficulties* or *problems* with government offices or officials about any of the following matters?" Whether or not standing in line for two hours to get a driver's license renewed is defined as a problem may be a function of such variables as amount of education and income level. If a person is used to waiting for caseworkers in welfare offices or for surplus food, or used to being stopped by police as looking suspicious (i.e., young, long-haired, black, etc.), it is possible that one would define a problem differently from the person who is used to receiving prompt and courteous service.

Collective Importance of Background Characteristics in Determining Constraint Agency Problems

Table 2.29 shows the results of a Multiple Classification Analysis which utilizes the previously considered nine independent variables to

Table 2.29

Partial and First Order Correlations Between
Demographic Characteristics and Difficulties
with Control Agencies

Predictor	Eta	Eta²	Beta	Beta²
Region	.098	.009	.051	.003
Sex	.145	.021	.130	.017
Age	.202	.041	.162	.026
Work status	.107	.015	.082	.007
Ethnicity	.092	.008	.072	.005
Education	.167	.028	.095	.009
Occupation	.116	.014	.062	.004
Income	.130	.017	.088	.008
Political party	.166	.028	.130	.017

Multiple R = .34 (population estimate = .28)
Variance explained (R^2) = 11.8% (population estimate = 8.0%)

Note: MCA can be utilized when the dependent variable is dichotomous. It is suggested, however, that the distribution be no greater than 80%-20%. In the present analysis, the proportion in the two groups is closer to 15% and 85%. Therefore, the results should be viewed with caution.

predict whether or not the respondent has had a problem with a constraint agency. Demographic factors predict constraint problems less well than they do service experiences. It is possible, however, that the results are depressed by the very skewed distribution of the dependent variable. Approximately 85 percent of the sample did not report any problems with constraint agencies. Age is the best predictor, either considered alone, or taken into account with the other eight predictors. The amount of variance explained by all nine predictors collectively is less than 12 percent.

TOTAL ENCOUNTERS WITH PUBLIC OFFICES

If we examine the background characteristics of all types of contact with government agencies (see Appendix C, Tables C.1-C.8), we find that the person having no encounters with either service or control offices is likely to be (1) female rather than male, (2) white rather than black, (3) a student or housewife rather than an employed person, (4) a white collar rather than a blue collar worker, (5) a comparatively high income rather than low income person, (6) a well-educated rather than a poorly educated person, and (7) a person residing in the South rather than the West. These differences, though statistically significant, are not of a high order of magnitude.

Age as a correlate of bureaucratic encounters gives a more mixed pattern. The youngest age category (18 to 20) shows a low incidence of contact with public office; the group over 60, a heavy incidence of contact; but the age group from 50 to 59 shows relatively little experience with government offices. The reasons for this pattern are not obvious.

The elderly are more likely to report only a service agency contact but no problems with constraint agencies. Whereas almost three out of four of those over 70 have had exclusively service agency contacts, one in five of the 18-20 year olds have had only service agency contacts. The poor are also more likely to have only service agency contacts—71 percent of those individuals with family incomes less than $3,000 as compared to less than 20 percent of those earning more than $20,000 yearly. The person with service agency experience is also more likely to be retired or permanently disabled, black, have a relatively low level of educational attainment, and a blue collar job.

Individuals with both a service and constraint experience are more likely to be young, unemployed males. They are not necessarily high school dropouts, however. Individuals with either academic or non-academic training beyond high school are more apt to report both service and constraint experiences. It is also interesting that blacks are less likely to report both types of experiences than whites or other non-whites.

Individuals who report only constraint experiences do not fall into a stereotyped pattern. They are more likely to be young, from the western states, have at least some college, and have over $20,000 a year in family income. Working status, race, and sex do not differentiate these persons well. One possible explanation is in the differences among the types of control agencies, which result in a range from income tax problems affecting the more affluent to police problems affecting the younger age group.

NON-USERS

Another perspective on the problem of utilization of public agencies has to do with non-users. How great is the discrepancy between expressed need and actual use? Who are the non-users and why did they not avail themselves of government services? How much of this failure is due to a lack of knowledge? And why did the knowledgeable people refuse to seek the help of an agency?

Overall, about a third of the people with a problem do not avail themselves of relevant government services (Table 2.30). There is a

Table 2.30

Utilization of Various Types of Public Agencies Related
to Knowledge about Agencies

	I. Total Sample			II. Sub-Sample		
	(A)	(B)	(C)	(D)	(E)	(F)
		Percent	Percent	Problem-people	Problem-people	Problem-people
	Percent	with problem	with	not using	Problem-people	knowing about
	using	not using	problem	agency	not knowing	agency but not
Problem	service	service	(A+B)	(B/C)	agency exists	using it
Finding a job	23.8%	9.3%	33.1%	29%	28%	72%
Job training	8.9	21.4	30.3	70	46	54
Workmen's compensation	7.6	5.3	12.9	41	49	51
Unemployment compensation	25.6	2.1	27.2	6	27	73
Public assistance	11.9	0.3	12.2	2	-	-
Hospital/ medical care	5.9	1.6	7.5	26	55	45
Retirement benefits	14.5	4.1	18.6	22	36	64
N	(1,431)	(1,431)	(1,431)			

great deal of variation, however, in that some 70 percent of those wanting job training did not seek government help; whereas only 2 percent of those needing public assistance failed to go to a public agency. And only 6 percent of those in need of unemployment compensation failed to contact a government office.

The urgency of the problem could be the simplest explanation of the differential use of government agencies. It could account for the almost complete utilization of public service for welfare and unemployment compensation in contrast to the very poor use of government agencies for job training or retraining. But the immediacy of the problem is only one factor.

There is also a high probability that some of those in need of monetary assistance report their need as one only for a job or job training. Hence our figures showing almost complete coverage of those needing public assistance may suffer from the way in which people report their needs.

As many as 26 percent of the people with medical and hospital needs did not go to a public office for help. They may not have been aware of recent legal changes that provide financial benefits as in the Medicaid program. Our findings show, in fact, that 55 percent of the non-users with medical problems did not know there was a government agency to which they could go. Lack of knowledge of the existence of an appropriate agency is also high for non-users in the areas of job training and workmen's compensation.

It could be argued that poor motivation is responsible for lack of knowledge with respect to job training, but the same argument does not hold for medical problems. Bureaucratic complexity, program inadequacies, and changing rules may be of major importance in accounting for non-utilization. There are the stubborn facts that, in spite of continuing publicity about social security benefits, some 28 percent of retirees do not seek government help, and of this number about a third do not know that an appropriate office exists. It should be noted that workmen's compensation is a special case in that the high percentage of non-users (41 percent) may be due to the lack of visibility of the role of the government for this service. Workmen's compensation is processed by private companies or state agencies under government guidelines.

As far as felt need is concerned, adult Americans expressed a far greater need for job finding and training (911 responses) than they did for welfare services (281 responses for public assistance or hospital and medical care). A program such as the Nixon Administration's Family Assistance Plan, in which the emphasis is on job training and job finding in an effort to reduce welfare roles, receives support from the people in need, as well as from politicians. However, lack of available jobs was cited by both Schiller (1973) and Mildred Rein (1972) as problematic for poor Americans. Evidence for laziness and disinterest in self-support is lacking in the present data. On the contrary, respondents have expressed a need for services which will enable them to be more self-sufficient.

It is interesting that 28 percent of those who are retired or expressed a need for retirement benefits are not receiving such benefits. This number may be reduced in the coming years as recent changes in the Social Security Act have incorporated new groups, such as non-profit organization employees and domestic workers, into the program.

Those knowledgeable individuals who had a problem but did not seek help from the agency were asked why not. In general, the reasons given were pragmatic and did not indicate negativism toward public bureaucracies. The dominant responses for all categories except job training were that the problem was somehow taken care of; e.g., the respondent decided to do something else, or the problem was solved by the respondent's own efforts or the efforts of another individual, such as spouse, child, neighbor, or boss.

For those for whom the problem remained, the reasons for not using the government agency were more often practical than ideological. More people said there was no available local agency, or it lacked the specific program they needed, than complained about the character of bureaucracy in general. Only 12 people out of 361 respondents said agencies were useless and wasteful, and only two refused to go because the government office was seen as discriminatory. Not a single person volunteered the reason that the agency personnel were rude or that the government pried too much. Ten people, however, did say that they did not go because they preferred a private agency, and another 11 just weren't interested in going to a public office.

For job training, the reasons for not utilizing government agencies ranged over a wide number of categories. Of the 160 knowledgeable non-users, 31 (19 percent) solved the problem themselves or through the help of a friend or relative. Another 25 (16 percent) felt they did not need the assistance of a public agency. But 20 respondents (13 percent) thought there was no provision in the program for people like them, and another 18 percent stated there was no local agency or that it was difficult for them to get to it. Failure to make contact with public agencies for job training, then, is not just a matter of clinging to the doctrine of individualism. For many people, training facilities appropriate to their needs are either not to be found in the public sector or there is no agency in their own community readily available to them. Their perceptions are in good part correct in that training programs are largely for blue collar positions rather than technical and professional ones.

Table 2.10 showed that job training has been utilized more by individuals with at least a high school diploma than their less educated counterparts. There seems to be a relatively high demand for job training by individuals who are already comparatively well educated. Some of these individuals find, to their disappointment, that job training programs are generally aimed at the least skilled or unskilled. For problems other than job training, non-users of government services who know about appropriate agencies do not turn away from these agencies because of negative feelings about them. Rather, it is a matter of trying other solutions first and turning to government offices as a last resort.

It is theoretically possible to express a need for all seven service areas under study and yet not utilize the services of any agency. Only 11 individuals, however, reported failure to use needed services for three or more of these areas. Tables 2.31 and 2.32 show that proportionately more males than females, and more blacks than whites, did not avail themselves of the services of government agencies for their problems, although males and blacks are both heavier utilizers of services than females or whites. The very young (18-20), more than any other age group, express a need for available services which they

Table 2.31

Relation of Sex to Failure to Utilize Agency for Seven
Service Areas

Discrepancy	Sex	
	Male	Female
No discrepancy between perceived need and utilization	63%	68%
Discrepancy in one service area between perceived need and utilization	27	25
Discrepancy in two or more service areas between perceived need and utilization	10	7
Total	100%	100%
N	(611)	(820)

Table 2.32

Relation of Race to Failure to Utilize Agency for Seven
Service Areas

Discrepancy	Race		
	White	Black	Other
No discrepancy between perceived need and utilization	67%	53%	72%
Discrepancy in one service area between perceived need and utilization	25	37	19
Discrepancy in two or or more service areas between perceived need and utilization	8	10	9
Total	100%	100%	100%
N	(1,246)	(126)	(57)

do not utilize (Table 2.33). It may be that the nature of the problem is significant here. To find a job and get job training are relatively high among the problems of the young, and these two areas are ones in which public agencies are the least successful and definitely not as well utilized. It should also be noted that a significant number of respondents aged 60 to 69 do not turn to public agencies for two or more of their problems.

Table 2.33

Relation of Age to Failure to Utilize Agency for Seven
Service Areas

Discrepancy	Age Group							
	18-20	21-24	25-29	30-39	40-49	50-59	60-69	70+
No discrepancy between perceived need and utilization	55%	71%	61%	61%	68%	71%	66%	69%
Discrepancy in one service area between perceived need and utilization	31 24	30	32	24	21	21	24	
Discrepancy in two or more service areas between perceived need and utilization	14	5	9	7	8	8	13	6
Total	100%	100%	100%	100%	100%	100%	100%	100%
N	(71)	(132)	(180)	(268)	(230)	(214)	(199)	(135)

It is not the poorly educated who show a discrepancy between perceived need for services and utilization of public agencies, but rather the group with a high school diploma and some non-academic training in which the discrepancy is most apparent (Table 2.34). It is also not the poorest group who report the greatest lack of utilization of public services, but the people in the $7,500 to $12,500 income brackets (Table 2.35). These findings suggest that relative rather'than

Table 2.34

Relation of Education to Failure to Utilize Agency for
Seven Service Areas

Discrepancy	Years of Education					
	Fewer than 8	8-11	12	12 + non-academic	1-3 college	B.A. or more
No discrepancy between perceived need and utilization	69%	65%	66%	54%	66%	75%
Discrepancy in one service area between perceived need and utilization	24	28	26	34	25	18
Discrepancy in two or more service areas between perceived need and utilization	8	7	8	12	9	7
Total	100%	100%	100%	100%	100%	100%
N	(277)	(234)	(291)	(198)	(261)	(163)

absolute deprivation may be operating to make the unmet needs for public services higher among the middle groups than among the

Table 2.35

Relation of Income to Failure to Utilize Agency for
Seven Service Areas

Discrepancy	Income Group							
	0-$2,999	$3,000 -4,999	$5,000 -7,499	$7,500 -9,999	$10,000 -12,499	$12,500 -14,999	$15,000 -19,999	$20,000 +
No discrepancy	70%	67%	66%	60%	62%	65%	65%	71%
Single discrepancy	20	25	28	29	32	27	25	18
Discrepancy of two or more	10	8	7	11	6	8	10	11
Total	100%	100%	100%	100%	100%	100%	100%	100%
N	(172)	(155)	(179)	(185)	(203)	(155)	(157)	(166)

poorly educated and low-income classes. There is some confirmation of this tendency among occupational groups in that craftsmen head the list in relative degree of needs for which agencies are not utilized (Table 2.36).

Table 2.36

Relation of Occupation to Failure to Utilize Agency for
Seven Service Areas

Discrepancy	Occupation						
	Professional & Technical	Managerial	Clerical & Sales	Skilled	Semi-skilled	Laborers	Farmers
No discrepancy	71%	61%	62%	55%	63%	58%	79%
Single discrepancy	23	27	28	34	28	32	21
Discrepancy of two or more	6	12	10	11	9	10	0
Total	100%	100%	100%	100%	100%	100%	100%
N	(158)	(74)	(284)	(149)	(193)	(186)	(28)

Working categories do not show substantial differences in failure to use public services save for the grouping which includes students and housewives (Table 2.37). This heterogeneous category is understandably low in discrepancy between need and utilization of government agencies. Geographic regions do not differ in non-utilization of public services for various problems (Table 2.38).

Table 2.37

Relation of Work Categories to Failure to Utilize
Agency for Seven Service Areas

Discrepancy	Work Status			
	Working	Unemployed	Retired/Permanently Disabled	Other
No discrepancy	63%	62%	58%	76%
Single discrepancy	28	30	30	18
Discrepancy of two or more	9	8	12	6
Total	100%	100%	100%	100%
N	(839)	(64)	(185)	(343)

Table 2.38

Relation of Geographic Region to Failure to Utilize
Agency for Seven Service Areas

| Discrepancy | Geographic Region | | | |
	West	North Central	Northeast	South
No discrepancy	65%	68%	63%	66%
Single discrepancy	29	22	29	27
Discrepancy of two or more	6	11	9	7
Total	100%	100%	100%	100%
N	(255)	(423)	(315)	(438)

KNOWLEDGE OF THE EXISTENCE OF SERVICE AGENCIES

As has already been indicated, part of the failure to utilize government services is due to ignorance concerning their existence. We will look at this problem more systematically on the basis of the answers to the question: "Is there a government office which helps in such matters?" This was asked for each type of service, both for people with a problem who had not contacted an agency and for people not having a problem. Knowledge that there is an appropriate public agency is very high across the nation for three of the seven service areas, namely, unemployment compensation, public assistance, and retirement (Table 2.39). But with respect to job training, four out of ten people do not know whether there is a government office to go to (or believe no such office exists), and three out of ten are similarly uninformed about hospital and medical services and about workmen's compensation.

People with problems of a given type are naturally more knowledgeable about the existence of relevant public agencies. In the area of job training, however, the difference between those expressing a need for training and those with no need is slight. Sixty-seven percent of the problem group know and 62 percent of the no-problem group know (Table 2.39). Although in an absolute sense the degree of knowledge among the problem people in other service areas is widespread, it leaves something to be desired when 11 percent of the population with medical and hospital needs do not even know if there is a public agency to which they can turn.

Table 2.39

Knowledge of Existence of Agency

Problem	Total sample who know	No-problem people who know*	Problem people who know**	Problem people not using service who know
Finding a job	82%	78%	93%	72%
Job training	59	62	67	54
Workmen's compensation	68	67	81	51
Unemployment compensation	91	89	98	73
Public assistance	91	91	100	-
Hospital/medical care	70	69	89	45
Retirement benefits	88	88	94	64

*These percentages may be inflated; people were only asked if a government agency was available rather than the name of the agency.
**Over 90% of respondents who said they tried for government help were able to name the agency contacted.

In an attempt to discover what sorts of people are knowledgeable about public agencies, the responses of the total sample to the knowledge questions were merged. Overall, women are relatively less knowledgeable of the presence of service organizations than are men (Table 2.40). There is very little difference between the sexes in knowledge about public assistance or hospital and medical benefits.

Table 2.40

Relation of Sex to Lack of Knowledge of Existence of Appropriate Agency

Problem	Sex	
	Male	Female
Finding a job	12.2%	20.0%
Job training	26.0	42.9
Workmen's compensation	22.7	36.3
Unemployment compensation	5.4	10.7
Public assistance	7.4	7.7
Hospital/medical care	27.0	30.1
Retirement benefits	8.0	13.3
N	(611)	(820)

Blacks, in larger proportion than whites, know about public assistance and hospital and medical benefits (Table 2.41). Whites are relatively more knowledgeable about most other services. It is interesting that although blacks are more likely than whites to receive job training services, they are less likely to realize that such government services exist.

Table 2.41

Relation of Race to Lack of Knowledge of Existence of
Appropriate Agency

Problem	Race		
	White	Black	Other
Finding a job	16.8%	15.8%	15.7%
Job training	34.6	45.2	40.3
Workmen's compensation	30.0	38.0	26.3
Unemployment compensation	7.3	15.9	15.8
Public assistance	7.5	4.8	15.8
Hospital/medical care	29.5	24.6	21.0
Retirement benefits	10.0	22.2	8.7
N	(1,246)	(126)	(57)

The youngest and oldest age categories are the least knowledgeable about three of the seven government services studied: job training, workmen's compensation, and unemployment compensation (Table 2.42). For finding a job, there is a negative relationship between age and knowledge if the 18 to 20 year olds are excluded.

There is a substantial difference in knowledge between those respondents with fewer than eight years of education and those with a bachelor's degree or more in all areas except hospital and medical benefits (Table 2.43). It is worthy of note that all of the respondents with a B.A. or more are aware of public assistance, whereas over 10 percent of those with less than a high school diploma are not. Some 50 percent of respondents with less than eight years of education are unaware of job training services; almost 40 percent are unaware of workmen's compensation; and over 30 percent are unaware of job-finding facilities. Overall, the expected correlation appears between education and knowledge of the existence of appropriate agencies. The discouraging aspect is that those most in need are those who are the least likely to know where to go for help.

Table 2.42

Relation of Age to Lack of Knowledge of Existence of
Appropriate Agency

Problem	Age Group							
	18-20	21-24	25-29	30-39	40-49	50-59	60-69	70+
Finding a job	15.5%	8.3%	10.6%	13.4%	16.9%	17.3%	21.6%	31.8%
Job training	47.9	32.6	28.9	28.7	34.8	37.4	42.7	43.7
Workmen's compensation	45.0	26.5	32.7	26.9	27.8	26.2	32.7	40.0
Unemployment compensation	14.1	3.9	8.9	5.6	7.4	4.7	11.1	19.3
Public assistance	8.5	8.3	9.3	6.0	5.7	6.1	8.5	16.3
Hospital/ medical care	31.0	28.0	28.9	28.0	29.6	31.8	26.6	27.4
Retirement benefits	16.9	9.1	11.7	9.7	13.9	11.7	7.0	11.9
N	(71)	(132)	(180)	(268)	(230)	(214)	(199)	(135)

Table 2.43

Relation of Education to Lack of Knowledge of
Existence of Appropriate Agency

Problem	Years of Education					
	Fewer than 8	9-11	12	12+ non-academic	1-3 college	B.A. or more
Finding a job	30.7%	20.0%	15.5%	11.6%	7.3%	11.0%
Job training	49.0	38.9	40.5	30.3	26.8	20.9
Workmen's compensation	39.4	32.9	34.4	30.3	22.6	18.4
Unemployment compensation	17.0	10.7	6.9	3.5	4.2	6.1
Public assistance	10.1	11.5	7.2	9.1	4.6	0.0
Hospital/ medical care	26.0	33.8	28.1	30.0	28.0	27.6
Retirement benefits	12.6	12.4	11.0	10.6	10.0	8.6
N	(277)	(234)	(291)	(198)	(261)	(163)

Occupation is less clearly related to knowledge. Although the sample only includes 28 farmers, Table 2.44 shows that farmers generally tend to lack knowledge of government services except retirement benefits. Since farmers pay their own social security, it is not surprising that those who are participating in the program would be aware of the services.

Table 2.44

Relation of Occupation to Lack of Knowledge of
Existence of Appropriate Agency

	Occupation						
Problem	Professional & Technical	Managerial	Clerical & Sales	Skilled	Semi-skilled	Laborers	Farmers
Finding a job	10.7%	8.1%	16.5%	12.1%	19.2%	16.1%	39.3%
Job training	21.5	22.9	39.4	28.1	36.8	40.8	42.9
Workmen's compensation	19.6	18.9	26.1	26.2	26.9	37.1	39.3
Unemployment compensation	6.3	4.0	6.0	4.4	6.3	9.1	21.4
Public assistance	1.3	4.1	8.5	6.7	9.3	5.4	17.9
Hospital/ medical care	25.3	17.6	25.3	33.6	33.2	27.4	32.1
Retirement benefits	8.2	5.4	10.2	10.7	10.4	10.2	7.1
N	(158)	(74)	(284)	(149)	(193)	(186)	(28)

Attention should be drawn to the large number of unskilled (41 percent) and semi-skilled (37 percent) workers who do not know about job training opportunities. The unskilled are also poor in knowledge of workmen's compensation. They are in jobs which pay poorly and are often hazardous compared to jobs held by skilled workers who benefit from unionization. Again the people most in need of services are the least knowledgeable about available public agencies.

Higher income is associated with more knowledge. Respondents whose annual family income is more than $20,000 were more knowledgeable in all areas except hospital and medical benefits compared to those whose family income is less than $3,000 (Table 2.45). This relationship is probably a function of education, but again the most needy, those with the lowest family incomes, are more likely to lack information on appropriate government agencies.

Table 2.45

Relation of Income to Lack of Knowledge of Existence
of Appropriate Agency

Problem	Income Group							
	0- $2,999	$3,000 -4,999	$5,000 -7,499	$7,500 -9,999	$10,000 -12,499	$12,500 -14,999	$15,000 -19,999	$20,000+
Finding a job	22.6%	21.3%	17.3%	15.6%	11.8%	16.1%	12.7%	12.0%
Job training	44.8	44.5	37.4	36.8	30.0	33.5	29.3	27.1
Workmen's compensation	40.7	38.7	32.4	29.2	28.6	30.6	18.5	23.5
Unemployment compensation	19.1	11.6	6.7	8.1	4.9	2.5	8.3	5.4
Public assistance	7.5	12.3	7.8	11.3	9.7	3.2	5.7	4.2
Hospital/ medical care	23.8	24.5	29.6	38.4	31.5	27.1	25.5	25.3
Retirement benefits	15.7	14.2	14.5	8.1	10.3	7.7	6.4	9.0
N	(172)	(155)	(179)	(185)	(203)	(155)	(157)	(166)

Housewives and students generally are relatively low utilizers of
government services; they also lack knowledge of services as Table
2.46 demonstrates. They have relatively less knowledge in all areas
than those who are in the labor force. The unemployed are relatively

Table 2.46

Relation of Work Category to Lack of Knowledge of
Existence of Appropriate Agency

Problem	Work Status			
	Working	Unemployed	Retired/ Permanently Disabled	Other
Finding a job	13.8%	12.5%	24.8%	20.0%
Job training	31.7	37.5	43.2	41.4
Workmen's compensation	25.0	37.5	33.0	41.3
Unemployment compensation	4.5	12.5	15.1	13.7
Public assistance	5.6	3.1	13.0	10.2
Hospital/medical care	28.6	25.0	24.3	32.4
Retirement benefits	8.9	20.3	11.3	14.3
N	(830)	(64)	(185)	(343)

aware of public assistance but 13 percent are not aware of job-finding services and 38 percent lack knowledge of job training. It is also worthy of note that some 11 percent of the retired and permanently disabled are not aware of social security or other retirement benefits.

Table 2.47 shows that, in general, people in western states are more knowledgeable than those in other parts of the country. They are particularly more likely to know about workmen's compensation than respondents from the rest of the country.

Table 2.47

Relation of Geographical Region to Lack of Knowledge
of Existence of Appropriate Agency

	Geographic Region			
Problem	West	North Central	Northeast	South
Finding a job	11.0%	21.7%	14.0%	17.1%
Job training	35.2	35.9	37.7	34.2
Workmen's compensation	17.6	36.1	30.4	32.6
Unemployment compensation	7.5	10.6	7.0	8.0
Public assistance	5.0	9.7	7.0	7.3
Hospital/medical care	27.1	32.1	35.2	21.9
Retirement benefits	6.7	10.4	13.7	12.3
N	(255)	(423)	(315)	(438)

In general, knowledge of hospital and medical benefits did not follow the pattern of knowledge of other services. It is possible that the relative newness of Medicare and Medicaid accounts in part for this divergence. Those who were eligible for either were so informed by the social security or welfare offices, but there has been relatively little publicity urging people to see if they are eligible for either of these benefits.

The data in Tables 2.40-2.46 suggest that for some services, such as job training, the greater the need, the less likely are people to know about available agencies, whereas for other services eligibility or potential eligibility means greater knowledge. First of all, it is not surprising that those respondents who are not in the labor force and have low levels of income and education are most likely to lack information about government services. They are the same people who generally lack knowledge in many areas, from the state of the economy to the names of their state senators. That these people are the most needy probably goes without saying. Our data would indicate that more effort should be expended in order to inform this segment of the society of the services available to them.

On the other hand, there is also evidence that user groups are likely to be informed about the agency. For example, males who are heavier utilizers than females are more likely to know about all seven service areas. Those respondents who are in the labor force are more likely than non-workers to know about unemployment compensation, workmen's compensation, and job-training services, which are all relevant to working people. And younger persons are more likely to know about employment services than are their elders. It seems probable that people learn about work-related benefits when they start a job and that job-locating offices at schools and colleges also inform potential users of benefits available.

SUMMARY

1. There is conspicuous underutilization of government services. On the average, about one-third of the people with problems for which government agencies provide help do not go to public offices.

2. Of the government programs studied, job training and employment services are the least utilized in relation to need, and unemployment compensation and public assistance are the most utilized in relation to need.

3. Lack of knowledge of the agency or the available program is the most important single reason for underutilization. For those who know of the existence of programs, the practical problems of getting to the appropriate office are more important than any negative feelings about public bureaucracy.

4. Knowledge of government services among the total sample ranged from 59 percent for job training to 91 percent for unemployment compensation and public assistance.

5. In spite of considerable lack of utilization in relation to need, government services are used by 58 percent of the national sample. The services most frequently patronized are unemployment compensation and employment services.

6. There is considerable variation in the types of services utilized within demographic categories. For example, although blacks are proportionately more likely than whites to utilize job-finding and job-training services, and public assistance, whites are more likely to utilize social security, retirement, and workmen's compensation. Young people are more likely to utilize job-training and job-finding services, whereas the elderly receive social security. This trend even

applies to income categories. While the poor are more likely to be recipients of public assistance and hospital or medical benefits, the higher income groups are not less likely than the poor to utilize unemployment insurance, workmen's compensation, job-finding, or job-training services, for example.

7. These findings suggest that the present system of social services does not involve a redistribution of wealth to the poor or uneducated. Rather, services are provided for various constituencies such as the unemployed or retired. The increased sophistication that comes with higher education and its concomitant, higher income, has enabled middle class persons to take advantage of services which are provided. On the other hand, structural considerations have also aided the middle and working classes. For example, only people who have been employed at a regular job are eligible for workmen's compensation, unemployment compensation, or social security retirement benefits. (In the case of social security, the widow or widower is also entitled to benefits.) Unionization is another structural factor which has helped.

8. Fifteen percent of our respondents reported difficulties in encounters with control agencies in problems concerning income tax, vehicular licenses, traffic violations, and police interference. Income tax was mentioned by 6.4 percent of the sample and traffic violations by 3.1 percent.

9. The most important determinant of problems with control agencies was age. People under 30 were more likely to report difficulties for all four types of constraint experiences than people over 30. Race, however, made no difference, and the percentage of blacks was almost exactly the same as the percentage of whites in encountering problems with officials. Women reported proportionately fewer such encounters than men.

Chapter 3

EVALUATION

In addition to questions about various aspects of their experiences on the occasion of their last contact with a service agency, people were asked directly about how satisfied they were with the way the office handled their problem. About two-thirds expressed satisfaction rather than dissatisfaction (Table 3.1), and almost half fell in the extreme category of *very satisfied* (43 percent). Only 14 percent took the opposite extreme, *very dissatisfied*. These figures seem, at first glance, to be impressive evidence of the effective functioning of public service agencies. This might be all the more true in that some of the dissatisfaction may be generated by the nature of the problem rather than by the way the public office handled it. Our question was directed solely at the latter issue, but not all individuals with problems make nice distinctions between the initial complaint and the difficulty of getting help, nor for that matter are such logical discriminations always possible in the pragmatic situation. The overall figures on satisfaction, however, can be interpreted more negatively in that the standard for many agencies might well be considerably higher than a satisfied clientele of 69 percent. A helping agency and the larger organization of which it is a part, or the public it serves, might propose a much more ambitious standard of performance—that all clients shall be satisfied, or that in an imperfect world, 100 percent satisfaction is unreasonable, but 90 percent is not.

Such external standards are in part value judgments, and involve data not presently available. Another way of seeking a better basis of interpretation for these findings is to examine comparative satisfaction with various offices and reactions to different aspects of agency functioning.

The various services were given markedly different evaluations by the respondents they served. Social security headed the list with 88 percent of the clients satisfied with the way their retirement problems were handled. Obtaining medical and hospital care was at the

Table 3.1

*"How Satisfied Were You with the Way the Office
Handled Your Problem?"*

| | Type of Problem | | | | | | | | |
Rating	Finding job	Job training	Workmen's Compensation	Unemployment Compensation	Welfare	Hospital/medical	Retirement	Other	Total
Very satisfied	35.1%	50.9%	52.5%	35.2%	27.2%	48.9%	64.2%	41.9%	42.6%
Fairly well satisfied	26.3	22.6	22.5	35.8	34.0	8.9	23.7	14.5	25.9
Somewhat dissatisfied	15.8	18.9	5.0	13.6	18.4	24.4	3.5	11.3	12.6
Very dissatisfied	19.9	5.7	10.0	11.7	18.5	17.8	2.9	29.0	13.5
D. K.	0	0	0	.1	0	0	.6	1.6	0
N. A.	2.9	1.9	10.0	3.1	1.9	0	4.6	1.6	5.1
Total	100%	100%	100%	100%	100%	100%	100%	100%	100%
N	(171)	(53)	(40)	(162)	(103)	(45)	(173)	(62)	(827)

bottom, with only 58 percent giving positive responses. Public assistance and employment services were also not highly regarded relative to other agencies, with about a third of their clients expressing dissatisfaction. On the other hand, the handling of workmen's compensation was seen as satisfactory by 75 percent of the people, and job training and unemployment compensation were favorably regarded by about three-fourths of their clients. Respondents who had contacted agencies outside of the seven major service areas were included in the "other" category. Because of the extremely heterogeneous nature of the miscellaneous group, these "others" were excluded from the analysis.

There is probably an objective basis for the highly favorable evaluation of social security benefits and the poor evaluation of medical and hospital care services. Government services for obtaining medical and hospital care are the least utilized of all public services, and there is less knowledge of the existence of public agencies in this field than in any other. Social security offices probably have a simpler, or at least a better-defined problem; certainly they have a better-defined clientele, and they have made determined efforts to make contact with retirees. Moreover, they administer a clearer program, with specifications and criteria for entitlement which can be readily followed by their many offices.

In addition to the direct question on satisfaction, respondents were asked to describe their most important experience with a service agency. Answers to this question were coded on a number of dimensions including (1) whether the problem was solved, (2) how favorably the client evaluated the procedures by which a solution was attempted, and (3) how fair he considered his treatment. Not enough information was furnished to code all respondents on these dimensions, but the differences among agencies are nevertheless instructive.

On the average, 83 percent of the clients could be coded as to whether or not they believed their problems were solved by the appropriate public agency. About one-fifth thought their problems were not taken care of by the government office in question (Table 3.2). Overall, a reported failure rate of this order seems low if one considers the difficult nature of some of the problems and the limitations under which some agencies must operate. With the evaluation of public agencies already reported, it should be interpreted as evidence of a high level of effective functioning. The breakdown of solutions by type of service agency (Table 3.2) again shows the functioning of retirement agencies at the head of the list in popular assessment. Problem solving with respect to medical and hospital benefits was not as highly evaluated, nor were the solutions offered by welfare and job-training agencies. Government employment services result in the least favorable outcomes.

Table 3.2

Summary Evaluation of Solutions

				Type of Problem					
Solution Rating	Finding job	Job training	Workmen's Compensa- tion	Unemploy- ment Com- pensation	Welfare	Hospital/ medical	Retirement	Other	Total
Favorable	32.2%	54.7%	65.0%	67.3%	62.1%	57.7%	80.9%	38.7%	58.8%
Neutral	1.2	0	0	1.2	1.9	2.2	1.7	9.7	2.0
Unfavorable	45.0	26.4	20.0	7.4	17.5	24.4	8.1	40.3	22.1
N. A.	21.6	18.9	15.0	24.0	18.4	15.5	9.2	11.3	16.7
Total	100%	100%	100%	100%	100%	100%	100%	100%	100%
N	(171)	(53)	(40)	(162)	(103)	(45)	(173)	(62)	(809)

Services for finding a job and job training were rated as satisfactory by many more people than reported agency success in solving their problems. Thus some respondents did discriminate between how the agency handled their difficulties and whether their problems were really taken care of.

The second dimension coded from free answers was the evaluation by the client of procedures required by the agency (the papers to be filled out, appointments made, red tape tied or untied). Respondents could be coded as positive, negative, or netural about procedures in about half the cases. In general, most of the references to procedures were neutral in tone. The ratio of favorable to unfavorable responses varied considerably from agency to agency (Table 3.3). For retirement benefits, there were twice as many favorable as unfavorable attitudes toward procedures. For unemployment compensation and welfare, there were almost three times as many negative as positive evaluations. Medical and hospital services and employment agencies also had more negative than positive responses, about two to one. The three services which were rated lowest in the way in which they handled problems were again low in favorable attitudes toward their procedures (medical and hospital services, welfare, and employment services).

Table 3.3

Summary Evaluation of Procedures

	Type of Problem								
Procedure Rating	Finding job	Job training	Workmen's Compensation	Unemployment Compensation	Welfare	Hospital/ medical	Retirement	Other	Total
Favorable	6.4%	11.3%	5.0%	2.5%	7.7%	13.3%	11.6%	6.5%	7.5%
Neutral	26.3	22.6	35.0	37.0	17.5	13.3	35.3	22.6	28.4
Unfavorable	11.7	11.3	5.0	8.0	20.4	24.4	6.9	27.4	12.6
N. A.	55.5	54.7	55.0	52.5	54.4	48.9	46.2	43.5	51.4
Total	100%	100%	100%	100%	100%	100%	100%	100%	100%
N	(171)	(53)	(40)	(102)	(103)	(45)	(173)	(62)	(809)

Specific questions were raised about certain aspects of the client's experience. The client was asked, "Was it hard to find an office or official who could handle your problem?" On the average, only 12 percent reported difficulty in finding an appropriate office or official (Table 3.4). Five percent said this was true for retirement benefits, but 31 percent found this to be the case for medical and hospital services. Once again we find these two types of service at the top and bottom levels of positive-negative evaluation. Public assistance, moreover, is next to medical and hospital services in relative frequency of unfavorable responses. It would appear that the poor showing of these two services on satisfaction with the handling of problems is not so much the difficulty of the problems, as the policies which the agencies administer and the resultant treatment of people. Both job-finding and job-training services were viewed as less able to solve problems than welfare or medical and hospital services, but the former were given better marks than the latter on perceived difficulty of finding a responsible office or officer.

Table 3.4

"Was It Hard to Find an Office or Official Who Could Handle Your Problem?"

| | | | | Type of Problem | | | | | |
Response	Finding job	Job training	Workmen's Compensation	Unemployment Compensation	Welfare	Hospital/medical	Retirement	Other	Total
Yes	10.5%	13.2%	10.0%	8.6%	18.4%	31.1%	4.6%	27.4%	12.3%
No	86.0	84.9	85.0	87.6	78.6	68.9	90.2	71.0	82.6
D. K.	0	0	2.5	0	1.0	0	1.2	1.6	.7
N. A.	2.9	1.9	2.5	3.7	1.9	0	3.5	0	4.4
Total	100%	100%	100%	100%	100%	100%	100%	100%	100%
N	(171)	(53)	(40)	(162)	(103)	(45)	(173)	(62)	(827)

Similar results appeared in answer to the question of how much effort agency people made to help the client. Overall, some 57 percent thought agency people made about the right amount of effort; 16 percent responded *more than they had to;* 12 percent *less than they should have;* and 9 percent *no effort at all* (Table 3.5). These findings accord with the high incidence of people reporting satisfaction with the way the agency handled their problems. Only 20 percent were critical of the representative of bureaucracy with respect to his effort on their behalf. Retirement services are seen in a favorable light by most people with one out of four commending agency personnel for doing more than they had to. Only 1 percent said they made no effort at all, and 5 percent said they made less than they should have. In contrast, 18 percent saw agency people who deal with medical and hospital problems as making no effort at all, and 13 percent as doing less than they should have. But there were 20 percent who were more fortunate and reported *more than they had to.* Employment and welfare services are also relatively low in their perceived efforts to help people.

Table 3.5

"How Much Effort Did the People at the Office Make to Help You?"

	Type of Problem								
Rating	Finding job	Job training	Workmen's Compensation	Unemployment Compensation	Welfare	Hospital/medical	Retirement	Other	Total
More than had to	12.3%	24.5%	25.0%	4.3%	10.7%	20.0%	26.0%	24.2%	15.9%
About right	56.7	56.6	45.0	71.0	59.2	48.9	61.3	38.7	57.4
Less than should have	15.8	7.5	2.5	13.0	21.4	13.3	5.2	17.7	12.3
No effort at all	11.7	7.5	12.5	8.0	6.8	17.8	1.2	16.1	8.5
D. K.	.1	0	2.5	.6	0	0	.6	1.6	.7
N. A.	2.9	3.8	12.5	3.1	1.9	0	4.6	1.6	5.2
Total	100%	100%	100%	100%	100%	100%	100%	100%	100%
N	(171)	(53)	(40)	(162)	(103)	(45)	(173)	(62)	(827)

Respondents were also asked to evaluate the efficiency of the agency with which they had been dealing. On the average, about one in five regarded the agency as *inefficient,* and half of this number responded *very inefficient* (Table 3.6). This was more than countered

Table 3.6

"How Efficient Did You Think the Office Was in Handling Your Problem?"

	Type of Problem								
Rating	Finding job	Job training	Workmen's Compensation	Unemployment Compensation	Welfare	Hospital/medical	Retirement	Other	Total
Very efficient	31.0%	45.3%	50.0%	37.0%	32.0%	51.1%	67.1%	40.3%	42.9%
Fairly efficient	38.6	28.3	32.5	40.7	38.8	12.5	21.4	19.4	31.0
Rather inefficient	13.5	13.2	5.0	8.0	12.6	13.3	2.3	11.3	9.2
Very inefficient	13.5	9.4	5.0	9.3	13.6	22.2	2.3	22.6	10.5
D. K.	.6	0	0	1.2	0	2.2	.6	3.2	.8
N. A.	2.9	3.8	7.5	3.7	2.9	0	5.8	3.2	5.6
Total	100%	100%	100%	100%	100%	100%	100%	100%	100%
N	(171)	(53)	(40)	(162)	(103)	(45)	(173)	(62)	(827)

by 43 percent who said *very efficient,* and 31 percent *fairly efficient.* These findings are in marked contrast to the popular image of officials bucking responsibility back and forth in offices cluttered with red tape. Medical and hospital services are seen as inefficient by 36 percent of the people having contact with them. Welfare and unemployment services are next in inefficiency. Retirement services are rated by the overwhelming majority (89 percent) as either very efficient or fairly efficient.

A different basis of evaluation of agencies derives from perceived fairness of treatment. On the average, three out of four said they felt they were treated fairly (Table 3.7). Only 13 percent responded they were treated unfairly, a smaller number than those critical of the efficiency of the agency (20 percent). The highest incidence of feelings of unfairness is found among clients of medical and hospital services (29 percent) and of public assistance (23 percent), and the lowest incidence is for retirement benefits (5 percent) and workmen's compensation (5 percent).

Table 3.7

"Do You Feel You Were Treated Fairly or Unfairly by the Office?"

Rating	Type of Problem								
	Finding job	Job training	Workmen's Compensation	Unemployment Compensation	Welfare	Hospital/medical	Retirement	Other	Total
Fairly	75.4%	84.9%	85.0%	81.5%	67.0%	64.4%	87.3%	58.1%	75.9%
Mixed	7.6	1.9	2.5	6.2	5.8	4.4	2.3	1.6	4.6
Unfairly	11.7	7.5	5.0	7.4	23.3	28.9	4.6	30.6	12.5
D. K.	2.3	3.8	0	0	0	0	1.2	8.1	2.2
N. A.	2.9	1.9	7.5	3.1	1.9	2.2	4.0	1.6	4.8
Total	100%	100%	100%	100%	100%	100%	100%	100%	100%
N	(171)	(53)	(40)	(162)	(103)	(45)	(173)	(62)	(827)

Though few of our respondents felt they themselves were unfairly treated, a larger minority (24 percent) thought that some kinds of people get better treatment than others from the office with which they had contact (Table 3.8). As many as one-third of the agency clients could not say whether there was preferential treatment, and some 39 percent felt definitely there was not.

Table 3.8

"Do Some Kinds of People Get Better Treatment Than Others from This Office?"

				Type of Problem					
Response	Finding job	Job training	Workmen's Compensa-tion	Unemploy-ment Com-pensation	Welfare	Hospital/ medical	Retirement	Other	Total
Yes	32.7%	22.6%	17.5%	17.9%	39.8%	37.8%	7.5%	32.3%	24.1%
No	37.4	47.2	25.0	40.7	30.1	31.1	50.9	32.3	39.3
D. K.	26.3	28.3	50.0	38.3	28.2	28.9	37.0	32.3	33.5
N. A.	3.5	1.9	7.5	3.1	1.9	2.2	4.0	3.2	3.3
Total	100%	100%	100%	100%	100%	100%	100%	100%	100%
N	(171)	(53)	(40)	(162)	(103)	(45)	(173)	(62)	(809)

Those who did think there was such inequity in the service provided by the agency were asked to specify which groups get better treatment and which groups get worse treatment. Of the people who felt there was preferential treatment, some 13 percent would not or could not name groups being favored, and 17 percent would not or could not name kinds of people getting worse treatment (Table 3.9). There was no focused target of groups getting better treatment with the most popular categories cited as *blacks* and *people who know someone*. Each of these groups was mentioned by only 14 percent of the respondents who believed that preferential treatment exists. Clients were in no greater agreement in specifying groups getting worse treatment.

The data suggest that most Americans do not perceive the service agencies with which they have had contact as functioning in an inequitable fashion. Very few complain that they themselves were treated unfairly. Even when the question is at the level of preferential treatment in general, three out of four did not believe some groups get better treatment than others. And among the one-fourth who believe that some groups fare better than others, there is a wide scattering of responses with no indication of systematic bias. Though there is no deep widespread negative feeling against service agencies on grounds of fairness, two types of services have aroused resentment of sufficient strength to warrant consideration of changes in policies and procedures, namely agencies concerned with public assistance and hospital and medical help.

There is a general tendency, then, for people to be more critical at a general than at a personal level. They report more favorably

Table 3.9

"What Kinds of People Get Better Treatment? What Kinds Worse Treatment?"

Types of People	Treatment	
	Better	Worse
White	9.2%*	12.8%*
Black	13.8	9.7
Minority	7.7	3.6
Rich	7.7	0
Poor	2.6	11.8
Educated	5.6	0
Uneducated	0	6.2
Unskilled	0	4.1
People who know someone	13.8	0
People who know system	4.1	0
People with less serious problem	4.1	0
No groups specified	13.0	17.0

*Percentages based upon number of people who believe some groups get differential treatment.

about their own experiences than about the agency operation for all people. They are more negative about the objective aspects of agencies, such as efficiency, than they are about fairness of treatment which is a more personal dimension.

Another way of getting at the respondent's perception of government offices was through a question about the people manning those offices, e.g., "Are the people in the office pretty much people like you?" If the client sees the office staff as a group of officious bureaucrats, disinterested professionals, exploitive politicians, or hostile representatives of an antagonistic class or race, he should answer in the negative. In fact, negative responses were about 17 percent (Table 3.10) of the total for all agencies. Only welfare services climbed over this mark, with 26 percent of welfare clients not identifying with agency personnel. Though the majority of people may have an image of a public bureaucracy set apart from themselves, they perceive the office personnel as individuals much like themselves. Again we encounter a personal level of response in which people, when talking about their own experiences with public offices and their own encounters with service personnel, are positive in their reactions.

Table 3.10

*"Are the People in the Office Pretty Much
People Like You?"*

				Type of Problem					
Response	Finding job	Job training	Workmen's Compensation	Unemployment Compensation	Welfare	Hospital/ medical	Retirement	Other	Total
Yes	70.2%	67.9%	55.0%	72.2%	64.1%	66.7%	75.1%	71.0%	70.2%
No	18.7	11.3	12.5	17.9	26.2	17.8	11.0	17.7	16.9
D. K.	6.4	17.0	25.0	5.6	5.8	15.6	6.9	9.7	8.7
N. A.	4.7	3.8	7.5	4.3	3.9	0	6.4	1.6	4.4
Total	100%	100%	100%	100%	100%	100%	100%	100%	100%
N	(171)	(53)	(40)	(162)	(103)	(45)	(173)	(62)	(809)

Those who saw the agency people as very much like themselves were asked, "In what ways are they like you?" The salient characteristics for agency clients were not group categories like race, religion, sex, or age, but personal attributes like friendliness, helpfulness, understanding, honesty (Table 3.11). Some 30 percent talked about one or more of these personality qualities, and only a total of 5 percent mentioned social class or income. Twenty-four percent, however, said just average, ordinary, common people; in similar fashion, 13 percent thought of agency people as workers like themselves ("they work too") and 7 percent as employees just doing their job. Identification with office personnel is not only the common response, but it is based upon perceived likeness of personal traits and of commonality of ordinary people working for a living.

Those who felt agency staff were not "people like themselves" were asked, "In what ways are they different?" There was no widely agreed upon perception of differences; a clear popular image of a bureaucracy set apart from its constituents is definitely missing at the level of personal experiences with service agencies. Again there was no heavy attribution of group characteristics, though this time 19 percent utilized age, race, or sex to make a distinction between themselves and agency personnel, with age as the most important of the three (Table 3.11). Another 7 percent mentioned income or social class. Sixteen percent spoke of the education, training, and skills of the agency personnel, and 6 percent mentioned their intelligence and

Table 3.11

"In What Ways Are They Like You?
In What Ways Different?"

	Comparisons and Contrasts	
Individual's Characteristics	Like You	Different from You
Race	2.4%	6.3%
Age	1.6	11.2
Sex	1.0	1.4
Marital status	0.7	0.7
Income	1.7	5.6
Social class	3.3	1.4
Education, skills	2.4	16.1
Intelligence	0.9	5.6
Values	5.8	4.2
Personality	24.4	21.7
Occupation	2.1	4.2
Working status	13.4	7.7
Neighborhood	1.6	0
Life style	2.3	2.1
Just doing their job	6.6	0
Average, ordinary people	24.1	0
D. K.	2.8	0.7
N	(573)	(143)

competence. Twenty-six percent saw the differences as due to other personal characteristics such as laziness or rudeness. Thus, even those who fail to identify with agency people are not in agreement about the qualities which distinguish client from bureaucrat. Nor are all attributions of differences unfavorable to the personnel of public offices, e. g., the skills, training, and competence of agency people. In spite of stereotyped conceptions of bureaucracy to be discussed in the next chapter, there is little evidence of social distance between the people being served and the people administering the services, at least from the point of view of clients. They regard agency people as fair in treating clients, as handling problems in a satisfactory fashion, and as being much like themselves in trying to do a job.

Still another appraisal of a bureaucratic office comes from people's beliefs about the possibility of recourse from their treatment at lower levels in the system. Accordingly clients were asked, "Was there someone at a higher level in the office to whom you could appeal for help if things were not working out all right?'' The modal response was in the affirmative, 47 percent overall, and only 14 percent felt there was no appeal within the agency (Table 3.12). But a large minority did not know whether there was a higher official to whom they could turn. Medical and hospital services, job training, and welfare were the agencies highest in incidence of belief about lack of appeal, as expressed by about one out of five of these clients. One reason why so many people do not know about making an appeal (some 37 percent of the clients) is that their satisfaction with agency services created no cause for appeal.

Table 3.12

"Was There Someone at a Higher Level in the Office to Whom You Could Appeal for Help if Things Were Not Working Out All Right?"

Response	Finding job	Job training	Workmen's Compensation	Unemployment Compensation	Welfare	Hospital/medical	Retirement	Other	Total
				Type of Problem					
Yes	51.5%	43.4%	42.5%	56.8%	40.8%	37.8%	42.2%	40.3%	46.6%
No	9.4	20.8	7.5	10.5	19.4	22.2	7.5	30.6	13.6
D. K.	36.3	34.0	42.5	29.6	37.9	37.8	45.7	27.4	37.0
N. A.	2.9	1.9	7.5	3.1	1.9	2.2	4.0	1.6	3.1
Total	100%	100%	100%	100%	100%	100%	100%	100%	100%
N	(171)	(53)	(40)	(162)	(103)	(45)	(172)	(62)	(809)

Despite the number of people who knew about the possibility of appealing, only a very low proportion actually tried that route (Table 3.13). Respondents with welfare experiences had the highest number who had appealed (31 percent) although they had the second smallest number of those who knew about the appeal process (41 percent). Respondents with experiences with medical and hospital services had the lowest proportion of people who knew about appeal procedures (38 percent), but had the second largest group to appeal (18 percent).

The ranking of agencies based on the percentage of clients taking an appeal to a higher level corresponds fairly well to their ranking in various measures of favorable evaluation of their funtioning. Retirement services head the list with the smallest percentage of appeals (8 percent), and public assistance is highest, as has already been noted.

Of all of those who had appealed, slightly more respondents (47 percent) were satisfied with the results of the appeal than were dissat-

Table 3.13

"Did You Try to Appeal?"

				Type of Problem					
Response	Finding job	Job training	Workmen's Compensation	Unemployment Compensation	Welfare	Hospital/ medical	Retirement	Other	Total
Yes	10.2%	8.7%	11.1%	10.8%	31.0%	17.6%	8.1%	30.8%	14.1%
No	89.8	91.3	88.9	89.2	69.0	82.4	91.9	69.2	85.9
N. A.	0	0	0	0	0	0	0	0	0
Total	100%	100%	100%	100%	100%	100%	100%	100%	100%
N	(89)	(23)	(18)	(94)	(43)	(17)	(74)	(26)	(384)

Note: Percentages are based on those who knew about an appeal possibility. (See Table 3.12.)

isfied (40 percent) (Table 3.14). The numbers of people making appeals became too small to make meaningful comparisons of satisfaction with the appeal process across agencies.

Table 3.14

"How Did the Appeal Turn Out?"

Rating	Total for All Types of Problems
(Mostly) satisfactory	47.3%
Mixed; some ways satisfactory and some not	5.5
(Mostly) unsatisfactory	40.0
Other	1.8
N. A.	5.5
Total	100%
N	(53)

Note: Percentages are based on those who tried to appeal. (See Table 3.13.)

It is sometimes assumed that people like to have options open to them, even in enlisting the aid of public agencies in working out their problems. Respondents who had had contact with a service agency were queried about whether they had to take what the office decided or whether they were given some choice. One out of four said they did have a choice (Table 3.15). This was especially true in employment-related areas of finding a job and getting job retraining, where about 50 percent felt they had had a choice. But the comparison of experiences with these services to those with public assistance or retirement benefits must be qualified in that job-related services are necessarily more individualized. The comparison between public assistance and retirement services again favors social security over welfare agencies. Though there should be more flexibility in public assistance than in social security, 11 percent more of the welfare clients than of retirees believe they have to take what the office decides.

Table 3.15

"Do They Give You Any Choice About Things at That Office or Do You Have to Take What They Decide?"

Rating	Finding job	Job training	Workmen's Compensa- tion	Unemploy- ment Com- pensation	Welfare	Hospital/ medical	Retirement	Other	Total
				Type of Problem					
Have a choice	50.9%	52.8%	17.5%	17.3%	10.7%	13.3%	16.2%	22.6%	25.8%
Take what they decide	36.8	43.4	70.0	74.1	87.4	80.0	76.3	62.9	65.6
D. K.	3.5	0	2.5	4.3	0	4.4	1.7	3.2	2.6
N. A.	8.8	3.8	10.0	4.3	1.9	2.2	5.2	9.7	5.8
Total	100%	100%	100%	100%	100%	100%	100%	100%	100%
N	(171)	(53)	(40)	(162)	(103)	(45)	(173)	(62)	(809)

The questions so far discussed have focused on a specific episode of the respondent's experience, his most important contact with a service agency. Respondents were also asked about the number of *other* contacts they had with the agency during the past two years and were further requested to give an overall evaluation of these experiences. The majority of clients had no other contacts than the one experience reported. This group was well satisfied with their sole experience with the agency as Table 3.16 attests. The more frequent users were asked to assess these other experiences as well as their most important contact. Their reports were dominantly favorable, indicating that their continuing experiences with the agencies generally did not result from the failure of the office to be helpful. A small group (about one in five of the frequent users and one in 20 of all clients), however, found their experiences very unsatisfactory. This raises the question once more about the interpretation which should be given these figures. A very dissatisfied group of only 5 percent could mean a highly effective public office, but not necessarily so if one seeks practically no *extreme* negative reactions. It is of interest in this connection that retirement services had no clients at all who said the agency was very unsatisfactory with respect to repeated experiences. Only 3 percent had expressed strong dissatisfaction as a result of the single contact with retirement services.

Table 3.16

Other Experiences with Same Agency

(a) Number of other contacts with
same office during past two years:

No contacts	68.0%
One contact	8.0
Two contacts	5.0
Three contacts	4.0
Four or more contacts	9.0
N. A.	6.0
Total	100.0%
N	(801)

(b) How satisfactory have these experiences been?

Very satisfactory	42.2%
Fairly satisfactory	29.9
Somewhat unsatisfactory	8.5
Very unsatisfactory	19.0
D. K.	0.4
Total	100.0%
N	(212)

RELATION OF DEMOGRAPHIC CHARACTERISTICS TO EVALUATION OF SERVICE AGENCY

A number of demographic variables were examined to determine their effect on respondents' perceptions of different facets of the encounter. The variables include age, race, sex, income, education, and occupation. The differences are significant unless otherwise mentioned.

Satisfaction with the Office's Handling of the Problem

Age and race were the only demographic variables significantly related to satisfaction with the way the service agencies handle clients' problems. As age increases, so too does satisfaction with agency treatment. The relationship is pronounced in the extreme categories of *very satisfied* and *very dissatisfied,* with 27 percent of those under age 30 very satisfied compared to 60 percent of those over age 70. Strong dissatisfaction is minimal in the older groups but includes a fourth of the clients under 30 (Table 3.17). One reason for the positive relationship between age and satisfaction may be higher levels of expectation among younger people, not only in relation to government services, but to everything. Another reason could be the selective nature of clients and their problems at the various age levels. Social security matters bring a majority of older people into contact with government offices, whereas the majority of younger people seeking help have problems about employment. It is the normal expectation to turn to social security in later years but not necessarily to seek government help about a job.

Table 3.17

Age Related to Satisfaction with Agency

Rating	Age Group				
	18-29	30-49	50-69	70+	Total
Very satisfied	26.7%	38.8%	53.0%	59.8%	42.6%
Fairly well satisfied	22.8	27.8	25.9	27.1	25.9
Somewhat dissatisfied	21.8	13.9	7.3	2.8	12.6
Very dissatisfied	24.8	14.2	7.3	3.7	13.5
D. K.	0	0.4	1.3	0	0.4
N. A.	3.9	5.0	5.2	6.5	5.1
Total	100%	100%	100%	100%	100%
N	(206)	(281)	(232)	(107)	(826)

Fewer blacks (32 percent) than whites (45 percent) are found in the very satisfied category (Table 3.18). This is a function of the type of problem experienced by the two groups. Blacks seek help much more frequently than whites in finding jobs, job retraining, and for public assistance.

Table 3.18

Race Related to Satisfaction with Agency

| | Race | | | |
Rating	White	Black	Other	Total
Very satisfied	44.6%	31.9%	30.6%	42.6%
Fairly well satisfied	26.0	24.2	27.8	25.9
Somewhat dissatisfied	11.6	19.8	13.9	12.6
Very dissatisfied	12.4	18.7	22.2	13.5
D. K.	0.4	0	0	0.4
N. A.	4.9	5.5	5.6	5.1
Total	100%	100%	100%	100%
N	(700)	(91)	(36)	(827)

Difficulty in Finding Office or Official Who Could Handle the Problem

Respondents who had the hardest time in finding assistance were more likely to be young than old, in the middle, rather than high or low, income group, and in the ethnic/racial category of "other" rather than white or black. There were no significant differences on the basis of sex, education, and occupation.

Difficulty in finding the right office or official seemed to be a direct function of age (Table 3.19). The 18-29 year olds had the worst

Table 3.19

Age Related to Difficulty in Finding Appropriate Office or Official

| | Age Group | | | | |
Response	18-29	30-49	50-69	70+	Total
Yes	22.3%	12.8%	6.5%	4.7%	12.3%
No	73.3	81.9	88.4	88.8	82.5
D. K.	0.5	1.1	0	1.9	0.7
N. A.	3.9	4.3	5.1	4.7	4.5
Total	100%	100%	100%	100%	100%
N	(206)	(281)	(232)	(107)	(826)

time. Twenty-two percent of them had encountered problems in locating the appropriate source of assistance. This compares to 13 percent of the 30-49 year olds, and 7 percent of the 50-69 year olds. The differences were significant among the three age groups. The difference between the 50-69 year olds and over 70 year olds was not significant.

Income appeared to be a U-shaped function in relation to the respondent's difficulty in finding an appropriate office or official (Table 3.20). The highest income group had the least trouble. Seven percent of this group had difficulty while the two middle income groups averaged about 16 percent. But the highest income group was not significantly different from the low income group of which about 11 percent said they had encountered problems.

Table 3.20

Income Related to Difficulty in Finding Appropriate
Office or Official

| Response | Income Group | | | | |
	0-$4,999	$5,000-9,999	$10,000-14,999	$15,000+	Total
Yes	10.7%	16.0%	15.2%	6.9%	12.6%
No	85.8	76.9	79.3	88.5	85.2
D. K.	0.8	0.9	0.5	0.8	0.7
N. A.	2.8	6.2	4.8	3.8	4.3
Total	100%	100%	100%	100%	100%
N	(253)	(225)	(184)	(130)	(792)*

*The total of 792 rather than 827 is due to the fact that the income category of 35 respondents could not be ascertained.

Race played a minor role in relation to the degree of difficulty in finding an appropriate office or official (Table 3.21). There was no significant difference between whites (11 percent) and blacks (15 percent). However, there was a slightly significant difference between whites and other ethnic groups (22 percent).

Effort Expended by Agency Personnel

Respondents least satisfied with efforts made in their behalf were

Table 3.21

Race Related to Difficulty in Finding Appropriate
Office or Official

	Race			
Response	White	Black	Other	Total
Yes	11.4%	15.4%	22.2%	12.3%
No	83.4	80.2	69.4	82.5
D. K.	0.7	0	2.8	0.7
N. A.	4.4	4.4	5.6	4.5
Total	100%	100%	100%	100%
N	(700)	(91)	(36)	(827)

more apt to be in younger groups, in the middle income brackets, of a higher education level, and in the "other" ethnic category. Sex and occupation showed no significant differences.

The respondents' ratings of the effort expended by agency personnel appeared to be a function of age, with the two youngest groups significantly different in their responses from the two oldest groups (Table 3.22). Only 12 percent of the 18-29 year olds and 13 percent of

Table 3.22

Age Related to Perceived Helpfulness of
Agency Personnel

	Age Group				
Rating	18-29	30-49	50-69	70+	Total
More than they had to	11.7%	12.8%	19.4%	23.4%	15.8%
About right	45.1	61.2	61.2	62.6	57.3
Less than they should have	24.3	10.0	9.1	2.8	12.3
No effort at all	14.6	10.0	3.9	2.8	8.5
D. K.	0	1.1	0.4	0.9	0.6
N. A.	4.4	5.0	6.0	7.4	5.4
Total	100%	100%	100%	100%	100%
N	(206)	(281)	(232)	(107)	(826)

the 30-49 year olds felt that agency personnel had done more than they had to. These proportions differ from those for the 50-69 year olds (19 percent) and the over 70 group (23 percent). The two youngest and the two oldest groups showed slight differences among themselves in the expected direction.

There was a tendency toward a U-shaped distribution for income groups in evaluating efforts made by agency personnel to help them (Table 3.23). Both the poor (those under $5,000) and the affluent (those over $15,000) perceived agency people as trying harder in comparison with middle income groups. A similar pattern appeared in the amount of satisfaction with the way the agency handled problems expressed by the various income groups, but it was not as pronounced.

Table 3.23

Income Related to Perceived Helpfulness of
Agency Personnel

	Income Group				
Rating	0-$4,999	$5,000 -9,999	$10,000 -14,999	$15,000+	Total
More than they had to	19.8%	13.8%	9.8%	20.8%	15.9%
About right	57.3	53.8	59.8	57.7	56.9
Less than they should have	10.3	16.0	14.1	7.7	12.4
No effort at all	7.5	9.8	9.8	7.7	8.7
D. K.	0.8	0	0.5	1.5	0.6
N. A.	4.4	6.7	5.9	4.6	5.2
Total	100%	100%	100%	100%	100%
N	(253)	(225)	(184)	(130)	(792)*

*The total of 792 rather than 827 is due to the fact that the income category of 35 respondents could not be ascertained.

Whites (75 percent) were slightly more positive than blacks (68 percent) in assessing agency personnel as trying hard to be helpful (Table 3.24). People from other ethnic minorities (Mexicans, Puerto Ricans, Indians) were most critical of the efforts of service agencies. Though their numbers in our sample were small, it is suggestive that relatively more than twice as many of them as whites thought agency people made little or no effort to be helpful.

Table 3.24

Race Related to Perceived Helpfulness
of Agency Personnel

| | Race | | | |
Rating	White	Black	Other	Total
More than they had to	16.9%	11.0%	8.3%	15.8%
About right	58.3	57.1	38.9	57.3
Less than they should have	11.4	14.3	25.0	12.3
No effort at all	7.7	12.1	13.9	8.5
D. K.	0.3	0	8.3	0.6
N. A.	5.4	5.5	5.6	5.4
Total	100%	100%	100%	100%
N	(700)	(91)	(36)	(827)

Education was related only slightly to reactions to agency personnel (Table 3.25). Clients who had not completed high school were somewhat less critical than those who had at least a high school diploma. There were no differences, however, among those with just a high school education and those who had had some college training.

Table 3.25

Education Related to Perceived Helpfulness
of Agency Personnel

| | Years of Education | | | |
Rating	Fewer than 12	12+ non-academic training	1-3 college	Total
More than they had to	14.3%	16.7%	17.2%	15.8%
About right	63.3	53.5	53.4	57.3
Less than they should have	9.0	16.0	13.1	12.3
No effort	7.8	8.6	9.5	8.5
D. K.	0.6	0	0.9	0.6
N. A.	5.1	5.2	5.9	5.4
Total	100%	100%	100%	100%
N	(335)	(269)	(221)	(827)

Efficiency of Office in Handling the Problem

Respondents who considered the office to be efficient were most likely older and female. Whites tended to be more extreme in their satisfaction compared to other groups, and blacks had a significantly higher proportion who said that they were very dissatisfied.

Age was a significant factor in the respondents' perceptions of agency efficiency with satisfaction clearly increasing with age (Table 3.26). The youngest group had a much smaller number of respondents feeling the agency had been very efficient (26 percent). The 30-49 year olds (37 percent) and the 50-69 year olds (55 percent) were higher in satisfaction, and the over 70 year olds (65 percent) were the most impressed. There was no significant difference between the two oldest groups. These findings are consistent with the results of the other questions of agency evaluation. Older people are less critical than younger people.

Table 3.26

Age Related to Perceived Efficiency of Agency

	Age Group				
Rating	18-29	30-49	50-69	70+	Total
Very efficient	25.7%	37.0%	54.7%	64.5%	42.8%
Fairly efficient	33.0	37.0	26.3	21.5	31.0
Rather inefficient	17.0	9.6	5.2	1.9	9.2
Very inefficient	18.4	10.7	6.0	4.7	10.5
D. K.	1.5	0.7	0.9	0	0.8
N. A.	4.4	5.0	6.9	7.5	5.7
Total	100%	100%	100%	100%	100%
N	(206)	(281)	(232)	(107)	(826)

Men and women differed in their perceptions of agency efficiency in their use of the extreme categories of the scale (Table 3.27). More women than men, 48 percent compared to 38 percent, regarded the agency as *very efficient,* and 9 percent of the women and 13 percent of the men thought the agency *very inefficient.* There was less difference between the sexes in the intermediate categories of *fairly efficient* or *rather inefficient.*

Table 3.27

Sex Related to Efficiency of the Office
in Handling the Problem

Rating	Sex		
	Male	Female	Total
Very efficient	37.6%	47.6%	42.8%
Fairly efficient	34.0	28.2	31.0
Rather inefficient	9.4	9.0	9.2
Very inefficient	12.7	8.5	10.5
D. K.	1.0	0.7	0.8
N. A.	5.3	6.0	5.6
Total	100%	100%	100%
N	(394)	(433)	(827)

In similar fashion the differences between blacks and whites were at the extremes of the scale. Proportionately four times as many whites considered the agency to have been *very efficient* as against *very inefficient*. On the other hand, only twice as many blacks characterized the agency with which they had contact as *very efficient* compared to *very inefficient* (Table 3.28).

Table 3.28

Race Related to Efficiency of the Office
in Handling the Problem

Rating	Race			
	White	Black	Other	Total
Very efficient	44.9%	34.1%	25.0%	42.8%
Fairly efficient	30.3	34.1	36.1	31.0
Rather inefficient	9.0	7.7	16.7	9.2
Very inefficient	9.4	17.6	13.9	10.5
D. K.	0.9	0	2.8	0.8
N. A.	5.5	6.6	5.6	5.7
Total	100%	100%	100%	100%
N	(700)	(91)	(36)	(827)

Income differences with respect to ratings of efficiency are similar to the U-shaped distribution reported on other questions, but the tendency toward this pattern is not clear and compelling (Table 3.29). The two middle income groups do total 26 percent and 24 percent in the inefficiency categories, and the two extreme income groups only 14 percent and 16 percent.

Table 3.29

Income Related to Efficiency of the Office
in Handling the Problem

	Income Group				
Rating	0-$4,999	$5,000 -9,999	$10,000 -14,999	$15,000+	Total
Very efficient	51.4%	36.4%	38.6%	40.0%	42.3%
Fairly efficient	28.5	30.2	29.9	39.2	31.1
Rather inefficient	5.1	11.6	13.0	8.5	9.3
Very inefficient	9.1	14.2	11.4	7.7	10.9
D. K.	1.2	0.4	1.6	0	0.8
N. A.	4.7	7.1	5.4	4.6	5.4
Total	100%	100%	100%	100%	100%
N	(253)	(225)	(184)	(130)	(792)*

*The total of 792 rather than 827 is due to the fact that the income category of 35 respondents could not be ascertained.

Table 3.30

Education Related to Efficiency of the Office
in Handling the Problem

	Years of Education			
Rating	Fewer than 12	12+ non-academic training	1-3 college	Total
Very efficient	49.5%	38.3%	39.4%	42.8%
Fairly efficient	29.3	32.7	31.2	31.0
Rather inefficient	7.2	11.0	9.5	9.2
Very inefficient	8.7	11.5	12.2	10.5
D. K.	0.9	0.4	1.4	0.8
N. A.	5.1	5.6	5.6	5.7
Total	100%	100%	100%	100%
N	(335)	(269)	(221)	(827)

The people who did not finish high school tend to be more favorable in their evaluation of agency efficiency than do the better-educated groups (Table 3.30). The same trend appeared in other questions about agency functioning.

Perception of Differential Treatment of Certain Types of People by the Agency

The perception of unfairness is more characteristic of young than old and of black than white, with young blacks most likely to state that some people received better treatment than others. Other demographic variables made little difference. Men and women responded almost identically to this question, and differences due to education and occupation were insignificant. People with middle class incomes ($10,000-$14,000) were less likely than others to report differential treatment and correspondingly more likely to report uncertainty about the question, but the differences were modest.

Once more, the age pattern reflects youthful criticism and elderly acceptance. More of the very young (35 percent) perceived discriminatory treatment than did any other age group. The proportions dropped consistently with increases in age, with only 11 percent of those 70 and over reporting bias. The small percentage in the oldest group reflects a somewhat larger proportion of people who weren't sure of the answer (38 percent), as well as a larger proportion convinced of agency fairness (Table 3.31).

Table 3.31

Age Related to Perception of Whether Some People
Receive Preferential Treatment

| Response | Age Group | | | | |
	18-29	30-49	50-69	70+	Total
Yes	35.0%	26.0%	16.8%	11.2%	23.7%
No	35.9	34.9	42.2	44.9	38.6
D. K.	24.8	34.2	34.9	38.3	32.5
N. A.	4.4	5.0	6.0	5.6	5.2
Total	100%	100%	100%	100%	100%
N	(206)	(281)	(232)	(107)	(826)

Blacks (34 percent) were significantly more critical than whites (22 percent) in terms of believing that certain groups received better treatment than others, a fact that presumably reflects their perception of racial discrimination (Table 3.32). Blacks are also seen by some whites as advantaged in their treatment by agencies. These conflicting views illustrate the difficulty agencies face in attaining perceived equity throughout society.

Table 3.32

Race Related to Perception of Whether Some People
Receive Preferential Treatment

| Response | Race | | | |
	White	Black	Other	Total
Yes	22.0%	34.1%	30.6%	23.7%
No	41.0	26.4	22.2	38.6
D. K.	31.9	34.1	41.7	32.5
N. A.	5.2	5.5	5.6	5.2
Total	100%	100%	100%	100%
N	(700)	(91)	(36)	(827)

Fairness of Treatment by Agency

Rumors are often more frightening than facts, and people often believe that the misfortunes of others will not befall them. Whatever the mechanism at work, there is a persistent tendency in our data for personal experience to be more positive than belief about the society at large. Thus, while about one-fourth of all respondents with agency experience thought that some people were treated better than others, only one-eighth felt that they had themselves received unfair treatment.

The pattern of differences among sub-groups is similar for this question and the more general one about fairness. Thus, age is the major explanatory factor among the demographic variables, with the proportion of people alleging unfair treatment dropping from 21 percent in the youngest age group to less than 4 percent among those over 70 (Table 3.33).

Table 3.33

Age Related to Perception of Fairness
of Treatment by Agency

		Age Group			
Rating	18-29	30-49	50-69	70+	Total
Fairly	64.1%	75.4%	80.6%	88.8%	75.8%
Mixed	6.8	6.4	2.6	0	4.6
Unfairly	20.9	12.5	9.1	3.7	12.5
D. K.	3.9	1.1	2.2	1.9	2.2
N. A.	4.4	4.6	5.2	5.6	4.8
Total	100%	100%	100%	100%	100%
	(206)	(281)	(232)	(107)	(827)

There is an apparent tendency for blacks (18 percent) to report unfair treatment in greater proportion than whites (12 percent), but the difference between the races is scarcely significant (Table 3.34). Certainly the more meaningful datum is the large proportion of whites and blacks who say they were treated fairly.

Table 3.34

Race Related to Perception of Fairness
of Treatment by Agency

		Race		
Rating	White	Black	Other	Total
Fairly	77.1%	68.1%	69.4%	75.8%
Mixed	4.6	4.4	5.6	4.6
Unfairly	11.7	17.6	13.9	12.5
D. K.	1.9	4.4	2.8	2.2
N. A.	4.7	5.5	8.3	4.9
Total	100%	100%	100%	100%
N	(700)	(91)	(36)	(827)

Differences among other demographic sub-groups were even smaller. The whole range of differences among occupational groups, for example, was only five percentage points among those who responded *fairly*, and only three points among those who reported *unfair* treatment. Differences between men and women were still smaller. Only with respect to income does another significant difference emerge, with the hint of a U-shaped distribution. There is a tendency for the middle income groups ($5,000 to $15,000) to be less satisfied with respect to fairness, with the $5,000 to $10,000 income group least satisfied, and the top income group most satisfied (Table 3.35).

Table 3.35

Income Related to Perception of Fairness of Treatment
by Agency

	Income Group				
Rating	0-$4,999	$5,000 -9,999	$10,000 -14,999	$15,000+	Total
Fairly	78.3%	70.7%	72.8%	82.3%	75.8%
Mixed	3.2	4.4	7.6	3.1	4.6
Unfairly	13.4	16.4	11.4	7.7	12.5
D. K.	0.8	2.2	3.3	3.1	2.2
N. A.	4.3	6.2	4.8	3.8	4.9
Total	100%	100%	100%	100%	100%
N	(253)	(225)	(184)	(130)	(792)*

*The total of 792 rather than 827 is due to the fact that the income category of 35 respondents could not be ascertained.

Similarity of Agency Workers and Self

Client and agency representatives confront each other in very different roles. On one side of the desk is the person in need of medical care, retirement benefits, or employment. He brings to the interview all the strength of that problem, his anxieties about it, and his hopes for its solution. Opposite him sits the agency representative, who must respond in terms of the rules and resources of the organization he represents. In these respects, client and representative are very different. In other respects, they may be very similar, i.e., two workers with a common culture and probably many of the same aspirations.

As we have seen earlier, most people think in terms of similarities rather than differences. More than two out of three said that the individuals they met in the agency were people pretty much like themselves. They seemed to be thinking in terms of observable personal characteristics, rather than the differences in their roles. If we were to attempt a demographic description of the clients most likely to report such feelings of similarity, it would specify women rather than men, white people rather than black, clerical rather than managerial or laboring occupations, and maturity rather than youthfulness. In short, people who report that agency representatives resemble them are probably being very literal about it. The point, of course, is not so much the accuracy of their perceptions as the evidence of comfort and, perhaps, ease of identification, rather than discomfort, social distance, and alienation. In general, demographic groupings were more impressive for their similarity in this respect than for their differences. However, race made a substantial difference, with 71 percent of the whites asserting similarity to staff people in the agency office and only 55 percent of the blacks giving the same response (Table 3.36). The response differences between men and women (65 and 72 percent, respectively), while significant, were not nearly so large (Table 3.37).

Table 3.36

Race Related to Perceived Similarity Between Agency
Personnel and Self

| | Race | | | |
Rating	White	Black	Other	Total
Similar	71.0%	54.9%	55.6%	68.6%
Not similar	14.6	29.7	25.0	16.7
D. K.	8.3	7.7	13.9	8.5
N. A.	6.1	7.7	5.6	6.2
Total	100%	100%	100%	100%
N	(700)	(91)	(36)	(827)

Among people over 50, almost three out of four felt that those working in the agency office were "like them," a response given significantly less often by 18-29 year olds. Even in this youngest age

Table 3.37

Sex Related to Perceived Similarity Between Agency
Personnel and Self

Rating	Sex		
	Male	Female	Total
Similar	64.7%	72.1%	68.6%
Not similar	19.8	13.9	16.7
D. K.	9.4	7.6	8.5
N. A.	6.1	6.4	6.2
Total	100%	100%	100%
N	(394)	(433)	(827)

group, however, 63 percent saw resemblances rather than differences
as they looked across the agency desk (Table 3.38).

Table 3.38

Age Related to Perceived Similarity Between Agency
Personnel and Self

Rating	Age Group				
	18-29	30-49	50-69	70+	Total
Similar	62.6%	66.9%	73.7%	72.9%	68.6%
Not similar	28.2	14.2	11.6	12.1	16.7
D. K.	5.8	12.5	6.5	7.5	8.5
N. A.	3.4	6.4	8.2	7.4	6.2
Total	100%	100%	100%	100%	100%
N	(206)	(281)	(232)	(107)	(826)

Among occupational groups, clerical and salespeople were most
likely to report positively in response to this question—80 percent of
them. Other occupational groups were undifferentiated in this respect, as were income and education groups.

Choice of Options Given to Client by Agency

The client's sense of choice during his experience with a service agency is almost certainly the result of many things. Agencies differ in the latitude and discretion that they are allowed by statute or budget; agency executives differ in establishing policies that invite or preclude client involvement in decisions affecting them; and agency staff differ in their enactment of policy. They differ as well in their behavior toward clients of a different background, who no doubt differ in turn with respect to their tolerance for accepting the decisions of others. All these factors are reflected in the statements of respondents that they do or do not have any choice about matters at the agency.

There is no ambiguity about the overall response pattern; two-thirds of the people say they had no choice about things at the agency office, and almost none were uncertain about it. Moreover, in every demographic sub-group the majority response is the same—no choice. There are some demographic differences, however. The likelihood of a person having some choice, or of feeling that he does, is three times as great if he is young rather than old; twice as great if he is highly educated (college) rather than little educated (less than high school); and twice as great if he is prosperous rather than poor. Other differences are of lesser magnitude, but in the expected direction. Men report more choice than women; professionals and managers more than laborers. Racial differences are insignificant, although the direction is as expected—26 percent of whites report having some choice, as compared to 20 percent of blacks.

The relationships of age, education, and income to perceived choice are quite linear, on the whole. The proportion of respondents who assert that they had some choice in dealing with the agency drops with each decade of age, from 31 percent among the 18-29 year olds to 11 percent among those over 70 (Table 3.39). The differences before age 50, however, are insignificant; the descent occurs thereafter. It is likely that the data reflect in part the involvement of the upper age groups with questions of retirement and with offices of the Social Security Administration. Both agency staff and clients are working within narrowly defined specifications of entitlement, and both may recognize these limitations as imposed externally. In any case, the older clients, who reported greater satisfaction with most aspects of the agency experience, also reported less choice in the process. Likewise, the greater degree of perceived choice by younger clients may be due to the fact that they frequent offices such as unemployment agencies which intrinsically offer more choice.

Table 3.39

Age Related to Perceived Choice

Rating	Age Group				
	18-29	30-49	50-69	70+	Total
Have a choice	31.1%	30.2%	20.7%	11.2%	25.3%
Take what they decide	56.8	60.5	69.8	78.5	64.6
D. K.	4.9	1.4	1.3	3.7	2.5
N. A.	7.3	7.8	8.2	6.5	7.6
Total	100%	100%	100%	100%	100%
N	(206)	(281)	(232)	(107)	(826)

The sense of choice increases consistently with education, although the significant break is between those who have graduated from high school and those who have not, 17 percent and 29 percent respectively (Table 3.40). Income shows a similar break between those earning less than $5,000 and those earning more, although the trend continues, and those with incomes above $15,000 report the greatest choice (Table 3.41).

Table 3.40

Education Related to Perceived Choice

Rating	Years of Education			
	Fewer than 12	12+ non-academic training	1-3 college	Total
Have a choice	17.3%	29.4%	32.6%	25.3%
Take what they decide	75.5	59.5	54.3	64.6
D. K.	2.1	3.0	2.7	2.5
N. A.	5.1	8.2	10.5	7.6
Total	100%	100%	100%	100%
N	(335)	(269)	(221)	(825)

Table 3.41

Income Related to Perceived Choice

	Income Group				
Rating	0-$4,999	$5,000 -9,999	$10,000 -14,999	$15,000+	Total
Have a choice	17.0%	28.0%	25.5%	34.6%	25.3%
Take what they decide	75.5	61.3	62.5	54.6	64.6
D. K.	2.8	2.7	2.7	1.5	2.5
N. A.	4.7	8.0	9.3	9.2	7.6
Total	100%	100%	100%	100%	100%
N	(253)	(225)	(184)	(130)	(792)*

*The total of 792 rather than 827 is due to the fact that the income category of 35 respondents could not be ascertained.

Knowledge of Opportunities for Appealing Agency's Decision

The question of choice in the client experience was at first posed in general terms. It was then given a more specific focus in terms of appeal: Did the client feel that there was recourse from an unsatisfactory decision? Fewer than half of all clients said yes to that question, but most of the others simply didn't know. One hopes this reflects satisfaction as well as lack of sophistication; the satisfied client has little motivation to search out appellate procedures, even for precautionary reasons.

Demographic determinants are more suggestive of sophistication and self-confidence than satisfaction per se as determinants of appellate knowledge. For example, in the most advantaged occupational and income groups (Tables 3.42 and 3.43), the majority of respon-

Table 3.42

Occupation Realted to Perceived Opportunity for Appeal

	Occupation					
Response	Professional & Managerial	Clerical & sales	Skilled and semi-skilled	Laborers	Other	Total
Yes	53.5%	45.9%	48.6%	44.6%	38.3%	45.7%
No	16.7	13.4	11.8	14.2	9.9	13.3
D. K.	24.6	37.6	33.5	39.2	44.0	36.0
N. A.	5.3	3.2	5.7	2.0	7.1	4.9
Total	100%	100%	100%	100%	100%	100%
N	(114)	(157)	(245)	(148)	(141)	(805)

Table 3.43

Income Related to Perceived Opportunity for Appeal

Response	Income Group				
	0-$4,999	$5,000 -9,999	$10,000 -14,999	$15,000+	Total
Yes	38.7%	47.1%	48.4%	56.2%	45.7%
No	13.0	12.9	16.8	9.2	13.3
D. K.	43.9	33.8	29.9	30.8	36.0
N. A.	4.3	6.2	4.8	3.8	4.9
Total	100%	100%	100%	100%	100%
N	(253)	(225)	(184)	(130)	(792)*

*The total of 792 rather than 827 is due to the fact that the income category of 35 respondents could not be ascertained.

dents say that some avenue of appeal was open to them, and about 25-30 percent say that they are not sure. In the least advantaged groups, the proportion who affirm the possibility of appeal drops below 40 percent, and the modal response is uncertainty. These differences are not dramatic, however, and differences between adjacent income and occupational groupings are not significant.

More whites than blacks thought they had the right of appeal within the agency; more of the blacks were uncertain (Table 3.44). Uncertainty also increased with age, not steeply but steadily, so that almost half of the elderly said they did not know what possibilities

Table 3.44

Race Related to Perceived Opportunity for Appeal

Response	Race			
	White	Black	Other	Total
Yes	47.6%	36.3%	33.3%	45.7%
No	13.4	11.0	16.7	13.3
D. K.	34.1	47.3	44.4	36.0
N. A.	4.9	5.5	5.6	4.9
Total	100%	100%	100%	100%
N	(700)	(91)	(36)	(827)

existed for appeal, and only 30 percent were confident of them (Table 3.45). Women were slightly less certain than men, and correspondingingly less confident that they could make an appeal; the proportion who were sure they did not—about one in seven or eight—was nearly the same for men and women.

Table 3.45

Age Related to Perceived Opportunity for Appeal

Response	Age Group				
	18-29	30-49	50-69	70+	Total
Yes	46.1%	45.9%	49.6%	30.4%	45.7%
No	20.4	12.1	9.5	10.3	13.3
D. K.	29.6	37.0	35.3	47.7	36.0
N. A.	3.9	5.0	5.6	5.6	4.9
Total	100%	100%	100%	100%	100%
N	(206)	(281)	(232)	(107)	(826)

Exercise of Appellate Prerogative

Knowledge of appellate procedures and the actual attempt to appeal an agency decision are, of course, related. Knowledge that appeal is possible facilitates the act of appealing, and the attempt to appeal generates knowledge of the possibilities and limits, whatever the initial naivete of the individual. It seems likely that dissatisfaction is the prime mover in the search for appeal and redress, and that knowledge is a facilitator of the process. Since the knowledgeable clients (high income, high education) are also the more satisfied by and large, the demographic predictors of actual appeal differ in interesting ways from the predictors of appellate knowledge. These differences are most apparent if we consider demographic variations in appellate behavior only among those who knew that appeals were possible.

The main point, of course, is that very few people appealed the initial agency decisions. Those who did were only 14 percent of those who knew appeal was possible, which means only 6 percent of those who had some agency contact. Among those who knew they could appeal, frequency of doing so varies more with age than any other demographic characteristic, from about 1 percent of those over 70 to

22 percent of the 18-29 year olds (Table 3.46). Differences between races are also substantial, with the proportion of appeals more than twice as high among blacks as whites (Table 3.47), though we are dealing here with a small number of cases in our black sample. Differences of the same order of magnitude are apparent in relation to income, but the relationship is not linear; it peaks in the $5,000-$10,000 group, in which 22 percent of those who knew appeal was possible in fact attempted to make one (Table 3.48).

Table 3.46

Age Related to Attempted Appeal

| | Age Group | | | | |
Response	18-29	30-49	50-69	70+	Total
Yes	21.6%*	12.9%	11.1%	7.5%	14.0%
No	78.4	86.4	86.3	92.5	86.0
N. A.	0	.8	2.6	0	1.0
Total	100%	100%	100%	100%	100%
N	(97)	(132)	(117)	(40)	(386)*

*Percentage based on those who knew of appeal procedure.

Table 3.47

Race Related to Attempted Appeal

| | Race | | | |
Response	White	Black	Other	Total
Yes	11.8%*	27.3%	38.5%	14.0%
No	87.0	72.7	61.5	85.0
N. A.	1.2	0	0	1.0
Total	100%	100%	100%	100%
N	(340)	(33)	(13)	(386)*

*Percentage based on those who knew of appeal procedure.

No systematic differences are apparent among occupational groups nor among people of different educational background.

Table 3.48

Income Related to Attempted Appeal

Response	Income Group				
	0-$4,999	$5,000 -9,999	$10,000 -14,999	$15,000+	Total
Yes	10.0%*	22.2%	11.8%	12.5%	14.0%
No	90.0	76.9	84.9	88.9	85.0
N. A.	0	.9	3.2	0	1.0
Total	100%	100%	100%	100%	100%
N	(100)	(108)	(93)	(72)	(373)*

*Percéntage based on those who knew of appeal procedure.

Women are less informed than men about appellate possibilities, but among people who are informed, men and women are equally likely to make appeals.

THE COMBINED EFFECT OF DEMOGRAPHIC VARIABLES ON SATISFACTION

The discussion to this point has centered largely on bivariate relationships among the major demographic variables, type of agency and different facets of the service agency experience. The resulting variations among different sub-populations and users of different service agencies raised the more fundamental question about the strength of the predictor variables in explaining the variance in criterion variables such as satisfaction with the experience. Because the seven service agencies attracted different types of clientele, as discussed in chapter two, the source of the discrepancies in user attitudes toward the specific service experience could not be adequately pinpointed in bivariate terms. Without further analysis it was unclear whether the variations in satisfaction, for instance, could be attributed to the quality of the functioning of the agency, the nature of the service rendered, or the type of clientele served.

In order to investigate the predictive power of selected variables and to account for the differences in respondents' evaluations of specific agencies, the data on service agency users were analyzed through the AID III program, similar to a step-wise analysis of variance. The AID technique determines a series of optimal dichotomous splits of sub-samples on predictor variables which successively explain the most variance in the criterion variable.

The AID program was run using seven variables to predict to satisfaction with the service agency experience. The predictor variables were: age, race, income, sex, education, occupation, and type of agency contacted. The analysis explained approximately 14 percent of the variance in satisfaction scores among service agency users, with age and type of agency as the strongest predictors.

The age factor appeared to be the most powerful determinant of satisfaction. The service agency users first split on the basis of age into an 18-29 year old group and a 30-and-over group, a dichotomy which explained 8 percent of the variance. The older respondents tended to be significantly more satisfied with the experience than the younger respondents.

The next split partitioned the 30-and-over group into social security clients and clients of other agencies; this dichotomy accounted for an additional 4 percent of the variance in overall satisfaction. The social security group was significantly more satisfied than the users of other agencies. The relation of social security experience to satisfaction, even after the major effect of age has been taken into account, can also be observed in the consistently higher degree of other positive attitudes of social security clients. The comparison of that group with respondents having contact with other bureaucracies has been discussed earlier in this chapter.

The AID analysis failed to produce a further split in the group of social security clients; in similar fashion, there is no further partitioning of the 18-29 age group.

Respondents over age 30 whose experiences were with agencies other than social security were further partitioned in terms of race. The explanatory contribution is very small, but the whites in this age/agency category were significantly more satisfied than the blacks.

The white group went on to dichotomize again into those respondents with welfare and medical care agency contacts and those with experiences with the remaining four agencies: employment, unemployment compensation, workmen's compensation, and job training. That partition also accounted for only 1 percent of the variance in satisfaction.

In conclusion, while the foregoing analysis suggests that being white, over 30, and having a social security experience are the best indicators of satisfaction, these variables are still weak predictors. The major splits accounted for only 14 percent of the variance. One explanation for their relatively weak predictive power may be due to the skewness of the criterion variable, the degree of satisfaction. This means that the variations between satisfaction ratings by different respondents tended to be too small to allow for the detection of significant variations among the different sub-populations. Our sub-groups were also very limited in reflecting the range of all the variables, e.g., the 140 blacks in the sample were too small a number to include all age groups patronizing various agencies. But the major reason for the small amount of variance accounted for by type of agency and demographic factors has already been suggested in chapter two. Different groups in the population use various agencies for different purposes. There is no one clientele being served by all government offices. Hence, it is very unlikely that the same demographic factors will predict to satisfaction across different types of agencies.

Because of the low amount of variance explained, the analysis did not include further manipulation of the data to determine proportional contributions to the variance by the major variables such as would be derived from a Multiple Classification Analysis (MCA). Nevertheless, the AID III results did substantiate certain trends discussed in chapter three, such as the greater dissatisfaction of the young respondents, and the high satisfaction of social security users.

AGENCIES OF CONSTRAINT

Agencies that constrain, regulate, or penalize, generate much more dissatisfcation than those that deliver services—a fact that will surprise no one, of course. No matter how convinced people may be that absolute individual freedom would produce chaos, no matter how fully people accept the necessity and legitimacy of regulations, the experience of being constrained is certain to involve frustration. And while frustration may not lead inevitably to aggression, it is likely to generate dissatisfaction and resentment. To encounter difficulty in getting a driver's license, to be called to court for an unpaid traffic ticket, or to have one's income tax return questioned, are common ways of encountering the agencies of constraint, and none of them is pleasurable.

When a citizen approaches a service agency, he does so typically because he has encountered a problem and believes that he is entitled to some kind of assistance with it. When he approaches an agency of constraint, he often does so because he has been summoned. In fact, our questions about constraint experiences asked about problems of difficulties with the agency, whereas our questions about service experiences emphasized contact. Thus, locus of the problem is different, the initiation of the episode is different, and the nature and direction of the transaction are different. Therefore, in drawing inferences from the constraint data, especially in relation to the service agencies, the intrinsically more negative bias of the constraint inquiry must be kept in mind.

Whereas three-fourths of the clients of service agencies reported satisfaction, about 40 percent of the constraint users were satisfied with the way agency staff handled their cases (Table 3.49). The difference is particularly striking in the most positive category, with 45 percent of the service users reporting their problems *very well* handled, in comparison to 9 percent of the constraint respondents. At the other end of the satisfaction spectrum, only 14 percent of the service agency users were very dissatisfied, compared to 26 percent of the constraint "clients."

Table 3.49

"Looking at the Whole Experience Would You Say that Government Officials Handled It Very Poorly, Poorly, Fairly Well, or Very Well?"

| | Type of Problem | | | | | |
Rating	Driver's license	Traffic violations	Tax	Police	Other	Total
Very well	9.8%	11.5%	11.3%	5.7%	5.5%	9.0%
Fairly well	26.8	30.8	23.9	17.1	32.4	25.7
Poorly	26.8	30.8	25.3	20.0	18.9	24.2
Very poorly	24.4	19.2	22.5	48.6	18.9	26.2
D. K.	2.4	0	2.8	0	0	1.4
N. A.	9.8	7.7	14.1	8.6	24.3	12.9
Total	100%	100%	100%	100%	100%	100%
N	(41)	(26)	(71)	(35)	(37)	(210)

As with the service agencies, the various constraint agencies were evaluated differently, with some faring worse than others. However, experiences with constraint agencies are not so widespread as those for service agencies, and the sample of constraint episodes is correspondingly small. Differences among agencies must, therefore, be interpreted tentatively. Moreover, differences in client attitudes toward various constraint categories were much smaller than differences for service agencies. The average was about 36 percent for satisfaction with constraint agencies, and the range was small except for experiences with police. Only 23 percent of the people had satisfactory experiences with law officers, and almost half (49 percent) thought that the police had, in fact, done a *very poor* job. The corresponding figure for other constraint agencies is only half as large—about 25 percent.

In addition to the direct questions on respondent experiences, two composite evaluations were developed: (1) a summary evaluation of procedures used by the agency, and (2) a summary evaluation of whether the agency had used threats and pressures. These evaluations were based on responses to open-ended questions, as they had been for service agencies.

The summary score for constraint procedures yielded a generally negative evaluation, with 59 percent of the respondents expressing negative attitudes (Table 3.50). An additional 10 percent were neutral. The greatest amount of criticism was directed at driver licensing bureaus (73 percent). Responses to other constraint agencies were approximately 60 percent negative. It should be noted that almost one-third of the respondents who experienced difficulties with constraint agencies could not be coded on their evaluation of agency procedures. This finding suggests that their experiences were not sufficiently critical to make them articulate about the way the agency operated. Nonetheless, there was more comment about procedures involved in constraint experiences than in service episodes, in that almost one-half of the people with service contacts could not be coded on reactions to procedures.

Table 3.50

Summary Evaluation of Procedures

	Type of Problem					
Rating	Driver's license	Traffic violations	Tax	Police	Other	Total
Favorable	0	3.8%	0	0	0	1.0%
Neutral	12.2%	7.7	15.5%	0	8.1%	10.0
Unfavorable	73.2	42.3	57.7	65.7	51.3	58.5
N. A.	14.6	46.2	26.8	34.3	41.0	30.5
Total	100%	100%	100%	100%	100%	100%
N	(41)	(26)	(71)	(35)	(37)	(210)

Respondents were also coded on whether their descriptions of their experiences with the constraint agency indicated pressures or threats from the agency. Almost 90 percent of those with experiences could be categorized on felt pressures and threats. Only a minority (22 percent), however, reported they had been pressured or threatened. This figure is surprisingly low since these are people who had had difficulty with agencies of control.

Experiences with various agencies produced significantly different responses about threats and pressure (Table 3.51). Respondents experiencing problems with police (54 percent) and traffic violations bureaus (46 percent) were most likely to report threats and pressures. At the other extreme, respondents dealing with driver licensing bureaus and tax offices were the least likely to have been subjected to pressure.

Table 3.51

Summary Evaluation of Threats/Pressures

	Type of Problem					
Rating	Driver's license	Traffic violations	Tax	Police	Other	Total
Threatened/ pressured	2.4%	46.2%	12.7%	54.3%	13.5%	21.9%
No threats/ pressures	92.7	46.2	73.2	45.7	64.9	67.6
N. A.	4.9	7.6	14.1	0	21.6	10.5
Total	100%	100%	100%	100%	100%	100%
N	(41)	(26)	(71)	(35)	(37)	(210)

As with service experiences, respondents were queried on specific aspects of their encounters with constraint bureaucracies. For instance, people were asked how much difficulty the constraint experience had created for them. More than 46 percent stated that it had presented at least *some difficulty*, and 42 percent said that it had presented a *great deal of difficulty* (Table 3.52). The differences among the groups were not statistically significant.

The trend was further supported in answer to the question of whether the constraint officials had made the problem worse by their way of handling it (Table 3.53). Almost 69 percent of the respondents who had had dealings with the traffic violations bureau stated that the

Table 3.52

"How Much Difficulty Did This Experience Make for You?"

	Type of Problem					
Rating	Driver's license	Traffic violations	Tax	Police	Other	Total
Great deal of difficulty	43.9%	50.0%	39.4%	45.7%	37.8%	42.4%
Some difficulty	34.1	34.6	28.2	25.7	27.0	29.5
A little difficulty	14.6	11.6	19.7	17.1	13.5	16.2
D. K.	0	0	1.4	2.9	0	1.0
N. A.	7.3	3.8	11.3	8.6	21.6	10.9
Total	100%	100%	100%	100%	100%	100%
N	(41)	(26)	(71)	(35)	(37)	(210)

problem had been worsened. This finding was closely followed by 66 percent of respondents who had problems with police. In comparison, 51 percent of the respondents with problems about a driver's license and 37 percent of those with tax problems felt that the situation was made worse by the way it was handled.

Table 3.53

"Did the Government Office or Official Make the Problem Worse by Their Way of Handling it?"

	Type of Problem					
Response	Driver's license	Traffic violations	Tax	Police	Other	Total
Yes	51.2%	69.3%	36.7%	65.7%	32.5%	47.6%
No	39.1	26.9	40.8	22.8	37.8	35.2
D. K.	2.4	0	5.6	2.9	0	2.9
N. A.	7.3	3.8	16.9	8.6	29.7	14.3
Total	100%	100%	100%	100%	100%	100%
N	(41)	(26)	(71)	(35)	(37)	(210)

The reluctant clients of constraint agencies were unimpressed with their efficiency. One could argue, of course, that the inefficiency of some government bureaucracies is the citizen's ultimate protection, but respondents were apparently complaining of the inability of the agency to "get it over with," rather than of its inefficiency in identifying violations in the first place. In this respect also, constraint agencies compared unfavorably with service offices. Approximately 46 percent of those who used agencies viewed them as being *very efficient*, but only 14 percent of respondents who came in contact with constraint agencies held such a positive opinion of them (Table 3.54). The difference is not as striking in the *fairly efficient* category. The difference between service and constraint respondents are similarly apparent at the negative end of the efficiency scale. While only 20 percent of users of service agencies viewed them as inefficient, over two times as many (49 percent) of the constraint agency respondents thought these offices were inefficient.

Table 3.54

*"How Efficient Was the Office
in Handling Your Problem?"*

| | Type of Problem | | | | | |
Rating	Driver's license	Traffic violations	Tax	Police	Other	Total
Very efficient	7.3%	38.5%	16.9%	5.7%	8.1%	14.1%
Fairly efficient	17.0	19.2	22.5	22.9	24.3	21.4
Rather inefficient	46.3	15.4	19.7	5.7	29.7	23.8
Very inefficient	22.1	23.1	25.4	40.0	21.7	26.1
D. K.	2.4	0	2.8	0	2.7	1.8
N. A.	4.9	3.8	12.7	25.7	13.5	12.8
Total	100%	100%	100%	100%	100%	100%
N	(41)	(26)	(71)	(35)	(37)	(210)

A question related to the perceived efficiency of constraint agencies dealt with the length of time the agency took to settle the matter. Almost one-third of the respondents (32 percent) felt that the constraint agency had spent a longer time than necessary on the problem (Table 3.55). Nine percent thought that settlement came about as soon as could be expected, and only 25 percent of the sample thought the matter had been settled quickly.

Respondents were most critical of the driver licensing agencies (39 percent) and the police (34 percent) for taking longer than was

Table 3.55

"Was the Matter Settled Quickly, or Did It Take Much Longer Than Was Really Necessary?"

	Type of Problem					
Rating	Driver's license	Traffic violations	Tax	Police	Other	Total
Quickly	22.0%	27.0%	28.2%	25.7%	18.9%	24.7%
As soon as could be expected	9.7	23.1	2.8	5.7	8.2	8.6
Longer than necessary	39.0	30.8	29.6	34.3	27.0	31.9
Other	0	3.8	1.4	0	0	1.0
D. K.	0	3.8	1.4	0	0	1.0
N. A.	29.3	15.4	38.0	34.3	45.9	33.8
Total	100%	100%	100%	100%	100%	100%
N	(41)	(26)	(71)	(35)	(37)	(210)

necessary to come to some kind of a decision. Responses to the question of time tended to be bi-modal; many respondents thought solutions took longer than necessary, but almost as many thought they were accomplished quickly; the middle judgement, *as soon as could be expected,* was mentioned least often.

Despite the negative context of constraint experiences, a surprisingly large proportion of people (48 percent) thought that they had been treated with consideration (Table 3.56). Respondents with police

Table 3.56

"Did the Government Officials Treat You with Consideration?"

	Type of Problem					
Response	Driver's license	Traffic violations	Tax	Police	Other	Total
Yes	43.9%	53.8%	53.5%	40.0%	43.3%	47.6%
No	43.9	42.4	26.8	51.4	24.3	35.7
D. K.	2.4	0	4.2	0	2.7	2.0
N. A.	9.8	3.8	15.5	8.6	29.7	14.7
Total	100%	100%	100%	100%	100%	100%
N	(41)	(26)	(71)	(35)	(37)	(210)

experience were least likely to report considerate treatment (40 percent), and respondents with tax and traffic violation problems showed the highest proportion (54 percent) who felt that they had received considerate treatment.

Another facet of the constraint experience had to do with respondents' perceptions of mistakes in the agency's handling of the problem (Table 3.57). Almost half of the users (45 percent) felt that mistakes had been made in their case. The police were perceived as the most prone to error by respondents (54 percent). Driver licensing bureaus, tax agencies, and traffic bureaus were seen as being slightly less prone to error (49 percent, 48 percent, and 42 percent respectively).

Table 3.57

*"Did the Agency Make Mistakes
in Handling Your Case?"*

| | Type of Problem | | | | | |
Response	Driver's license	Traffic violations	Tax	Police	Other	Total
Yes	48.8%	42.3%	47.9%	54.3%	27.0%	44.7%
No	41.5	46.2	29.6	37.1	43.3	37.5
D. K.	2.4	3.8	5.6	0	0	2.9
N. A.	7.3	7.7	16.9	8.6	29.7	15.2
Total	100%	100%	100%	100%	100%	100%
N	(41)	(26)	(71)	(35)	(37)	(210)

Respondents were further asked whether the agencies had been willing to correct any errors on their part. Fewer than half the people who claimed that mistakes had been made felt that the agencies were willing to do anything about correcting errors (Table 3.58). Police were seen as the most arrogant of the officials in this respect; none of the 18 who felt that the police had made mistakes in their case stated that the police had been willing to correct such mistakes. The numbers are small, but 54 percent of the respondents who had reported problems with police felt that the police had made errors in handling the situation. Other agencies were seen as more willing to correct mistakes, particularly tax bureaus (50 percent) and driver licensing agencies (65 percent). There is no implication in all this that the people summoned to constraint agencies are unbiased observers of the situation. Independent measures of agency performance are

Table 3.58

"If They Made Mistakes in Handling Your Case, Were They Willing to Correct Them?"

Response	Type of Problem					
	Driver's license	Traffic violations	Tax	Police	Other	Total
Yes	65.0%	33.3%	50.0%	0	54.5%	41.7%
No	35.0	58.4	41.1	94.7	45.5	53.1
D. K.	0	0	5.9	5.3	0	3.2
N. A.	0	8.3	3.0	0	0	2.0
Total	100%	100%	100%	100.0%	100%	100%
N	(20)	(12)	(34)	(19)	(11)	(96)

needed, and future research should provide them. One can argue, however, in a democratic society that an appropriate aim for government agencies—even agencies of constraint—is to have the affected citizens feel that they were treated fairly, promptly, and appropriately.

The question of equitable treatment was a particularly significant indicator of the quality of the constraint experience as contrasted with a service one. A much lower proportion of constraint agency clients (45 percent compared to 75 percent) felt that they had been treated fairly (Table 3.59). Within the constraint group, police once more came out at the bottom with only 34 percent of respondents perceiv-

Table 3.59

"Did the Government Office or Official Treat You Fairly?"

Response	Type of Problem					
	Driver's license	Traffic violations	Tax	Police	Other	Total
Yes	51.2%	50.0%	45.0%	34.2%	45.9%	45.2%
No	43.9	46.2	28.3	54.3	29.8	38.2
D. K.	0	3.8	12.7	2.9	2.7	5.7
N. A.	4.9	0	14.0	8.6	21.6	10.9
Total	100%	100%	100%	100%	100%	100%
N	(41)	(26)	(71)	(35)	(37)	(210)

ing fair treatment from them. Traffic violations offices (50 percent) and driver licensing bureaucracies (51 percent) were considered to be more equitable. Forty-five percent of the tax respondents said that they had been treated fairly.

The issue of equitable treatment is further illuminated by responses to the question of whether certain groups of people receive better treatment than others in relation to the agencies. The data give further support to the perception of unfair treatment by constraint agencies. Almost two times as many respondents perceived constraint bureaucracies as operating on a preferential basis (41 percent) as service agencies (24 percent). The police were considered to be the most biased, with 71 percent of those respondents who had contact with them believing that certain people fared better than others in relation to the police (Table 3.60). Traffic violation agencies were seen as the next worse offenders by those who had used them, with 65 percent of that sample perceiving preferential treatment of certain groups. Tax agencies (27 percent) and license bureaus (29 percent) were believed to be much more impartial.

Table 3.60

"Do Some Kinds of People Get Better Treatment Than Others from this Office?"

| Response | Type of Problem | | | | | |
	Driver's license	Traffic violations	Tax	Police	Other	Total
Yes	29.3%	65.4%	26.8%	71.4%	35.2%	40.8%
No	43.9	19.2	26.8	5.8	24.3	25.1
D. K.	21.9	15.4	33.8	11.4	24.3	23.7
N. A.	4.9	0	12.6	11.4	16.2	10.4
Total	100%	100%	100%	100%	100%	100%
N	(41)	(26)	(71)	(35)	(37)	(210)

The users of service agencies saw no particular groups as receiving either positive or negative treatment. The clients of constraint agencies, on the other hand, were in some agreement as to who received favored treatment and who, the opposite. Of the constraint agency users who believed in the existence of preferential treatment, 35 percent were convinced that the *rich* received the best treatment (Table 3.61). Of the service agency users, only 8 percent felt that way. Among constraint agency users, 29 percent believed the next most favored group were those *people who knew someone,* compared to 14 percent in the service group who felt this way. The racial issue was less important, with only 11 percent feeling that in dealing with constraint agencies, whites were favored. This was similar to the service agency response in which 9 percent saw favoritism toward whites. On the other hand, about as many respondents (14 percent) said blacks were at an advantage in dealing with the service agencies; almost no one thought that blacks received better treatment from constraint agencies.

Table 3.61

"What Kinds of People Get Better Treatment? What Kinds Worse Treatment?"

	Better Treatment	Worse Treatment
Whites	10.5%*	2.3%
Blacks	2.0	9.3
Rich	34.9	0
Poor	0	25.6
Politicians- People in Government	7.0	0
People who know someone	29.1	0
People who don't know someone	0	15.1
No groups specified	7.0	10.5

*Percentages based upon number of people who believe some groups get differential treatment.

However, since constraint *problems* are compared with service *experiences,* it is difficult to compare levels of satisfaction. One would expect somewhat less satisfaction among people who report problems with constraint agencies than among those who receive some form of service. Nevertheless, the differences between the two sets of experiences are not as great as one would expect, despite the fact that people are receiving assistance in the one situation and are being pressured to do something in the other. In fact, it is only a minority of those having problems with constraint agencies, though sometimes a sizable minority, who are clearly critical of these offices.

The experiences of respondents with service and constraint agencies do not show similar patterns, especially with respect to the issue of equitable treatment. The overall evaluation of the agencies can be viewed as reflecting two major aspects of client experience—one having to do with operational competence, the other with the more personal matters of consideration and fairness of treatment. Constraint agencies are judged to be more negative on both dimensions than the service agencies. Service agency clients were somewhat critical of the effectiveness of those agencies, but they did credit the service bureaucracies with rather equitable treatment. Constraint bureaucracies are seen as being much less fair in their operations, and less effective as well.

The questions on the awareness of the right of appeal and the results of going to higher levels shed further light on public perception of the constraint bureaucracy. Perhaps as a reflection of the respondents' more precarious positions in relation to constraint agencies, more constraint than service respondents knew about the existence of an appeal process (Table 3.62). Over one-half of the constraint sample were aware of appellate possibilities, compared to less than half of the service respondents. The proportion of knowledgeable respondents in constraint categories varied from 46 percent for tax and driver license problems to 69 percent for traffic violations.

Table 3.62

"Was There Someone at a Higher Level in the Office to Whom You Could Appeal for Help if Things Were Not Working Out All Right?"

	Type of Problem					
Response	Driver's license	Traffic violations	Tax	Police	Other	Total
Yes	46.3%	69.2%	46.5%	60.0%	45.9%	51.3%
No	19.5	15.4	12.6	17.2	27.1	17.5
D. K.	29.3	15.4	29.6	11.4	13.5	21.8
N. A.	4.9	0	11.3	11.4	13.5	9.4
Total	100%	100%	100%	100%	100%	100%
N	(41)	(26)	(71)	(35)	(37)	(210)

Not only did a higher proportion of constraint agency users know about the appellate process, but more availed themselves of the possibility in comparison to the service users. Of the 109 constraint agency respondents who were aware of options to appeal, 25 (about one-quarter) exercised this privilege (Table 3.63). This compares to 14 percent of the service utilizers who had gone to the trouble of appealing. Respondents were more likely to contest or appeal the initial constraint decision in police matters than with tax offices.

Table 3.63

"Did You Yourself Make Such an Appeal?"

	Type of Problem					
Response	Driver's license	Traffic violations	Tax	Police	Other	Total
Yes	21.1%	27.8%	14.7%	33.3%	23.5%	22.8%
No	78.9	72.2	79.5	66.7	76.5	75.2
D. K.	0	0	2.9	0	0	1.0
N. A.	0	0	2.9	0	0	1.0
Total	100%	100%	100%	100%	100%	100%
N	(19)	(18)	(34)	(21)	(71)	(109)

According to their own perceptions, more of the respondents in contact with service agencies than of those in contact with constraint agencies see themselves as similar to agency personnel. While almost 70 percent of the service agency users perceived the workers of those agencies as being like them, only about 50 percent of the constraint group felt similarly inclined (Table 3.64). The police seemed to be the

Table 3.64

"Are the People in the Office Pretty Much Like You?"

	Type of Problem					
Response	Driver's license	Traffic violations	Tax	Police	Other	Total
Yes	58.5%	46.2%	54.9%	34.2%	56.7%	51.4%
No	29.3	50.0	16.9	45.7	21.6	29.0
D. K.	7.3	3.8	16.9	3.6	3.4	8.6
N. A.	4.9	0	11.3	16.5	18.3	11.0
Total	100%	100%	100%	100%	100%	100%
N	(41)	(26)	(71)	(35)	(37)	(210)

most distant, with only 34 percent of the respondents perceiving similarity. Traffic violations personnel were seen as being slightly more like respondents (46 percent). Driver license personnel (59 percent) and tax agency workers (55 percent) had the highest perceived likeness to respondents.

Since only 41 respondents reported problems with driver licensing bureaus, 26 respondents problems with traffic violations, 71 tax problems, and 35 police interference with individual rights, an analysis of problem areas by background characteristics such as race, age, or education is not justified. Furthermore, although few respondents experienced difficulties with constraint agencies, the agencies studied were a sufficiently heterogeneous group that different agencies were salient for different groups, i.e., the types of individuals who experienced problems with the police were generally *not* the same persons who had tax problems. Therefore, it is not particularly meaningful to examine background characteristics across all four constraint experiences, nor are there sufficient cases to examine background variables within each constraint experience.

SUMMARY

Several patterns are apparent in the statements of respondents about their encounters with service agencies. For one thing, agencies differ in the satisfaction ratings they receive. A generally consistent pattern placed social security as the most positive service experience.* Medical and hospital care agencies and public assistance agencies were seen most negatively. The four work-related agencies were arrayed somewhere in between the two extreme positions, depending on the question.

Our data also contradict certain stereotypes about service bureaucracies. One of these commonly held beliefs is that bureaucratic encounters tend to be unpleasant and that clients are typically dissatisfied. Our results point in a more positive direction, with two-thirds of the respondents expressing satisfaction with their most important encounter. To say that common beliefs about the nature of bureaucracy are unduly derogatory, however, does not mean that service agencies are functioning at an acceptable degree of effectiveness. A

---

*Throughout this report, the Social Security Administration has been referred to for retirement benefits. There are, however, other public retirement benefit programs. While over 80 percent of respondents listed social security as the source of benefits, others mentioned such diverse programs as railroad retirement, state pension, teachers pension, Veteran's Administration, and the like.

majority of satisfied clients may leave a sizable minority dissatisfied. Even a 75 percent level of satisfaction may be low for some programs in which 90 percent or higher is desirable and feasible. In a population of 200 million, small percentages are large numbers.

In addition to rather high degrees of satisfaction elicited from those with service agency experiences, three out of five clients felt that their situations had been improved or their problems resolved by the agency they visited.

The stereotype of the elusive bureaucrat was also unsupported by our data. Such people exist, but only one in ten clients had encountered difficulties in finding the right person or agency. Clients were also more positive in their evaluation of the amount of effort expended by the people they dealt with in the agency. Three out of five respondents felt that agency personnel had done about the right amount of work to help them. An additional 16 percent felt that bureaucratic workers had gone beyond the call of duty. And yet, one in five felt that the personnel had done less than they should have or nothing at all. The stereotype of bureaucratic inefficiency was also called into question by the study. Only one in five clients evaluated an agency as having been inefficient.

Most respondents tended to view the service bureaucracies as operating on an equitable basis. Three out of four felt that they had been treated fairly, and only one in four felt that some groups of people received preferential treatment. Furthermore, clients who felt that an agency exercised discriminatory procedures did not share a focused impression as to which groups were advantaged or disadvantaged.

As far as having options or alternative courses of action, one out of four clients felt that he was offered no alternatives by the agency. However, a large majority felt that an opportunity to appeal an unfavorable decision existed. Slightly more than one in ten felt that they had no recourse vis-a-vis the agency. Nevertheless, despite the large proportion of people who were aware of the appellate process, only 15 percent actually exercised that prerogative.

The satisfactions and dissatisfactions that people experience with government services are not explainable to any great extent in terms of demographic variables. While the most satisfied respondents were likely to be older, white, female, in the lowest or highest income brackets, and relatively well-educated, the predictive power of each of these variables was quite low when others were held constant. Overall, age was the most consistent predictor, with young people highest in dissatisfaction.

In describing the constraint experience, the frame of reference shifted from asking respondents whether they had ever sought help from a service agency to asking them whether they had ever encountered problems in dealing with a constraint agency, a formulation that probably tends to evoke negative responses. Indeed, the results showed that agencies that constrained or penalized people generated many more negative evaluations by respondents than did agencies offering services. The results of constraint experiences also tended to support at least some of the negative stereotypes of bureaucracies.

A majority of the constraint agency respondents felt negatively about the procedures used by those agencies. One-fifth of the constraint group stated that they had been subjected to threats and pressures, although there was wide variation across the four constraint areas. Half of the respondents with police and the traffic violation experiences reported such treatment, compared to 13 percent of those who had been called in for tax problems, and almost none of those who had driver licensing problems. Approximately one-third of the respondents felt that the constraint experience had created some difficulty, and about two-fifths felt that the agency had created a great deal of difficulty. Furthermore, almost one-half of the constraint agency clients felt that agency personnel had made the problem worse by the way they had handled it.

On the question of equitable treatment, a much lower proportion of contraint agency respondents than service agency respondents felt that they had been treated fairly (45 percent as opposed to 76 percent). In addition, almost two times as many constraint agency clients perceived constraint bureaucracies as operating on a preferential basis. Moreover, the constraint agency respondents who thought that differential treatment existed were in considerable agreement as to who received better treatment. *The rich* and *those who knew someone* were seen as being in a more advantageous position.

On the question of appeal, approximately one-half of the constraint sample were aware of appellate possibilities, and almost one-fourth of those aware clients exercised the privilege.

Chapter 4

SYSTEM SUPPORT

Our examination of people's encounters with service and control agencies did include an evaluation of specific offices based upon the personal experiences of respondents. We were also interested in the more abstract level of attitudes toward government agencies and leadership in general. These generalized evaluations, moreover, should interact with the experiences of people with particular offices, but we do not expect any close correspondence between these levels in spite of some mutual influence of one upon the other.

The generalized evaluations are an important subject for investigation and, in recent years, speculation and research have grown about the extent of involvement, withdrawal, and disaffection in a bureaucratized society. Trend figures on apathy, anomie, and alienation for the country as a whole and for various sub-groups have been suggested as significant social indicators. But measures of individual disaffection which are not tied either to aspects of the social system or to related behaviors are not very useful or theoretically valuable. Unless it is known what people are alienated from, or what the behavioral consequences are, trend figures on percentages of alienation merely point to a problem.

Generalized attitudes, then, need to be considered in relation to some specific level or aspect of system functioning rather than as free-floating expressions of individual happiness or distress. For a more meaningful social approach, it is necessary to analyze the cognitive object of attitudes as they relate to dimensions of system support. Attitudes can vary in their strength and favorability as people move from one level of the system to another as David Easton (1965) suggests in his model of political structure. We will examine in greater detail the problem of different structural levels in the second section of this chapter. First, however, we will follow up the account in chapter three of basic satisfaction and dissatisfaction in the experiences of respondents with specific offices, with a discussion of attitudes toward administrative agencies in general. The specific experi-

117

ential level and the general evaluation of administrative machinery constitute two dimensions of system support in our own framework.

GENERAL ATTITUDES TOWARD ADMINISTRATIVE AGENCIES

The attitudes of American people toward their political system are complex. On the one hand, they accept the conventional criticisms of public bureaucracy which characterize government offices as arbitrary, impersonal, wasteful, and officious. On the other hand, they think that most government agencies are fair in their treatment of people and are considerate in dealing with them. And some of the same people who have little confidence in the competence and integrity of government leadership in general believe that their own congressman or local political leaders can be very helpful in getting a government agency to do something about a problem. A look at the specifics of these responses is in order before attempting an interpretation of the apparent inconsistencies.

Questions directed at the functioning of government offices in general draw more favorable than unfavorable responses. To the opening question, "By and large do you think most government offices do a good job?", some 61 percent answered affirmatively, 28 percent negatively (Table 4.1). The interpretation of these figures depends upon one's frame of reference. To carry an election, a bare majority or even a plurality may suffice. But to function effectively in the administration of policy, government agencies in a democratic system may need a much higher level of acceptance.

Table 4.1

"By and Large, Do Most Government Offices Do a Good Job?"

Response	Percent of Sample
Yes	60.7%
Mixed	1.8
No	28.3
D.K.	9.2
Total	100.0%
N	(1,414)

People were asked to be more specific in their reactions and were asked to rate government offices from very bad to very good on six characteristics: (1) giving prompt service; (2) really taking care of the problem; (3) giving considerate treatment to people; (4) giving fair treatment; (5) avoiding mistakes; and, (6) correcting mistakes. On these six criteria, there were more positive than negative ratings on four, and more negative than positive ratings on two (Table 4.2).

Table 4.2

Ratings of Government Offices on Various Criteria

				Criteria		
Rating	Giving prompt service	Really taking care of problem	Considerate treatment	Fair Treatment	Avoiding Mistakes	Correcting Mistakes
1 Very bad	8.0%	6.4%	5.3%	5.1%	6.5%	6.9%
2	10.1	9.9	7.3	7.1	9.6	10.0
3	19.0	18.7	15.4	13.8	17.2	15.3
4	30.5	32.0	29.1	28.1	26.1	24.3
5	19.1	18.7	24.2	25.2	20.2	19.2
6	6.4	7.7	10.7	12.4	12.3	13.5
7 Excellent	3.9	3.0	4.2	4.7	4.3	5.8
D.K.	3.1	3.7	3.8	3.7	3.9	5.0
Total	100.0%	100.0%	100.0%	100.0%	100.0%	100.0%
N	(1,422)	(1,419)	(1,419)	(1,418)	(1,420)	(1,414)

Some 10 percent of the respondents gave government offices high marks on prompt service, and 18 percent gave low ratings, with the great majority falling in the middle categories. In *really taking care of the problem* the distribution of responses was similar, with 10 percent very favorable and 16 percent very critical. But in evaluating the consideration shown by agencies, there were more positive than negative ratings, 39 percent as against 28 percent, though extreme ratings show only a 3 percent difference. Similarly, with respect to fair treatment, 42 percent were favorable and 26 percent critical, with a 5 percent difference between extreme scores. There is a slight difference with more favorable than unfavorable responses on *being careful to avoid errors* and a similarly slight, but significant, differential on *correcting errors*. In summary, government offices get bad marks from between 26 percent to 37 percent of the public, depending upon the characteristic being evaluated. On no criterion, however, does this evaluation fall into the two extreme negative categories for more than 18 percent of the people.

These responses indicate, then, that while less than one in five persons is strongly critical of government offices, the great majority are also not enthusiastic. Most people assign intermediate ratings to various aspects of the functioning of public agencies. They tend to be more critical of the services public offices provide on the basis of promptness, and more positive about fair and considerate treatment.

GENERAL EVALUATIONS COMPARED
WITH SPECIFIC EXPERIENCES

When we compare the overall distribution of evaluations of agency experiences with attitudes toward the functioning of agencies in general, there is a consistent trend toward a more positive picture at the level of personal experience with a particular service office. The difference is slight in comparing responses of satisfaction about the way the service agency handled the problem with general responses about how good a job government offices do (Table 4.3). It is marked, however, on the parallel questions of problem solution where 71 percent of the clients report a successful outcome in their own case whereas only 30 percent give the government office good marks on being able to take care of problems generally. It is also marked in reports of fairness, 80 percent in personal encounters compared to 42 percent in general evaluation. Considerate treatment was indicated by 77 percent for their own experiences, and by 39 percent for government offices in general. While 72 percent of clients thought the agency had functioned efficiently for them, respondents were rather evenly divided in responding positively or negatively on how most agencies functioned in general with respect to prompt services and avoiding errors. It is clear that for many respondents there is a separation of generalized attitudes from specific attitudes concerned with an individual's own experience.

Assessments of personal experiences with service agencies are thus considerably more favorable than evaluative attitudes toward the general functioning of public offices. But the more general responses about government offices may have been provided in reference to agencies of constraint as well as agencies of service. If we compare constraint experiences with general attitudes, there is greater correspondence between the two than between service experiences and general attitudes in overall distributions (Table 4.4). Responses of considerate treatment give the same figures for constraint experiences

Table 4.3

Comparison of Two Levels of Response: Personal
Experience with Service Agencies and General
Evaluation of Government Offices

Personal Experience		General Evaluation of All Agencies	
A. *Service agency's handling of own problem*		*Do most government offices do good job?*	
Very satisfied	44.8%	Yes	60.7%
Fairly well satisfied	27.3	Mixed	1.8
Somewhat satisfied	13.2	No	28.3
Very dissatisfied	14.3	D.K.	9.2
D.K.	0.4		
Total	100.0%	Total	100.0%
N	(785)	N	(1,414)
B. *Service agency taking care of personal problem*		*Rating of government offices on taking care of problem*	
Problem solved	70.8%	7 Excellent	3.7%
Problem pending	2.4	6	7.7
Problem not solved	26.8	5	18.7
		4	32.0
Total	100.0%	3	18.7
N	(671)	2	9.9
		1 Very bad	6.4
		D.K.	3.7
		Total	100.0%
		N	(1,419)
C. *Treated fairly*		*Fairness of government offices in general*	
		7 Excellent	4.7%
Fairly	79.8%	6	12.4
Mixed	4.8	5	25.2
Unfairly	13.0	4	28.1
D.K.	2.3	3	13.8
		2	7.1
Total	100.0%	1 Very Bad	5.1
N	(787)	D.K.	3.7
		Total	100.0%
		N	(1,418)

D. *Amount of effort shown by agency personnel*

More effort than required	16.7%
About right	60.5
Less than they should have	
No effort at all	8.9
D.K.	0.8
	———
Total	100.0%
N	(783)

Ratings of considerate treatment by agencies

7 Excellent	4.2%
6	10.7
5	24.2
4	29.1
3	15.4
2	7.3
1 Very Bad	5.3
D.K.	3.8
Total	100.0%
N	(1,419)

E. *Efficiency in handling own problem*

Very efficient	44.8%
Fairly efficient	27.3
Rather inefficient	13.2
Very inefficient	14.3
D.K.	0.4
	———
Total	100.0%
N	(785)

General ratings of promptness of service

7 Excellent	3.9%
6	6.4
5	19.1
4	30.5
3	19.0
2	10.1
1 Very bad	8.0
D.K.	3.1
Total	100.0%
N	(1,422)

and general attitudes. Efficiency in dealing with problems was also very comparable for constraint experiences and for general evaluation save that the comparison favored the general attitudes slightly. Similarly, those people who had contacts with control agencies were almost as likely to report their treatment as fair as those who referred to government offices in general. Only in making mistakes and correcting errors did experiences with control agencies show a significantly more unfavorable distribution of responses than the general reactions. The discrepancy between reports of experiences with service agencies and reports of general attitudes thus does not seem to be due to the possible negative weighting of general attitudes by encounters with control agencies. This seems true despite the fact that only problem experiences are included in the category of constraint encounters. Some light may be shed on the question by looking at the relationship between the answers of the same people when talking about personal experiences and about their general ideas of agency functioning.

Table 4.4

Comparison of Two Levels of Response: Personal Experience with Constraint Agencies and General Evaluation of Government Offices

Personal Experience		General Evaluation	
A. *Fairness of own treatment*		*Ratings of government offices in fairness*	
Fair	50.8%	7 Excellent	4.7%
Unfair	42.8	6	12.4
D.K.	6.4	5	25.2
		4	28.1
Total	100.0%	3	13.8
N	(187)	2	7.1
		1 Very bad	5.1
		D. K.	3.7
		Total	100.0%
		N	(1,418)
Preferential treatment			
Some people treated better	45.5%		
No preferential treatment	28.0		
D.K.	26.5		
Total	100.0%		
N	(189)		
B. *Considerate treatment in own contact with agency*		*General ratings of considerateness of agencies*	
Treated with consideration	55.6%	7 Excellent	4.2%
Not treated with consideration	41.7	6	10.7
D.K.	2.7	5	24.2
		4	29.1
Total	100.0%	3	15.4
N	(180)	2	7.3
		1 Very Bad	5.3
		D.K.	3.8
		Total	100.0%
		N	(1,419)

C. *Efficiency in handling own case*

		General ratings of efficiency of offices	
Very efficient	16.3%	7 Excellent	3.9%
Fairly efficient	24.5	6	6.4
Rather inefficient	27.2	5	19.1
Very inefficient	29.9	4	30.4
D.K.	2.2	3	19.0
		2	10.1
Total	100.0%	1 Very Bad	8.0
N	(184)	D.K.	3.1
		Total	100.0%
		N	(1,422)

D. *Mistakes made by agency in personal contact*

		General rating of taking care to avoid mistakes	
No mistakes made	44.1%	7 Excellent	4.3%
Mistakes made	52.5	6	12.3
D.K.	3.4	5	20.2
		4	26.1
Total	100.0%	3	17.2
N	(179)	2	9.6
		1 Very Bad	6.5
		D.K.	3.9
		Total	100.0%
		N	(1,420)

E. *Willingness to correct mistakes*

		General rating of correction of mistakes	
Willing to correct mistakes	42.6%	7 Excellent	5.8%
Not willing to correct		6	13.5
mistakes	54.3	5	19.2
D.K.	3.1	4	24.3
		3	15.3
Total	100.0%	2	10.0
N	(94)	1 Very Bad	6.9
		D.K.	5.0
		Total	100.0%
		N	(1,414)

People's perceptions of the fairness of their own treatment by a service agency are related to their evaluation of government offices in general, but only if their own experiences have been unfortunate. Those who report fair treatment are no more positive in their general evaluation of agencies than those who have had no experience with public service agencies (Table 4.5). The distributions of the ratings of public agencies by the fair treatment group and the no-experience group are very similar, with 47 percent of the former and 47 percent of the latter assigning good marks to the agencies. Twenty-five percent of the fairly treated group and 21 percent of the inexperienced gave unfavorable responses. For those receiving unfair treatment, some 57 percent evaluated agencies unfavorably, but as many as 20 percent did not generalize their experience to poor agency functioning.

Table 4.5

Perception of Fairness of Personal Treatment in Service
Agencies Related to Ratings of Fairness of Public
Agencies in General

Ratings of Fairness of Government Agencies	Personal Treatment					
	Treated fairly	Mixed treatment	Treated unfairly	Total with with experience	No experience	Total sample
1 Very bad	3.5%	15.8%	19.6%	6.4%	4.2%	5.1%
2	6.5	23.7	15.7	8.6	5.0	7.1
3	14.8	13.2	21.6	15.7	12.3	13.8
4	27.7	26.3	23.5	27.0	30.0	28.1
5	28.3	5.3	17.6	25.7	27.7	25.2
6	13.3	13.2	2.0	11.8	13.8	12.4
7 Excellent	5.8	2.6	0	4.9	5.2	4.7
D. K.						3.7
Total	100.0%	100.0%	100.0%	100.0%	100.0%	100.0%
N	(600)	(38)	(102)	(740)	(573)	(1,418)

People's perceptions of the fairness of treatment of other clients follows the same pattern. In general, those respondents utilizing government services who feel that certain sub-groups receive preferential treatment rate government agencies low in fairness. However, those who have had contact with a government agency and do not feel preferential treatment is given to specific groups do not rate government offices in general as more fair than do those respondents with no experience (Table 4.6).

Table 4.6

Perception of Differential Treatment in Service
Agencies Related to Ratings of Fairness of Public
Agencies in General

Ratings of Fairness of Government Agencies	Personal Treatment				
	Preferential treatment	No preferential treatment	Experience	No experience	Total
1 Very bad	11.9%	3.6%	6.1%	4.2%	5.0%
2	13.4	6.8	9.0	5.1	7.0
3	24.2	9.7	15.9	12.2	13.7
4	25.8	26.5	27.5	31.4	27.7
5	18.0	31.1	24.7	28.2	24.9
6	4.6	15.2	12.2	13.8	12.2
7 Excellent	15.4	7.1	4.7	5.2	4.7
D. K.					4.6
Total	100.0%	100.0%	100.0%	100.0%	100.0%
N	(194)	(309)	(790)	(574)	(1,364)

It appears, then, that bad experiences with specific agencies lower the individual's general appraisal of public offices, but good experiences do not raise it above the norm. A plausible interpretation is that general attitudes toward administrative agencies have little specific experiential basis and derive from the cumulative impact of the mass media and the accepted beliefs in the culture. These stereotyped conceptions are not impervious to certain types of personal experiences. Unpleasant occurrences result in lowered evaluations, whereas pleasant encounters have little impact. Another interpretation would be that those who have a very negative orientation toward government offices interpret their specific encounters negatively no matter how well they are treated. We shall return to a fuller consideration of these alternative explanations after considering more of the findings on the correlates of satisfaction with agencies.

Constraint agency experiences and attitudes show the same relationship between specific encounters and general evaluations as was true of service agencies. There is little difference in attitudes between the people who report fair treatment in their own constraint experiences, and those who have had no problems with a control agency with regard to a general rating of government offices on fairness of treatment (Table 4.7). Encountering fair treatment does not raise the level of favorable assessment. Specific contacts perceived as unfair, however, are associated with a more negative evaluation of the overall fairness of government agencies. Again we find a separation of appraisal at the level of personal experience and at the level of agencies as a whole. At the personal, particularistic level, responses are more favorable than at the general, more remote, level. There is an interaction between the two levels for bad experiences but not for good experiences.

Table 4.7

Perception of Fairness of Personal Treatment in
Constraint Agencies Related to Ratings of Fairness of
Public Agencies in General

Ratings of Fairness of Government Agencies	Personal Treatment				
	Treated fairly	Not treated fairly	Total experience	No experience	Total sample
1 Very bad	4.4%	14.3%	8.9%	4.8%	5.1%
2	6.6	16.9	11.3	6.7	7.1
3	17.6	20.8	19.0	13.6	13.8
4	26.4	28.6	27.4	29.1	28.1
5	28.6	18.2	23.8	26.4	25.2
6	9.9	0	5.4	14.2	12.4
7 Excellent	6.6	1.3	4.2	5.2	4.7
D. K.					3.7
Total	100.0%	100.0%	100.0%	100.0%	100.0%
N	(91)	(77)	(168)	(1,163)	(1,418)

The consistency of this trend in the findings is apparent in Table 4.8, in which a specific question on preferential treatment is related to general assessment of fairness. Respondents who had encounters with control agencies were asked about the specific office with which they were involved: "Do some kinds of people get better treatment from this office?" Those who felt the office did give preferential treatment were more likely to give government agencies poor ratings on fairness than were other respondents. But those who in their own experience found the office handling matters equitably for all people were no more favorably disposed to give good marks to public offices on fairness than were those not having any difficulties with control agencies. Good experience is the equivalent of no experience.

Table 4.8

Perception of Differential Treatment in Constraint
Agencies Related to Ratings of Fairness of Public
Agencies in General

Ratings of Fairness of Government Agencies	Personal Treatment				
	Preferential treatment	No preferential treatment	Experience	No experience	Total
1 Very bad	12.2%	3.8%	8.9%	4.7%	5.1%
2	14.6	7.5	11.9	6.7	7.1
3	19.5	15.1	17.8	13.6	13.8
4	28.0	32.1	29.6	29.2	28.1
5	20.7	26.4	23.0	26.4	25.2
6	2.4	11.3	5.9	14.1	12.4
7 Excellent	2.4	3.8	3.0	5.2	4.7
D. K.					3.7
Total	100.0%	100%	100%	100%	100%
	(82)	(53)	(135)	(1,161)	(1,418)

Since service and constraint experiences have been considered separately, it is possible that the foregoing findings may be due to the effects of the type of experience not considered in the separate analyses. For example, people who report fair treatment by a service agency may have felt unfairly treated by a control agency and so they evaluate the fairness of all governmental agencies negatively. To check on this possibility, we examined the relationship between service and constraint experiences. Of those who reported fair treatment by a constraint agency, only 14 respondents said they were treated unfairly by a service agency. Of those who reported fair treatment by a service agency, only 30 respondents reported unfair treatment by a constraint agency. These numbers are much too small to be responsible for the relationships cited.

Considerate treatment of clients by agency personnel is another area in which parallel questions were asked about the functioning of agencies in general and about the personal experience of the client. Every respondent was asked to rate government offices on considerate treatment, and clients were asked about how much effort people at the agency had made to be helpful. The clients who thought that agency people had put forth adequate or more than adequate effort in their behalf were no more generous in their general ratings of agencies on considerate treatment than were the people who had no contact with service agencies (Table 4.9). Nor was there any appreciable difference between those who thought the effort was about right and those who felt the effort was beyond the call of duty. But those who felt that agency people had done nothing at all, or less than their roles required, were much more likely to give government agencies a low rating on considerate treatment. Once more, the unfortunate experience is associated with low evaluation, whereas the favorable experience has no impact. It is almost as if agency people can do nothing to improve the general public image of government offices through consideration of clients and fairness of treatment, but they can do a great deal to impair it by unfair and inconsiderate handling of clients.

The generalization about the greater potency of unpleasant experiences holds for people having difficulties with control agencies. Those who say they were not treated considerately are the most

Table 4.9

Personal Experience with Service Agency Helpfulness
Related to General Ratings of Considerate Treatment by
Public Agencies

General Ratings of Considerate Treatment	Amount of Effort				Experienced with Agency	No experience with Agency	Total Sample
	More effort	About right	Less effort	No effort			
1 Very bad	4.0%	4.0%	9.9%	26.1%	6.9%	3.8%	5.3%
2	10.3	5.4	10.9	21.7	8.5	6.1	7.3
3	15.1	17.4	20.8	15.9	17.3	13.3	15.4
4	27.0	29.5	35.6	24.6	29.4	31.8	29.1
5	22.2	25.2	17.8	7.2	22.0	29.3	24.2
6	15.1	13.2	3.0	4.3	11.3	11.1	10.7
7 Excellent	6.3	5.4	2.0	0	4.6	4.5	4.2
D. K.							3.8
Total	100.0%	100.0%	100.0%	100.0%	100.0%	100.0%	100.0%
N	(126)	(448)	(101)	(69)	(744)	(576)	(1,320)

critical of agency functioning, with 59 percent of them assigning poor ratings to government offices in this respect (Table 4.10). For this question, however, even those who were treated with consideration according to their own account are less positive in their general evaluations than are people having no encounters with enforcement offices. The very fact of running into difficulty with a constraint office has a negative effect which is not completely removed by considerate treatment and which is intensified by lack of consideration. Again, personal experience generalizes more readily to attitudinal orientation when it is unpleasant than when it is pleasant.

Table 4.10

Personal Experience with Constraint Agency
Considerateness Related to General Ratings of
Considerate Treatment by Public Agencies

General Ratings of Considerate Treatment	Own Treatment		Experienced with Agency	No experience with Agency	Total Sample
	Treated considerately	Not treated considerately			
1 Very bad	10.4%	20.5%	14.8%	4.1%	5.3%
2	6.3	15.1	10.1	7.1	7.3
3	22.9	23.3	23.1	14.8	15.4
4	22.9	24.7	23.7	31.3	29.1
5	21.9	11.0	17.2	26.2	24.2
6	9.4	2.7	6.5	11.9	10.7
7 Excellent	5.3	1.2	4.7	4.5	4.2
D. K.					3.8
Total	100%	100%	100%	100%	100%
N	(96)	(73)	(169)	(1,160)	(1,419)

The questions so far examined have concerned fairness and considerateness on the part of agency people in relation to the evaluation of government offices. People were also asked to give their opinion of how efficiently the office with which they had been in contact had handled their problem. There was no comparable question on general ratings of agencies, but people were asked to evaluate agencies on promptness of service. The correlation of the answers to this question with those of the perceived efficiency of handling a personal problem is significantly positive (Table 4.11). Forty-two percent of the clients of service agencies in the *very efficient* response category gave positive ratings to public offices for prompt service as against only 8 percent in the *very inefficient* response category. In this instance there seems to be some direct effect of favorable experience. Those treated in *very efficient* fashion give public offices a higher rating than do those with no experience with service agencies. The no-experience people are more favorable than those treated in *fairly efficient* fashion, though only slightly so.

Table 4.11

Personal Experience with Service Agency Efficiency
Related to General Ratings of Promptness of Service of
Public Agencies

General Ratings of Considerate Treatment	Own Experience				Experienced with Agency	No Experience with Agency	Total Sample
	Very efficient	Fairly efficient	Rather inefficient	Very inefficient			
1 Very bad	6.7%	8.8%	22.7%	22.1%	10.8%	4.8%	8.0%
2	7.3	12.4	9.3	19.8	10.6	9.9	10.1
3	19.6	17.7	22.7	24.4	19.8	19.2	19.0
4	24.9	34.1	29.3	25.6	28.5	35.8	30.5
5	26.0	18.1	9.0	8.1	19.5	19.6	19.1
6	7.9	5.2	4.0	0	5.7	7.5	6.4
7 Excellent	7.6	3.6	4.0	0	5.1	3.2	3.9
D. K.							3.1
Total	100%	100%	100%	100%	100%	100%	100%
N	(342)	(249)	(75)	(86)	(752)	(577)	(1,422)

On this more objective aspect of agency functioning, both positive and negative experiences are effective. Experiences with constraint agencies, however, show a different pattern (Table 4.12). The most positive ratings of all government offices came from those having no difficulties with control offices. Even if the enforcement agency was efficient in handling the problem, people were more negative than positive in their evaluation. This does not seem to be due to a difference in the interpretation of efficiency with regard to a control agency as compared to a service agency (i.e., an efficient tax office could be resented because of its efficiency in taking one's money). The people who report the enforcement agency as inefficient give government offices the lowest evaluation in promptness of service.

Table 4.12

Personal Experience with Constraint Agency Efficiency
Related to General Ratings of Promptness of Service of
Public Agencies

Ratings of Prompt Service	Own Experience		Experienced with Agency	No Experience with Agency	Total Sample
	Efficient	Inefficient			
1 Very bad	13.9%	21.2%	18.2%	6.5%	8.0%
2	11.1	15.5	13.6	9.5	10.1
3	18.1	21.2	19.9	19.5	19.0
4	36.1	26.1	30.1	31.9	30.5
5	9.7	12.5	11.4	21.2	19.1
6	4.2	2.9	3.4	7.2	6.4
7 Excellent	6.9	0.1	3.4	4.1	3.9
D. K.			—		3.1
Total	100%	100%	100%	100%	100%
N	(72)	(104)	(176)	(1,173)	(1,349)

GOVERNMENT AND PRIVATE ENTERPRISE COMPARED

We have interpreted the less favorable orientation toward government offices at the general level than at the personal level as reflecting a stereotyped image of bureaucracy. Personal experiences are only one factor in accounting for the schemata people employ. Consistent with this interpretation are the findings from questions which ask people to make comparative evaluations of government and business organizations on six criteria, e.g., which was better (in giving prompt service, taking care of a problem, etc.), or were they about the same. The modal response for the total sample on five of the six aspects of organizational functioning was to equate public agencies and private enterprise (Table 4.13). Only on the criterion of fair treatment was the modal response *business organizations better.* On giving prompt service, the modal response of *both the same* was also a majority response. Among those who did not equate public and private performance, however, more people viewed private enterprise as superior to public agencies. The ratio in favor of business was highest for prompt service, 5 to 1, and lowest for fair treatment, 2-1/2 to 1. These findings are congruent, however, with the popular conception in the mass media that business organizations are more efficient and effective than government agencies. They suggest that some of the favorable evaluations of government services on the rating scales were only mildly favorable, and once a framework of comparison was provided, their lukewarm character became apparent. The opposite interpretation already suggested would be that the superiority of private to public organizations is a stereotype which tells little of people's feelings about how they would like their problems handled.

Table 4.13

Comparison of Government with Business

	Government Versus Business					
Ratings	Government better	The same	Business better	D.K.	Total	N
Giving prompt service	7.0%	54.4%	36.0%	2.7%	100%	(1,393)
Really taking care of problem	11.5	45.9	39.0	3.6	100%	(1,417)
Considerate treatment	11.5	47.8	37.5	3.0	100%	(1,420)
Fair treatment	18.8	33.6	44.5	3.0	100%	(1,415)
Avoiding errors	14.6	45.0	36.7	3.6	100%	(1,413)
Correcting errors	14.3	45.9	35.9	3.9	100%	(1,374)

Support for this second point of view comes from the answers to another battery of questions in which respondents were given a list of eight problems and then asked what kind of office or agency could handle it best. They could specify business rather than government and, if government, the level of government: town or city, county, state, or federal. For every type of problem the overwhelming response was in favor of a public agency rather than private enterprise (Table 4.14). It is not surprising that relief for the needy should be regarded as something which can best be handled by public agencies (only 3 percent thought private enterprise should deal with this problem). But even retraining for better jobs, which might be regarded as an appropriate function for private industry and which, in fact, some industrial enterprises do carry on, was seen as something which could be handled better by government agencies. Some 21 percent thought private enterprise the better agent to handle job retraining, and this was the highest percentage selecting business organizations for any of the eight problem areas. Only 5 percent selected private enterprise rather than a government agency for dealing with environmental pollution, and only 9 percent made a similar choice for safety standards for automobiles.

Table 4.14

Best Agency for Handling Problem

Problem	Agency							
	Business	Government						
		Town	County	State	Federal	D. K.	Total	N
Unemployment compensation	6.4%	18.0%	10.6%	40.4%	14.8%	9.8%	100%	(1,421)
Payment for health & medical services	9.7	8.5	13.7	27.6	33.6	9.7	100%	(1,419)
Retraining people for better job	21.2	11.8	10.7	28.5	18.8	8.9	100%	(1,416)
Retirement benefits	16.3	3.3	3.0	22.2	47.3	7.9	100%	(1,413)
Relief for needy and dependent children	2.8	16.0	16.6	30.3	27.9	6.4	100%	(1,416)
Controlling crime	1.4	34.3	10.4	19.4	27.7	6.8	100%	(1,406)
Preventing environmental pollution	4.7	14.8	8.6	24.0	40.7	7.3	100%	(1,412)
Safety standards for autos	9.1	3.7	1.8	23.8	54.1	7.6	100%	(1,417)

Clearly, then, while there is a popular conception of private enterprise as more effective than public agencies, there are also widely held beliefs that public agencies should handle problems of public concern. There would be no basic inconsistency between the two belief systems if people made their judgments about the appropriateness of the problem for government offices only on some clear criteria of public interest. And the findings do indicate that the rank order of percentages of people selecting private over public agencies for the various problems declines as the problem is more obviously in the public sphere—1 percent for controlling crime and 21 percent for retraining people for better jobs. It is also true that people may be responding on the issues of current practices which place these problems under the jurisdiction of public agencies.

Nonetheless, something of a puzzle remains as to why people who see business as better than government in taking care of problems efficiently and fairly do not also feel that government should stay away from as many problem areas as possible. Presumably they should be against government encroachment and so should want the automobile industry to deal with safety problems in cars and the broader industrial complex to cope with problems of environmental pollution. And they should be jealous of industry's role in job retraining. Obviously this is not the case, for people accept both sets of beliefs. It may well be that attitudes about the superiority of business organizations are general stereotypes, but when particular problems have to be met, people turn to the agency that seems related to the problem either because it has handled it in the past or it seems appropriate for it to do so. People thus have two modes of response: the ideological and the pragmatic. Social scientists have given insufficient recognition to these two modes, though some of the earliest studies of the nature of attitudes showed that people would accept specific measures while rejecting the general labels appropriate to them (G. W. Allport, 1929; G. W. Hartmann, 1936). R. Stagner (1936), for example, demonstrated that people who renounced the label of fascism would still accept many of its specific recommendations. Likewise today, people may oppose the idea of a welfare state, but still approve of receiving unemployment compensation while laid off, or workmen's compensation when injured on the job.

Another instance of these two attitudinal levels occurs in reactions to federal and local government. To the general question, "Would you like to see the people of this community have more or less control of governmental offices?", two-thirds of the sample predictably said *more control*. Some 18 percent, curiously, were not willing to commit themselves on the issue. When, however, people were asked about what level of government should handle a given problem, the federal and state levels were heavily preferred over city or county levels (Table 4.14). In only one of the eight problem areas did the city or town level get more votes than other levels—namely, for controlling crime. Some 34 percent felt this way, but 28 percent thought that even this traditional area of local jurisdiction should be taken care of by the federal government. In four of the seven other problem areas, the federal level was selected by more respondents than any other level, and in the remaining three areas the state government was selected as the best agency for taking care of matters. Though local control is a socially popular response in talking generally about public policy, when asked about particular problems, people realistically would rather see them handled at a higher level in the system. Pragmatism prevails over ideology in the reactions of the American public.

OTHER GENERAL ATTITUDES TOWARD PUBLIC BUREAUCRACY

In addition to having people evaluate the functioning of agencies on such specifics as giving prompt service and fairness of treatment, we asked respondents about their degree of agreement and disagreement with some general criticisms of public offices as well as with some statements favorable to such offices. For example, the list included such statements as "It is becoming difficult for an individual to have any private life because government pries and interferes," and "The people in government offices are usually very helpful."

The great majority of people avoided taking extreme positions, and on eight of the ten questions the sum of the respondents in both *strongly agree* and *strongly disagree* categories was less than 15 percent (Table 4.15).

Table 4.15

General Attitudes Toward Public Bureaucracy

Characteristics of Bureaucracy	General Attitudes						
	Strongly agree	Agree	Disagree	Strongly disagree	D. K.	Total	N
Too many officers doing same thing	19.5%	58.7%	13.3%	0.7%	7.6%	100%	(1,412)
Abuse their authority	7.0	30.1	54.6	3.0	5.3	100%	(1,409)
No official takes responsibility	8.6	47.6	37.0	1.6	5.2	100%	(1,417)
No official takes an interest in your problem	7.3	39.8	45.5	1.8	5.5	100%	(1,411)
Government pries into private life	9.9	33.5	48.6	5.2	2.7	100%	(1,419)
Officials gain most	10.5	47.6	33.8	1.6	6.5	100%	(1,413)
Government workers try to do good job	4.7	66.9	22.6	3.2	2.5	100%	(1,418)
Government workers helpful	2.1	66.2	25.1	2.5	4.0	100%	(1,411)
Good deal of money for public assistance never gets to people who need it	27.0	56.4	11.4	0.8	4.3	100%	(1,415)
Better off with government services as they are	14.1	73.3	9.9	1.1	1.6	100%	(1,414)

The two items which did draw a more extreme opinion found 27 percent strongly agreeing with the statement, "A good deal of the money for public assistance never gets to the people who really need it,"and 20 percent strongly agreeing that "There are too many government offices doing the same thing." Moreover, these two statements were also the most widely endorsed of all the items critical of government offices. Among the minority of people taking extreme positions, those critical of the government were more numerous than those supportive.

It is interesting, however, that while many people bewail the absence of an official who will take responsibility, there was an even division of opinion about finding someone in an agency who takes an interest in one's problems. Whether the majority of the people were favorable or unfavorable to government offices depended very much on the specific nature of the item. On the ten questions, five elicited more positive than negative responses, four more negative than positive, and one about the same. The two most heavily endorsed criticisms were aimed at the bureaucracy rather than the bureaucrats. The other two criticisms which also have majority support were aimed at bureaucrats: "The people who gain the most from government are the officials who run the agencies" and "The trouble with government offices is that no official is really willing to take responsibility for anything." Of the five statements in which the majority were supportive of public offices, four concerned agency personnel. People, by and large, did not feel that officials abused their authority or that the government pried unduly into their personal affairs. Moreover, 72 percent thought that, "Most of the people who work for government offices work hard and try to do a good job," and 68 percent said that, "People in government offices are usually very helpful." These responses accord with the favorable accounts clients give of their experiences with considerate, fair, hard-working agency personnel whom they see as people like themselves trying to do a job.

Finally, there is support for our thesis that ideology and pragmatism are not necessarily consistent. A majority did criticize the government for duplication, for not getting assistance to the right people, for permitting their own personnel to benefit more than their clients, and for not having responsible officials. Nonetheless, when the practical issue was raised about dispensing with government services, only 12 percent of the people said we would be better off without government services as they now are. Many of the same people who believed private enterprise superior to public agencies on many counts still think society is much better off with present government services than without them.

Nor does an entrepreneurial philosophy override practical considerations about taxes. Only 10 percent objected to an increase in government services if it meant no increase in taxes (Table 4.16). And two-thirds would not want public services cut back even if it meant lowered taxes. A majority, however, opposed extended services if it meant higher taxes (57 percent). Sixty-six percent were in agreement with the fairness of the principle whereby the affluent pay higher taxes to help the needy.

Table 4.16

Attitudes Toward Expansion or Reduction of
Government Services

	Rating						
Attitude	Strongly agree	Agree	Disagree	Strongly disagree	D. K.	Total	N
Government should do *less*, if it means lower taxes	7.4%	25.4%	54.5%	10.5%	2.2%	100%	(1,413)
Government should do *more*, if taxes not increased	34.3	55.0	8.3	1.6	0.8	100%	(1,415)
Rich should pay higher taxes to help needy	20.0	41.4	28.4	4.1	1.0	100%	(1,406)

In spite of the popularity of some criticisms of bureaucracy and bureaucrats, the great majority of people approve of the way in which administrative agencies function. They are especially appreciative of the people who work for agencies. They would not like to see major problems of public interest handled by private enterprise much as they pay lip service to the superiority of business. Their criticisms are directed at relatively few agencies. Only public assistance and medical and hospital services draw much fire. Relatively few people have had difficulties with agencies of constraint—about 15 percent—and less than one-half of this group felt they had been unfairly treated.

DIMENSIONS OF SUPPORT FOR THE POLITICAL SYSTEM

Attitudes toward government, both at the specific level of agency functioning and the more general level of the evaluations of public bureaucracy, are indications of public support for the national political system. The psychological sources of system support are complex and manifold, and are differentially tied to various activities related to continuity or disruption of system functioning. Theoretical attempts to provide a framework for the identification of important variables and their interrelationships have been overly general as in Parsons' (1960) model of values, norms, and roles, or in Easton's (1965) differentiation of three levels of system support. Easton does move us ahead, however, in addressing himself more specifically to the political system. He distinguishes among (1) a sense of political community at the interpersonal level such that people will cooperate with one another toward some common objective, (2) regime support or allegiance to the particular authorities in power, and (3) governmental support or commitment to the basic constitutional form of the political system. Easton, thus, is more concerned with the targets or referents of attitude and behavior than with their psychological basis.

Starting at the empirical end of the problem, Arthur Miller and his colleagues (1972; 1973) in the Center for Political Studies, Institute for Social Research, employed a large battery of questions of possible relevance to political involvement and disengagement in a number of surveys. Factor analyses of these data gave unusually clear-cut and consistent outcomes in three separate surveys conducted in 1964, 1968, and 1970. In the 1964 survey the following six factors emerged:

1) *Confidence in government leadership.* The authors, taking a negative perspective, label this *political cynicism*. The questions which constitute this factor have to do with the integrity of government leaders, their competence and their efficiency, and whether the government is run to benefit all the people. This index of confidence falls between Easton's levels of system support and regime support. It is not specifically addressed to the particular adminstration in power and yet is not general enough to deal with institutional factors.

2) *Confidence in democratic mechanisms.* The four questions which comprise this factor asked about congressmen's concern with the needs of their constituents, the role of political parties in government responsiveness to people's needs, the attention paid by government leaders to the needs of people, and the effect of elections on governmental responsiveness to public concerns. The high correlations among these questions and their relative independence of other items calls attention to a significant dimension of system support, namely, trust in political institutions for making the system responsive to the needs of the people.

3) *A sense of personal political efficacy.* A logically related, but psychologically independent, factor is a person's sense of his own efficacy in political matters. One can believe that congressmen are responsive to their constituents and yet not feel that he can personally affect them. The items hanging together to make up this factor are: (a) "People like me don't have any say about what the government

does," (b) "Voting is the only way that people like me can have any say about how the government runs things," (c) "Sometimes politics and government seem so complicated that a person like me can't really understand what is going on," and (d) "People like me don't have any say about what the government does."

4) *Interpersonal trust.* Easton postulated that an elementary level of system support required trust in one's fellows, or otherwise cooperative activity would be impeded. Three questions reflect this factor and have to do with whether most people can be trusted, whether most people try to be helpful, and whether most people do not take unfair advantage.

5) *Personal competence.* This factor reflects a personality variable which conceivably could be related to system involvement. It is based upon questions about whether a person can plan his life effectively, as in the Rotter measure of internal control of reinforcement.

6) *Ego strength.* A logically related personality variable emerged as a separate factor based upon the individual's own evaluation of the strength of his convictions and ability to win arguments.

In the 1968 survey the questions on ego strength were dropped, and questions were added on political protest. The factor analyses of the questions which were repeated showed a striking similarity to the 1964 analysis. Again, the same five factors emerged. Not even a single item was displaced from one factor to become part of another factor, and the factor loadings were very close to the 1964 pattern. The three new questions on the politics of protest intercorrelated strongly for an important additional factor.

The 1970 results again supplied confirmation of the same factor structure even though the questions on interpersonal trust were not used. In the three surveys of 1964, 1968, and 1970, four relatively independent dimensions were found with very similar factor loadings for their component factors, specifically: *confidence in government leadership, confidence in democratic mechanisms, sense of personal efficacy,* and *feeling of personal competence* (internal control). *Interpersonal trust* and the *politics of protest* emerged as additional factors in two of the three surveys and did not appear a third time merely because the questions relevant for their measurement were omitted in one of the studies.

These empirical findings do not invalidate Easton's framework, but they do indicate the difficulty of fitting a theoretical model to the actual cognitive structures of the members of the political system. We would suggest, therefore, that a more discriminating analysis of the problem of system support should specify more explicitly the referent of the individual's response. Accordingly, we believe the following six dimensions, or levels, should be taken into account:

1) Sense of political community, as in Easton's model. The referent here is other people, which can be measured by the degree of interpersonal trust.

2) Confidence in the fairness and competence of the specific offices and personnel in the individual's own encounters with administrative agencies, i.e., the experiential level. Government is not only a remote group of leaders in Washington, but is something encountered in specific offices and officials who administer services or enforce the law. The referent here is a particular administrative office and its personnel.

3) Support for public administration agencies as a system and not just as a mechanism operated by human beings. Here the referent is not a specific set of agency people doing their job, but an impersonal institution.

4) Confidence in the democratic mechanisms of the system, i.e., in representative democracy. The referents here are the representatives of the people in their responsiveness to people's needs and wishes.

5) Confidence in national political leadership in general, i.e., in the government in Washington. In the surveys previously cited, the referent was described in some questions as the government in Washington, and in others as the people running the government. The wording seems to make little difference in the responses of the American public. Apparently, respondents think of the political power structure and personalize it as "those characters in Washington in charge of things." The reference is more system-oriented than personality-oriented.

6) Commitment to national symbols, such as the flag or the national anthem. In the past, the individual attachment to symbols which stand for the unity of the nation and the identity of the people as a group has been a significant source of support for the national political system.

These dimensions omit four factors appearing in the Miller analyses: namely, personal competence, ego strength, sense of political efficacy, and the politics of political protest. All four have some relevance to system support, but they are not specifically tied to a given level of system functioning. People high in personal competence or high in ego strength can either strongly reject or accept different aspects of the present political system. A sense of political efficacy is more directly relevant, but is covered more adequately by confidence in democratic processes.

Dimensions of Support Used in the Present Study

Unfortunately, in the 35-minute interviews of the present investigation, it was not possible to get adequate measures of all of the six dimensions. Since the study centered on experiences with particular agencies, most of the questions dealt with the second and third dimensions of specific evaluation of agencies and with general attitudes toward public bureaucracy. We did retain, however, the scales used by Miller and his associates for interpersonal trust and confidence in national leadership. Finally, we added four questions to get at attachment to national symbols, an inadequate coverage because of the lack of previous use of these items in national samples. We also made no attempt to cover the dimension of confidence in democratic mechanisms. In short, five of our six levels were reflected in the questions employed, but not with comparable thoroughness.

Factor analysis of the answers to the many questions in our survey resulted in nine rather than five factors (Tables 4.17 and 4.18). As in the studies of Miller and his associates, the two dimensions of *confidence in national leadership* (political cynicism) and *interpersonal trust* again appeared as factors in their own right. In addition, the four questions on nationalism constituted another independent cluster.

Specific Attitudes and General Evaluations

With respect to specific attitudes toward administrative agencies and general evaluations of public bureaucracies, the findings are more complex. In this general area we found not two, but six factors. The experience with service agencies was not significantly related to experience with control agencies (Table 4.18). Hence, when we speak of supportive attitudes toward administrative functioning, we need to take account of the type of agency salient in the respondent's experience. The general evaluation of public bureaucracy yielded four factors rather than one, though some of them were highly interrelated. The factors are (1) general attitudes toward bureaucracy (factor I); (2) comparison of public offices with private enterprise (factor II); (3) rejection of negative stereotypes of bureaucracy (factor III); (4) positive attitudes toward the helpfulness of government (factor IV) (Table 4.17). Thus, at the third level of confidence in the administrative agencies of government, four sub-dimensions appeared as separate factors. Their independence of one another is relative, especially factors I, III, and IV. General evaluation of agency functioning correlated with positive attitudes toward government agencies (.53), and with rejection of criticism (.52).* Positive attitudes are correlated with rejection of criticism (.50). But comparative evaluation of government with private enterprise correlated only .37, .25, and .30 with factors I, III, and IV. Moreover, in examining the relationships between these

Table 4.17

Factor Loadings of Attitudinal Items

	Factor I	Factor II	Factor III	Factor IV
	General attitudes	Public vs. private preference	Rejection of negative stereotype	Government helpful
Rating of government offices				
Prompt service	-.740	-.174	-.014	-.132
Problem situation	-.758	-.132	-.049	-.092
Considerate treatment	-.753	-.118	-.054	-.171
Fair treatment	-.769	-.066	-.035	-.054
Accuracy	-.717	-.172	.020	-.064
Correcting error	-.732	-.240	.006	-.030
Government better than business				
Prompt service	.121	.708	.071	.069
Problem situation	.083	.752	.009	.084
Considerate treatment	.094	.700	-.039	.106
Fair treatment	.102	.643	-.087	.054
Accuracy	.157	.728	-.061	-.020
Correcting error	.161	.757	-.095	-.055
Negative stereotypes				
Officials gain most	-.102	.004	.561	-.221
Duplication of service	-.090	-.122	.514	-.005
Abuse authority	-.188	-.031	.664	-.124
No one responsible	-.174	-.129	.688	-.030
No interest in problem	-.200	-.072	.677	-.103
Government pries	-.149	-.023	.509	.062
Government helpful				
Government doing good job	.263	.147	.024	.278
Government workers try	.174	.134	-.204	.675
Government workers helpful	.351	.164	-.239	.535
Better with Gov't service	.172	.027	.005	.384

*See Table 4.30 for intercorrelations of factors. Factor I = C, Factor II = D, Factor III = G, Factor IV = L, Factor V = I, Factor VI = E, Factor VII = H, Factor VIII = A, and Factor IX = B.

Table 4.17 (continued)

Factor Loadings of Attitudinal Items

	Factor V	Factor VI	Factor VII
	Confidence in national leadership	Symbolic nationalism	Inter-personal trust
Confidence—Cynicism			
Amount tax waste	-.593	.081	.059
Amount trust	.678	.054	.084
Government for big interests	-.703	-.039	-.097
Competence of leaders	.357	-.022	.047
Integrity of leaders	.582	-.047	-.120
Responsiveness to elections	.481	-.090	.192
Nationalism			
Punish draft evaders	.183	.615	.081
Reaction to foreign criticism	-.016	.576	-.063
Patriotism in schools	.085	-.558	-.025
Respect for national anthem	-.114	-.732	-.107
Interpersonal trust			
People trustworthy	.079	.028	.792
People helpful	.110	.019	.803
People fair	-.117	-.054	-.770

four factors and other measures, Factors I, III and IV give highly similar patterns. They show the same level of correlation with such variables as interpersonal trust, confidence in national leadership, helpfulness of local leaders, and helpfulness of political leaders. Factor II, however, behaves differently on these variables. Hence, we would group factors I, III, and IV as part of the same basic dimension, namely general confidence in administrative agencies. Factor II, the comparative assessment of public and private organizations, we would not consider a direct measure of system support. It reflects a frame of reference with respect to evaluating government offices. People can see private enterprise as more efficient than government offices and still be supportive of the political system.

Before exploring in greater detail the relationships of these different levels of system support to one another and to background variables, we will examine the distribution of responses to questions directed at confidence in national leadership, interpersonal trust, and symbolic nationalism, as has already been done for bureaucratic experiences and general attitudes toward administrative agencies.

Table 4.18

Factor Loadings of Experience Items

	Factor VIII Service	Factor IX Constraint
Service		
Procedures good	.704	-.182
Personnel good	.902	.012
Problem solved	.648	.012
Handled well	.880	.004
All contacts satisfactory	.718	-.202
Constraint		
Amount of difficulty	-.116	-.325
Government worsens problem	-.044	-.656
Fair treatment	.084	.598
Settled quickly	-.174	.764
Considerate treatment	-.023	.606
Government made mistakes	.039	-.733
Handled poorly	-.051	-.757
Handled efficiently	.010	.790

Confidence in National Leadership

The questions on confidence in national leadership are of special interest because these are trend questions which show a consistent decline since they were first used in 1958. Moreover, our survey was in the field in April and May of 1973 when the Watergate hearings were in full swing, but before their disclosures were complete. As Table 4.19 indicates, there was a further erosion of confidence after the 1972 pre-election and post-election surveys on four of the six questions used. After the 1972 election, the modal response to the query, "How much of the time do you think you can trust the government in Washington to do what is right?" was *most of the time* (48 percent). In April and May of 1973, it was *some of the time* (50 percent). In 1972 (post-election), the majority thought the government was run by a few big interests, and in 1973 the majority had increased by 5 percent to 58 percent. Opinion about the competence of the leadership also declined during this period by about 5 percent, with 48 percent of the public in the spring of 1972 believing that the people who run the government are smart people who know what they are doing. The greatest loss was on the question about the responsiveness of government to elections. In the spring of 1973 survey, some 16 percent fewer people said that elections made the government pay attention to what people think, compared to the post-election survey

Table 4.19

Trends in Confidence in National Political Leadership
(Political Cynicism) 1958-1973

"How much of the time do you think you can trust the government in Washington to do what is right–just about always, most of the time, or only some of the time?"

	1958	1968	1972 Pre-election	1972 Post-election	Apr/May 1973*
Always	15.5%	7.1%	6.8%	5.3%	7.5%
Most of the time	55.6	51.9	44.9	47.7	38.1
Some of the time	28.8	35.3	44.7	44.2	49.9
None of the time	0	0.2	0.5	0.6	1.1
D. K.	6.1†	5.5†	2.2	2.1	3.4
Not ascertained			0.8	0.8	0
Total	100.0%	100.0%	100.0%	100.0%	100.0%
N	(1,450)	(1,557)	(2,705)	(2,191)	(1,433)

"Would you say the government is pretty much run by a few big interests looking out for themselves or that it is run for the benefit of all the people?"

For benefit of all	74.0%	49.1%	43.4%	37.5%	34.2%
Few big interests	17.1	38.5	48.4	53.0	58.0
Other; depends	1.0	4.5	2.5	2.5	2.0
D. K.	7.9†	7.9†	5.0	6.4	5.8
Not ascertained			0.8	0.5	0
Total	100.0%	100.0%	100.0%	100.0%	100.0%
N	(1,450)	(1,557)	(2,705)	(2,191)	(1,433)

*"Not ascertained" excluded from percentages in Apr/May survey.
†"Not ascertained" and "Don't know" combined in 1958 and 1968 surveys.

Table 4.19 (continued)

Trends in Confidence in National Political Leadership
(Political Cynicism) 1958-1973

"Do you feel that almost all of the people running the government are smart people who usually know what they are doing, or do you think that quite a few of them don't seem to know what they are doing?"

	1958	1968	1972 Pre-election	1972 Post-election	Apr/May 1973*
Know what they are doing	56.0%	56.2%	52.8%	54.7%	47.9%
Don't know what they are doing	36.2	36.1	41.9	39.9	45.3
Other; depends	1.2	1.8	1.0	1.0	0
Obvious sarcastic answer	0	0	0	0	1.7**
D. K.	6.6†	5.9†	3.6	4.0	5.1
Not ascertained			0.8	0.4	0
Total	100.0%	100.0%	100.0%	100.0%	100.0%
N	(1,450)	(1,557)	(2,705)	(2,191)	(1,433)

"And how much do you feel that having elections makes the government pay attention to what people think—a good deal, some, or not much?"

A good deal	***	57.3%	57.2%	54.4%	38.7%
Some		27.7	28.9	35.6	38.5
Not much		8.3	11.9	7.5	19.8
D. K.		6.7†	1.2	2.2	3.0
Not ascertained			0.8	0.3	0
Total		100.0%	100.0%	100.0%	100.0%
N		(1,557)	(2,705)	(2,191)	(1,433)

*"Not ascertained" excluded from percentages in Apr/May 1973 survey.
**The occurrence of the Watergate scandal elicited a number of obviously sarcastic responses to this question.
***This question was not asked in the 1958 survey.
†"Not ascertained" and "Don't know" combined in 1958 and 1968 surveys.

Table 4.19 (continued)

Trends in Confidence in National Political Leadership
(Political Cynicism) 1958-1973

"Do you think that quite a few of the people running the government are a little crooked, not very many are, or do you think hardly any of them are crooked at all?"

	1958	1968	1972 Pre-election	1972 Post-election	Apr/May 1973*
Hardly any	25.6%	18.4%	16.0%	14.0%	18.2%
Not many	42.7	49.3	46.1	45.1	43.1
Quite a lot	23.4	24.8	34.3	35.8	34.5
D. K.	8.3†	7.5†	2.6	4.3	4.2
Not ascertained			1.1	0.7	0
Total	100.0%	100.0%	100.0%	100.0%	100.0%
N	(1,450)	(1,557)	(2,705)	(2,191)	(1,433)

"Do you think that people in the government waste a lot of the money we pay in taxes, waste some of it, or don't waste very much of it?"

	1958	1968	1972 Pre-election	1972 Post-election	Apr/May 1973*
Not much	10.0%	4.2%	3.0%	2.3%	3.6%
Some	41.3	33.1	27.1	30.0	31.2
A lot	42.3	57.4	67.7	65.8	62.3
D. K.	6.4†	5.3†	1.5	1.8	2.9
Not ascertained			0.8	0.1	0
Total	100.0%	100.0%	100.0%	100.0%	100.0%
N	(1,450)	(1,557)	(2,705)	(2,191)	(1,433)

*"Not ascertained" excluded from percentages in Apr/May survey.
†"Not ascertained" and "Don't know" combined in 1958 and 1968 surveys.

in 1972.* Curiously, there was no change in the percentage of people who believed that quite a few of those running the government were crooked.

---

*This question does not theoretically belong to the level we have designated, confidence in national leadership. Rather, it belongs to the level of confidence in democratic mechanisms. We did not have enough interview time to explore this dimension with a battery of questions. In our factor analysis the attitude on the effect of elections did show a high loading on confidence in national leadership and is considered here with other trend questions.

Earlier we documented the thesis that people's responses to their own encounters with bureaucracy were more favorable than their more generalized evaluations of government offices. The experiential level, in other words, was more positively toned than the attitudinal level. We lack parallel questions at the more remote level of confidence in national leadership to those directed at more specific targets. Nonetheless, we can make rough comparisons for some questions. These comparisons show an extension of the same principle; namely, the more. removed the referent is from the individual's own experience, the more his response is colored by unfavorable popular beliefs. Three areas of questioning reveal this tendency. (1) At the most general level, respondents were asked about whether the government in Washington could be trusted to do what is right—always or most of the time. Fifty-one percent answered in the negative. But when asked about how fairly government offices treat people, only 26 percent gave them poor marks, and only 18 percent of service agency clients thought they themselves had been treated unfairly by a government office.* (2) The competence of national leaders was also called into question by an inquiry about whether the people running the government were smart people. At this very general level, 47 percent of the sample thought that government leaders did not really know what they were doing. But when the referent was government offices and their handling of problems, only 35 percent of the respondents felt they were doing a bad job. And at the experiential level, only 27 percent of service agency clients reported that their own problems had not been solved by the agency serving them. (3) At the general level, people were asked about the wastefulness of government, and 62 percent thought people in government wasted a lot of money. But only 37 percent gave government agencies low ratings for promptness of service, and 33 percent gave low ratings on being careful and avoiding mistakes. In appraising the efficiency of the service agency with which they had contact, only 28 percent regarded it as inefficient.

Granted that the lack of parallel questions makes our comparison imprecise, the pattern of findings is clear. The greatest incidence of critical responses occurs at the most global level, namely confidence in unspecified national leaders (people running the government). The most favorable responses occur at the experiential level where people

---

*The people having difficulties with control agencies had 42 percent of their number reporting unfair treatment. This is a special group, however, in that it was defined originally as those reporting difficulties with enforcement agencies and comprised only 15 percent of the total sample.

speak of the specifics of their bureaucratic encounters. Intermediate is the level of the evaluation of administrative agencies on given criteria.

Symbolic Nationalism

We included four questions to tap people's attitudes toward national symbols. At an earlier period in American history, one source of support for the national system was the emotional involvement of individuals in symbols of national identity. It has been argued that, in a developed technological bureaucratic society, such involvement has lost much of its force and that the patriotic outbursts of the hard hats are a flash of a dying fire. Nonetheless, we thought that it would be worthwhile to call attention to the problem of national involvement by the use of these questions:

> 1) What do you think the government should do about young men who evaded the draft? Should they be sent to prison, should they be made to serve their country in some way, or should they be given amnesty—that is, no punishment?

> 2) If a foreigner visiting this country were to criticize many things about America, what would your reaction be? Would you feel that he is being insulting; that he is just showing bad manners; or would you feel that he has every right to express his own opinion?

> 3) Do you think that our schools are putting enough emphasis on teaching children to be patriotic Americans?

> 4) How do you feel about Americans who won't rise when the "Star Spangled Banner" is being played? Do you strongly approve, approve, don't care, disapprove, or strongly disapprove?

Factor analysis of the many attitudinal items showed that these four items did comprise a separate factor. Though not highly intercorrelated, they all loaded on one factor and on no other. The findings suggest that we have a measure of a dimension worthy of further investigation with an expanded battery of questions. The distribution of responses to these items is of some interest in that they indicate that symbolic patriotism is not dead, though it is probably not as strong today as it was in the past (Table 4.20). Sixty percent felt that not enough emphasis is placed upon teaching children to be patriotic Americans in school. Eighty-four percent disapproved of Americans who won't rise when the national anthem is played, and a majority of the group are in the *strongly disapprove* category. In spite of the unpopularity of the Vietnam war, only 15 percent of the people would grant draft evaders amnesty. Very few people, however, wanted them sent to prison, and the great majority agreed that they should be made to serve their country in some way. Only on criticism by a foreigner was the patriotic response muted, with only 18 percent reacting strongly to such criticism. How much real feeling was elicited by these questions is problematic. Even if we are dealing with a mechanical response, it can be of significance in indicating a social climate of opinion which affects public policy.

Table 4.20

Symbolic Nationalism

Treatment of Draft Evaders		Interpretation of Criticism by Foreigner	
Sent to prison	12.5%	Insulting	18.1%
Made to serve country	69.1	Bad manners	26.2
Given amnesty	15.2	Expresses own opinion	55.1
Other	0.5	D. K.	0.5
D. K.	2.6	Total	100.0%
Total	100.0%	N	(1,414)
N	(1,400)		

Enough Emphasis on Teaching School Children to Be Patriotic Americans		Failure to Rise for National Anthem	
Yes	32.6%	Strongly approve	1.3%
No	60.2	Approve	2.3
D. K.	7.2	Don't care	12.1
Total	100.0%	Disapprove	34.4
N	(1,414)	Strongly disapprove	49.6
		D. K.	0.3
		Total	100.0%
		N	(1,419)

Interpersonal Trust

Basic to the functioning of any system is, to use Easton's term, a sense of political community, a mutual trustfulness and willingness of people to cooperate with one another on common tasks. Confidence in national leadership, faith in various institutional arrangements, and a favorable evaluation of the mechanisms of government are helpful societal bonds, but they can vary over time without social disintegration as long as people trust one another sufficiently to live and work together. The effect of increases in crime, in addition to its other costs, is the erosion of mutual trustfulness, with people seeking refuge in fortified conclaves as they move into condominiums and other retreats. We did not explore the sense of political community adequately but we did use three questions on interpersonal trust which constituted a relatively independent factor in earlier studies of the Center for Political Studies. Factor analysis of our data confirm the earlier investigations in that the questions on trust load heavily on the same factor and on nothing else.

A comparison of the 1973 findings with studies conducted over the past ten years shows some decline in interpersonal trust, but not as much as the drop in support for national political leadership (Table 4.21). On the question of whether most people can be trusted, there is a drop of between 8 and 10 percent from 1964, most of which has occurred in the past five years. A slight majority (55 percent) now believe that one cannot be too careful in dealing with people. There is very little change, however, on the question assessing the helpfulness of others. But on the belief that others would take advantage of you, there has been a shift of 7 percent in the pessimistic direction since 1964. Nevertheless, a majority (62 percent) still feel that most people would try to be fair and not seize an opportunity to exploit another person. The overall level of interpersonal trust is thus not high in that the various questions show substantial numbers of people distrusting their fellows.*

---

*Similar questions on interpersonal trust have been asked of national samples in other countries. In four of the six republics in Yugoslavia, people were asked in a 1968 survey whether most people could be trusted and whether, in the majority of cases, people were willing to help others. Fifty-two percent answered in the affirmative, a proportion not essentially different from the 55 percent so responding in the U. S. in the same year. The total Yugoslav figure, however, covers over substantial differences in the four republics studied, with Serbia some 22 percent higher than Slovenia. On the question of people being helpful, however, the affirmative answers in Yugoslavia were much higher than in the U.S.—73 percent compared to 58 percent (Katz, unpublished data).

Table 4.21

Trends in Interpersonal Trust

"Generally Speaking, Would You Say That Most People Can Be Trusted?"

	1964	1966	1968	1972	1973
Most people can be trusted	53.4%	52.9%	55.2%	45.8%	44.8%
Other, depends	1.4	1.0	1.6	0	0
Can't be too careful	44.7	45.6	43.2	52.4	54.8
D. K.	0.6	0.5	0	1.8	0.4
Total	100.0%	100.0%	100.0%	100.0%	100.0%
N	(1,446)	(1,284)	(1,343)	(2,179)	(1,421)

"Would You Say That Most Of The Time People Try To Be Helpful Or That They Are Mostly Just Looking Out For Themselves?"

Try to be helpful	54.3	51.9	58.2	46.9	52.6
Other, depends (both boxes checked)	3.9	1.9	2.6	0	0
Just look out for themselves	41.3	45.7	38.6	48.9	44.3
D. K.	0.5	0.5	0.6	4.2	3.0
Total	100.0%	100.0%	100.0%	100.0%	100.0%
N	(1,445)	(1,285)	(1,344)	(2,174)	(1,411)

"Do You Think Most People Would Try To Take Advantage Of You If They Got A Chance Or Would Try To Be Fair?"

Would try to be fair	67.3		66.8	58.9	61.5
Other, depends (both boxes checked)	3.2		2.7	0	0
Would take advantage of you	28.6		30.1	36.8	36.0
D. K.	1.0		0.5	4.3	2.4
Total	100.0%		100.0%	100.0%	100.0%
N	(1,443)		(1,342)	(2,179)	(1,401)

POTENTIAL CLEAVAGE LINES AND SYSTEM SUPPORT

Alienation or support for the political system for most individuals is not an all-or-none affair. The many dimensions of system support can mean that there is a substitutability of societal bonds such that people weak on one can be moderately strong on another. Some persons can be very distrustful of national political leadership in Washington and still be positively committed to the national system because of their trust in their fellow citizens and their confidence in the specific governmental agencies with which they have had contact. Furthermore, it is conceivable that some groups, such as the highly educated, have higher levels of expectations for the functioning of the political system and hence require support on several levels in order to feel positively committed to the system. On the other hand, other societal groups may have lower expectations of the political system, and it is only when almost all types of support break down for these groups that there is a serious condition of alienation or anomie. Blacks, for example, may feel more alienated from the political system today than they did in the past although they may be tied into the system at more levels today; however, they also expect more from the system today. The protests of upper middle class college students in the 1960's may be explained in terms of their expectations of the political sphere relative to the number of levels in which they are tied into the system. Alienation results from a combination of expectations of the political system and the amount of perceived support from various political levels.

It is worthwhile to look, then, at the four groups which are often seen as alienated in our society: (1) the socially and economically deprived, (2) the young, (3) the blacks, and (4) women. How do these groups stand relative to the rest of the population on various levels of system support?

Socially and Economically Deprived

Three measures of economic and social deprivation are available: income, education, and occupation. When income is used as an indication of deprivation, the very poor (under $3,000) and the poor ($3,000 to $5,000) differ very little from the affluent (over $15,000) on most indices of system support (Table 4.22). The poor are more cynical with respect to national political leadership than are the affluent, but not more so than people of modest income levels ($5,000 to $12,500). The poor are no less nationalistic than those with higher incomes. They are more likely than the affluent to accept stereotypes

Table 4.22

Income Related to Types of System Support

Income	Service experience*		Trust in local political leaders		General attitudes toward bureaucracy		Public vs. private preference		Government helpful		Rejection of bureaucratic stereotypes		Confidence in national leadership		Symbolic nationalism		Inter-personal trust	
	Unfav	Fav	Unfav	Fav	Unfav	Fav	Unfav	Fav	Unfav	Fav	No	Yes	Unfav	Fav	Low	High	Low	High
Under $3,000	16.9%	38.4%	14.5%	27.3%	20.9%	29.1%	20.3%	34.9%	13.4%	39.0%	18.6%	13.9%	22.6%	24.4%	20.9%	20.4%	36.7%	25.0%
3,000 to 4,999	16.8	40.0	21.1	25.8	23.2	26.4	15.5	36.1	14.2	40.0	20.6	11.0	29.1	25.1	18.7	22.5	38.1	21.2
5,000 to 7,499	20.1	21.8	16.2	25.1	23.5	21.2	25.1	28.5	24.5	41.3	22.4	20.6	26.3	22.9	15.1	16.7	31.3	30.7
7,500 to 9,999	18.9	20.0	14.1	25.4	29.2	20.5	29.2	26.0	22.2	34.1	19.5	13.5	25.4	26.0	21.1	17.3	36.8	33.5
10,000 to 12,499	16.8	19.2	22.2	34.5	20.2	22.1	30.0	25.6	19.7	45.3	20.2	15.8	20.7	27.6	18.3	22.7	25.6	33.5
12,500 to 14,999	16.1	12.9	19.3	23.8	25.2	14.2	29.0	20.6	22.6	43.2	19.3	16.8	18.1	27.7	20.6	16.8	23.2	36.8
15,000 to 19,999	12.1	19.1	13.4	29.9	19.8	18.5	34.3	19.1	20.4	45.9	18.5	17.8	15.3	31.2	9.5	17.8	19.1	47.1
20,000+	7.8	14.1	16.8	27.2	21.0	18.7	38.5	13.8	22.8	36.7	22.3	26.5	16.9	35.6	16.8	15.1	19.9	56.8

*Percentages combine two extreme positions at favorable or unfavorable ends of the scale. Total N's for each column vary from 220 for service experience (unfavorable) to 574 for government helpful (favorable).

of bureaucracy, save that they are much less likely to accept conventional beliefs about the superiority of business over government (public vs. private preference). It is the wealthy who believe that private enterprise can do things better than government. The poor have more confidence in public than private bureaucracy. Nor do the poor show any less support than the rich in terms of their positive attitudes toward government agencies or their general evaluation of agency functioning. In fact, it is the very poor who are most likely to be the most positive in their assessment of agency operations. And at the level of specific service encounters, relatively more of the poor than of the other income groups report favorable, as compared with unfavorable, experiences. Only on one measure do the economically deprived show signs of alienation; they are much lower in interpersonal trust than are those in better economic conditions. Only 22 percent of those with incomes under $5,000 trust their fellow creatures, whereas 57 percent of those with incomes over $20,000 are trustful. In fact, it is not just the extreme groups which show the relationship. As income rises, interpersonal trust goes up. It is almost as if one can increasingly afford to be trustful if he has a greater margin of economic security.

The lack of disaffection among the poor was also found in the Harris survey (1973) in which respondents were asked about their confidence in the people running various branches of government as well as non-governmental institutions. The low income groups expressed as much confidence in almost all governmental offices and types of service as did the high income groups save for local trash collection. In the private sector the poor were more supportive of such institutions as organized religion, TV news, and organized labor, but less trusting toward big business.

Since education is positively correlated with income, the same pattern of involvement can be expected for education as was true of income. In general, this expectation is realized. There are no sharp differences on measures of system support for the various educational groups save for interpersonal trust (Table 4.23). The poorly educated are more inclined than the well-educated to evaluate agency functioning favorably, to accept negative stereotypes of government bureaus while regarding public bureaucracy as superior to business, to report favorable experiences with service agencies, to have positive attitudes toward public offices (government helpful), and to be low in interpersonal trust. The only differences in relationships for educational as compared to income groups were on symbolic nationalism and evaluation of own service experience.

Table 4.23
Education Related to Types of System Support

Years of Education	Service experience*		Trust in local political leaders		General attitudes toward bureaucracy		Public vs. private preference		Government helpful		Rejection of bureaucratic stereotypes		Confidence in national leadership		Symbolic nationalism		Interpersonal trust	
	Unfav	Fav	Unfav	Fav	Unfav	Fav	Unfav	Fav	Unfav	Fav	No	Yes	Unfav	Fav	Low	High	Low	High
8 years or fewer	11.5%	35.7%	12.3%	23.8%	15.5%	30.0%	14.8%	44.7%	13.7%	42.2%	19.9%	15.5%	15.2%	26.0%	15.5%	23.1%	36.8%	23.8%
9 - 11 years	13.6	24.4	10.2	27.5	24.8	26.1	21.7	32.4	15.4	39.3	20.1	11.5	23.5	26.9	17.5	19.3	36.3	26.9
High School	15.1	19.6	16.2	28.8	25.4	20.2	28.2	26.1	19.6	44.7	22.0	19.2	21.3	28.2	15.2	21.3	29.5	35.8
High School +	21.2	21.7	16.7	32.8	23.7	22.8	28.8	22.2	25.2	44.4	21.7	16.8	22.8	28.8	14.2	18.2	29.8	34.3
Some College	18.0	21.9	22.9	28.7	26.1	12.6	38.0	11.9	25.6	34.4	20.7	18.4	19.5	24.9	21.1	15.7	19.5	42.2
B. A. +	14.1	13.5	19.7	18.4	19.1	15.9	39.8	11.7	23.3	34.3	15.3	21.4	14.7	30.7	24.0	11.1	14.1	58.3

*Percentages combine two extreme positions at favorable or unfavorable ends of the scale. Total N's for each column vary from 220 for service experience (unfavorable) to 574 for government helpful (favorable).

Nationalism showed little relationship with income but there was a clear tendency for the poorly educated to be more nationalistic than the well-educated. Some 23 percent of those in the lowest education category (eight years and less of schooling) against 11 percent of college graduates were very high in the patriotism index. The difference in evaluation of service experience was slight but seemed to indicate that education rather than income was related to critical standards for public service. In general, the differences between educational groups were greater than between income groupings on the various indices of system support. The contingency coefficients were higher on seven of the eight measures of system support in relation to education as against income. Nonetheless, the educationally deprived can hardly be considered an alienated group if all those with eight years or less of education are included in this category.

Occupational groups show some differences in degree and type of support for the political system, but no group shows a pattern of disaffection (Table 4.24). The semi-skilled are the most disaffected of all the occupational groupings in that they have negative general attitudes toward bureaucracy, accept negative stereotypes of bureaucracy, and are high on interpersonal distrust. But they are closely followed by laborers in the latter two categories. And skilled workers are also close to the other groups of blue collar workers in negative attitudes in their acceptance of negative stereotypes and in their lack of confidence in national leadership. Nevertheless, all three blue collar groups feel that the government is generally helpful, and their experiences with service agencies have been rewarding. Nor do they really stand out against other occupational groups in critical attitudes save for their low levels of interpersonal trust. Of the other groups, the managerial people are the most generally supportive of the political system. They are the highest of any occupational group in confidence in national leadership and nationalism, the least accepting of negative stereotypes of bureaucracy, and the highest in interpersonal trust. Their own experiences with service agencies, however, have not been as positive as was the case with some of the other occupational groupings. They are second to the professional people in their wide agreement about the superiority of business to government in handling problems. That managers and owners should be most supportive of the system suggests the validity of our approach in looking at a number of dimensions of support. The establishment people should be most favorable to the establishment on almost all dimensions. Though the professional group was also positive on most measures, it was more critical than the managerial people on general attitudes toward bureaucracy and nationalism.

Table 4.24

Occupation Related to Various Types of System Support

Occupation	Service experience*		Trust in local political leaders		General attitudes toward bureaucracy		Public vs. private preference		Government helpful		Rejection of bureaucratic stereotypes		Confidence in national leadership		Symbolic nationalism		Inter-personal trust	
	Unfav	Fav	Unfav	Fav	Unfav	Fav	Unfav	Fav	Unfav	Fav	No	Yes	Unfav	Fav	Low	High	Low	High
Professional	10.1%	19.2%	19.6%	19.0%	21.5%	12.0%	39.9%	12.0%	29.1%	38.6%	16.4%	19.6%	20.2%	26.6%	20.3%	10.1%	15.8%	51.2%
Managers	15.8	17.1	14.9	31.1	16.3	14.9	40.6	18.9	19.0	29.7	16.3	21.7	18.9	28.4	12.2	20.3	16.3	58.1
Clerical & Sales	14.9	16.3	17.2	27.8	22.2	20.8	30.6	22.9	19.7	44.7	21.1	23.2	20.1	27.8	17.0	15.9	24.7	40.8
Craftsmen	12.6	25.4	16.1	32.9	27.6	22.1	30.8	29.5	25.5	38.3	26.8	8.1	30.8	24.8	19.5	19.5	33.6	22.8
Operatives	17.5	31.6	18.7	22.8	30.5	18.6	24.3	32.1	22.3	38.3	25.9	13.0	24.3	22.8	17.1	20.8	40.9	23.8
Laborers	20.7	25.9	15.6	29.0	23.1	23.2	22.1	30.1	17.7	36.6	22.5	11.9	26.9	25.2	20.4	17.3	36.7	22.6
Farmers	22.6	26.9	7.1	39.3	10.7	46.4	17.9	42.8	21.4	28.6	25.0	10.7	3.6	25.0	3.6	28.5	32.2	39.2
Non-working	10.1	19.2	14.1	27.7	17.6	25.8	20.1	29.5	13.2	44.6	14.4	19.2	16.6	31.8	15.1	23.3	26.4	37.1

*Percentages combine two extreme positions at favorable or unfavorable ends of the scale. Total N's for each column vary from 220 for service experience (unfavorable) to 574 for government helpful (favorable).

Our findings thus indicate that objective measures of deprivation such as income, education, and occupation do not reveal any deprived group as significantly alienated on measures of system support with the exception of interpersonal trust which is low among the poor, the uneducated, and the blue collar workers. It is interesting that the various groups are tied into the system in different ways. People in the lower strata are stronger than managerial groups in their favorable account of their own experiences with service agencies and higher in their nationalism than the professional group. No one group from the socio-economic categories, however, departs consistently from the others in negative attitudes toward the political system.

There has been a growing body of literature which recognizes the importance of relative rather than absolute deprivation. Modern social science has almost caught up with Marxian theory which took account of the relativity of need satisfaction in describing the psychological impact of depression after a boom period. It also saw the skilled workers, rather than the lumpen proletariat, as the advance guard of the revolution. The measures considered so far of income, education, and occupation are differences in an objective sense. They reveal that certain people are better off than others, but not whether different income groups compare themselves with one another. Individuals do not necessarily use as a reference group those who are better off than they are. The poor may not consider themselves disadvantaged if they compare themselves with other poor people. Hence, we used as a measure of relative deprivation, the discrepancy score between education and income. Our assumption was that the college graduate in the middle income category would be more likely to be disaffected than would the person who had not completed high school. In general, the index based upon discrepancy between education and income did show some of the expected relationship to the various measures of system support, but in meager fashion (Table 4.25). The relatively deprived were the least positive in their attitudes and feelings about political leadership and government offices. But the differences were small, and on no measure did relative deprivation show as large a relationship as did objective deprivation (level of income).

Although relative deprivation and status congruence measures did not show strong relationships with measures of system support, we attempted to see if these indices added predictability over and above measures of education and income. Consequently, we partialed out income, then education, and finally relative deprivation, and examined the relationships remaining. For most indices there was no relationship between various measures of system support and rela-

Table 4.25

Relationship of Relative Deprivation to Various Types of System Support

Relative Deprivation	Service experience*		Trust in local political leaders		General attitudes toward bureaucracy		Public vs. private preference		Government helpful		Rejection of bureaucratic stereotypes		Confidence in national leadership		Symbolic nationalism		Inter-personal trust	
	Unfav	Fav	Unfav	Fav	Unfav	Fav	Unfav	Fav	Unfav	Fav	No	Yes	Unfav	Fav	Low	High	Low	High
1 (More education than income; relative deprivation)	14.7%	13.9%	12.7%	11.4%	:2.1%	8.5%	11.0%	6.8%	11.3%	9.2%	9.8%	8.6%	13.3%	11.2%	14.8%	10.2%	9.8%	11.0%
2	10.1	11.1	12.3	7.1	12.4	10.9	9.7	9.4	9.5	7.9	12.7	9.0	9.7	6.7	11.5	9.2	10.6	8.7
3	19.8	10.3	13.6	13.2	15.6	9.2	13.1	12.8	16.7	11.8	13.4	11.6	14.3	8.3	12.3	10.5	13.1	11.0
4 (Equal education and income; no deprivation)	21.2	30.1	22.4	23.2	17.8	25.9	18.1	29.3	17.5	23.5	19.6	20.6	20.3	22.4	21.8	25.8	26.3	19.3
5	20.7	13.6	18.4	16.1	17.8	19.5	20.9	14.0	21.5	20.1	17.8	20.6	18.7	23.2	20.6	15.2	16.2	21.0
6	5.5	9.5	9.6	14.6	10.2	14.3	16.0	12.3	11.6	13.8	10.1	16.3	9.7	13.9	9.5	13.3	10.4	15.4
7 (More income than education)	7.8	11.1	11.0	14.3	14.0	11.6	11.3	15.4	12.0	13.6	16.7	13.3	14.0	14.4	9.5	15.6	13.6	13.7

*Percentages combine two extreme positions at favorable or unfavorable ends of the scale. Total N's for each column vary from 220 for service experience (unfavorable) to 574 for government helpful (favorable).

tive deprivation with income held constant. Relative deprivation, with income partialed out, shows the effect of relative deprivation without the effects of income, per se. There are only two indices of system support that show any relationship to relative deprivation with income held constant. People who are relatively deprived (with the effects of income removed) feel that government is somewhat better than private enterprise (r=.21) and are slightly higher in interpersonal trust (r=.15). Status congruence, with income held constant, shows no relationship to system support. Relative deprivation, with education held constant, shows little relationship to our indices. There is a slight tendency (r=.12) for the relatively deprived, with the effects of education removed, to be lower in interpersonal trust. Thus, removing the effects of income, thereby increasing the salience of education, yields a positive relationship between relative deprivation and trust; and removing the effects of education yields a negative relationship between deprivation and trust. Status congruence once again shows almost no relationship to measures of system support.

The most interesting relationships were found when education was examined with relative deprivation held constant. Removing the effects of relative deprivation eliminates the variance in the relationship between education and income; i.e., it removes people who are status incongruent. While status congruence in itself is not predictive of measures of system support, those people who are status congruent and are high in status (income and education) are higher in personal trust than are those who are low in status (r=.25). Such people also prefer private to government agencies (r=.30).

It is worth noting that partialed measures of relative deprivation and status congruence are related to interpersonal trust and confidence in democratic mechanisms (government vs. private), but are not related to specific agency experiences or attitudes toward agencies. Relative deprivation and status congruence operate on a fairly abstract rather than concrete level of system support. There are three possible explanations for the failure of our index of relative deprivation to be predictive.

First, it may be that, in American society, level of income is perceived as relative to the broader society rather than to one's own group. The mass media and mass merchandizing make clear to almost everyone what an abundant life can be. Expectations escalate as information spreads. Thus, it does not take a college education to feel deprived on a modest income.

Second, a related explanation is that our discrepancy index does not discriminate sufficiently among people in various stages of the life cycle and with various types and levels of aspirations. The college graduate under 30 may not be affluent, but he may see an open road ahead toward his objectives. Hence, the discrepancy between education and income needs to be adjusted on the basis of perceived progress toward one's goals. We lacked the questions and the numbers of people in sub-categories for such an analysis.

Third, theories of relativity in psychology hold for middle ranges and run into problems of absolute values at the ends of the continuum. One can still feel cold when the temperature drops or hungry when his diet is inadequate even though he is no worse off than other individuals in his neighborhood. It is possible that, in spite of an affluent society, people on incomes of $4,000 and less a year are hurting, not because they compare themselves with the middle income groups, but because they are deprived in an absolute sense.

Another measure of socio-economic deprivation is working status—whether unemployed, employed, or outside the labor force. Here we came closer to an alienated group in that negative responses for the unemployed outweighed positive responses on confidence in national leadership, nationalism, general attitudes toward bureaucracy, evaluation of own experience with service offices, and interpersonal trust (Table 4.26). Only on attitudes toward the helpfulness of government and preference for public over private agencies did the unemployed show more favorable than unfavorable reactions. The people most supportive of the system were not the people presently employed, but those not working for pay—retirees, the disabled, and housewives.

Age Related to Types of System Support

The new political leftism and the counter culture have had their strengths among the young. Hence, it is instructive to look at a national sample rather than at elite groups to see how age groupings differ in their support for the establishment and its agencies (Table 4.27). In confidence in national political leadership, the 18-24 age group does not differ from any other age category save its immediate seniors (25-29). The 25-29 years olds are less supportive, whereas people at all other ages are more likely to be positive than negative toward national leaders. To the injunction, "Do not trust anyone over 30" should be added the amendment, "or anyone under 25," if only this one index of confidence in the system is considered. On symbolic nationalism, however, the 30 year division does apply, in that both the 18-24 and 25-29 groups are low in attachment to national symbols, with the 18-24 group being lower than the 25-29 year olds. Those 30 to

Table 4.26
Working Status Related to Types of System Support

Work Status	Service experience*		Trust in local political leaders		General attitudes toward bureaucracy		Public vs. private preference		Government helpful		Rejection of bureaucratic stereotypes		Confidence in national leadership		Symbolic nationalism		Interpersonal trust	
	Unfav	Fav	Unfav	Fav	Unfav	Fav	Unfav	Fav	Unfav	Fav	No	Yes	Unfav	Fav	Low	High	Low	High
Working	17.1%	18.9%	18.2%	27.8%	25.2%	17.6%	31.7%	23.4%	23.6%	38.3%	23.1%	22.0%	22.5%	26.0%	18.2%	16.2%	29.7%	35.3%
Unemployed	32.8	17.2	18.7	25.0	28.1	19.7	23.5	28.1	18.8	32.8	17.2	14.1	31.2	25.0	29.7	14.1	42.2	32.8
Retired/Disabled	11.4	55.2	10.8	22.7	16.2	29.7	23.3	33.0	15.6	43.2	18.3	19.4	22.7	25.9	11.8	24.9	22.7	33.6
Other (Housewife, student)	10.2	18.9	13.2	28.5	18.0	25.4	20.7	28.0	13.7	44.3	14.6	22.7	16.6	31.8	16.6	22.1	25.9	37.3

*Percentages combine two extreme positions at favorable or unfavorable ends of the scale. Total N's for each column vary from 220 for service experience (unfavorable) to 574 for government helpful (favorable).

Table 4.27

Relationship of Age and Various Types of System Support

Age Group	Service experience*		Trust in local political leaders		General attitudes toward bureaucracy		Public vs. private preference		Government helpful		Rejection of bureaucratic stereotypes		Confidence in national leadership		Symbolic nationalism		Inter-personal trust	
	Unfav	Fav	Unfav	fav	Unfav	Fav	Unfav	Fav	Unfav	Fav	No	Yes	Unfav	Fav	Low	High	Low	High
18-24	23.6%	14.8%	24.1%	22.2%	30.0%	14.8%	27.6%	17.7%	22.7%	32.5%	41.9%	26.6%	20.7%	26.1%	28.1%	7.4%	39.9%	21.7%
25-29	25.6	10.0	25.6	26.1	26.1	18.3	26.1	25.0	31.7	35.6	50.0	25.6	27.2	26.7	27.2	13.9	32.2	28.9
30-39	19.8	19.8	19.0	25.4	27.2	20.1	28.4	26.1	21.6	42.5	38.1	31.0	19.8	24.6	19.4	19.0	34.0	34.7
40-59	10.4	19.4	11.7	31.1	21.8	20.5	29.1	25.0	17.6	40.3	34.2	30.9	21.8	28.8	14.2	21.6	24.8	41.2
60+	8.1	44.3	9.6	27.2	12.9	29.9	25.7	32.6	14.1	44.9	40.4	26.9	19.5	28.7	8.7	24.0	20.1	40.4

*Percentages combine two extreme positions at favorable or unfavorable ends of the scale. Total N's for each column vary from 220 for service experience (unfavorable) to 574 for government helpful (favorable).

39 are evenly balanced in high and low nationalism scores, and the scales tip toward higher scores as age increases. There is support here for the thesis that symbolic nationalism is on the decline in our technological society.

In the general attitudes toward bureaucracy there is a steady progression with age of more favorable assessment. The sharp differences are between the extreme age groups—18 to 24 years olds and those 60 and over—and they are in the expected direction. In accepting negative stereotypes of public bureaucracy, these extreme groups come together as equally critical of government offices. The most positive of the age groups are the people between 40 and 59 and the most negative, those between 25 and 29. Another attitudinal measure, that government is helpful, shows considerably more favorable than unfavorable responses for all age groupings save the 25 to 29. The oldest respondents (60 and over) are the highest in this response ratio. In evaluating business as superior to government, the main difference is between the age groups at the extremes (18-24 and 60 and over). At the experiential level, both groups of young people (18-24 and 25-29) are more dissatisfied with their agency encounters than are those 40 and over. The oldest age group has relatively few dissatisfied people in this respect.

When it comes to trusting others, the very young (18-24) show a ratio of two to one in their beliefs that people can't be trusted as compared to beliefs that people can be trusted (40 percent to 22 percent). Those 60 and over have the same ratio but in the opposite direction (40 to 20 percent). If all age groups are considered, trust increases progressively from one group to another. In short, there may be some projection in the admonition, "Don't trust anyone over 30," in that young people tend to be much more distrustful than their elders.

In general, there is suggestive evidence here that the mechanisms which have worked to tie people to the system in the past are no longer as potent for the newer citizens. The newcomers tend to be lower in nationalism, in confidence in national leadership, in interpersonal trust, in general attitudes toward bureaucracy, and in favorable encounters with the bureaucracy. Do these findings reflect a change in culture, or are they a function of age? In other words, will they persist as younger people grow older, or will younger people change toward the norms of their parents as time goes by? There are no definitive answers, but on some of the dimensions, cultural change is operative and on others, transient age differences. For example, the dissatisfactions with specific agencies expressed by young people have to do with their seeking job training and job placement. As these same clients grow older and turn to other agencies for other types of service, their reactions may change. On the other hand, the decline in potency of attachment to symbolic patriotism looks like a stable cultural change. At other times in history, age as such would have predicted more emotional involvement among the young than among the old.

Other studies have also reported small differences but not drastic cleavages between age groups in the population (V. L. Bengtson and M. C. Lovejoy, 1973). The Harris study (1973) showed significant percentage differences between those under 30 and those over 50 in confidence in local government, especially the police and local tax assessment. Curiously, there was less disaffection among the young for higher levels in the government, save for the military, than for the local level. The young, moreover, were more negative about big business and organized religion than their elders.

Though young people are in general less supportive of the establishment, age differences are not so consistent or so sharp as to permit labeling any age group alienated or anomic. When we speak of differences among the young, the middle-aged, and the old, we are dealing with percentage variations of only a few points. Even where statistically significant, these differences do not account for a great deal of the variance on measures of system support.

Race Related to Types of System Support

Race is also viewed as an important determinant of integration into the national system. Blacks, Spanish-speaking Americans, and Indians, as deprived minorities, would not be expected to be as supportive of the existing social order as are members of the white majority. Data analyses show sizable differences between blacks and whites on a number of dimensions (Table 4.28). Three times as many blacks (39 percent) are highly critical of national political leadership as are strongly supportive (13 percent). This is the reverse of the ratio for whites, where 20 percent are highly critical and 28 percent strongly supportive. On the individual items making up this index of confidence in national political leadership, blacks showed the greatest differences from whites on the two questions: "How much of the time do you think you can trust the government in Washington to do what is right?" and "Do you think that *quite a few* of the people running the government are a little crooked, *not very many* are, or do you think *hardly any* of them are crooked at all?"

Table 4.28

Relationship of Race to Various Types of System Support

Race	Service experience*		Trust in local political leaders		General attitudes toward bureaucracy		Public vs. private preference		Government helpful		Rejection of bureaucratic stereotypes		Confidence in national leadership		Symbolic nationalism		Inter-personal trust	
	Unfav	Fav	Unfav	Fav	Unfav	Fav	Unfav	Fav	Unfav	Fav	No	Yes	Unfav	Fav	Unfav	Fav	Unfav	Fav
White	13.9%	23.8%	15.6%	27.5%	21.2%	21.8%	28.1%	24.6%	19.6%	41.1%	19.2%	17.3%	19.6%	28.4%	16.7%	19.1%	24.6%	38.9%
Black	25.4	21.4	17.4	27.7	31.8	19.8	21.4	36.5	19.8	34.1	23.0	15.8	38.9	13.4	27.0	11.1	54.0	11.1
Other	26.3	22.8	22.8	19.3	29.8	21.1	31.6	28.1	28.0	29.8	35.1	10.5	22.8	33.3	14.1	26.3	54.4	14.0

*Percentages combine two extreme positions at favorable or unfavorable ends of the scale. Total N's for each column vary from 220 for service experience (unfavorable) to 574 for government helpful (favorable).

Blacks were also low in symbolic nationalism, with only 11 percent at the high end of the scale. Whites were also low in nationalism scores (19 percent), but more of them were in the middle of the scale. Some 10 percent more of blacks than of whites evaluated government agencies very unfavorably, and 7 percent fewer blacks had positive attitudes toward public bureaucracy. Nevertheless, the distribution of blacks on this index showed many more on the positive than on the negative end of the scale. In terms of their own experiences, there are slightly more negative than positive responses among blacks, reversing the pattern for whites. Nonetheless, some 12 percent more of blacks than of whites regard the government as superior to business in conducting their affairs. The blacks are not happy about public bureaucracy, but they are even less happy about private enterprise. In the Harris survey the targets for trust were more differentiated with respect to kinds of public offices and blacks like young people had less confidence in local than in higher levels of the system. In fact, blacks had more trust in the Supreme Court than whites and tended to be more supportive of non-governmental institutions with the exception of big business and law firms.

The largest margin of difference between blacks and whites is on interpersonal trust. Fifty-four percent of the blacks as against 25 percent of the whites were low in trusting other people, and 11 percent of the blacks compared to 39 percent of the whites made high scores on the trust dimension. In summary, the blacks are the most alienated of any of the groups we have examined, though the racial differences are not large save on interpersonal trust. Our group of other racial minorities (Spanish-speaking people and Indians) is too small to yield anything but suggestions about relationships (N=57). These minority individuals resemble blacks more than whites in attitudes about lower levels in the system. But they are much closer to whites than to blacks in confidence in national political leadership and in symbolic nationalism. It would seem that many of these people are not as yet sufficiently politicized to reject the highest levels of authority.

The wide differences between blacks and whites on interpersonal trust may have something to do with the fact that blacks are not as negative toward the system as might be expected. If people do not trust one another, then they are not likely to be supportive of one another in a common revolutionary objective. A condition for drastic social change would be disillusionment with existing institutions but confidence in the motives of one's fellows. It is true that our questions did not ask about trust in people in their own neighborhood, social class, age group, or race. But respondents had no difficulty in responding about whether most individuals would treat them fairly, take advantage of them, and so forth. Our assumption is that if there had been a developed class consciousness, they would have responded differently. A further assumption is that members of a frustrated group, whether the young or the blacks, have to trust one another for widespread collective attack upon the system.

Sex Related to Types of System Support

Though women have been regarded as an exploited and frustrated group in modern society, they seem in no way alienated from the political system (Table 4.29). Just as many women as men express confidence in national political leadership, and just as many women as men are nationalistic (though neither sex is high in nationalism). Women tend to be slightly more favorable than men in general attitudes toward bureaucracy, to be less accepting of negative stereotypes of bureaucracy, to show positive attitudes toward the helpfulness of government, to have had fewer negative experiences with public offices, and to give public bureaucracy better marks than business. Both groups are alike on the index of interpersonal trust. The women's movement at the present time seems to lack a political base in that women and men are very much alike in their support for national leadership and are slightly more supportive of the agencies of government. The base of the movement is both cultural and economic, and as yet these sources for change have not been systematically linked to methods for political change. In fact, our findings indicate that such linkage has little going for it in the attitudinal differences between men and women.

Overall, our findings do not necessarily indicate a high degree of support for the political system on all dimensions. But the disaffection that does exist is neither concentrated in a single dimension nor in a single discontented group. The most disaffected segments of the population are blacks and young people, but they are basically more like the rest of the population than they are different. The economically deprived are also less happy with the existing state of affairs, but not consistently or uniformly so. In order to put together a strong dissident group, one would have to look for people with all these characteristics—non-white, young, and poor.

Interrelationships of Dimensions of System Support

How do the various dimensions of system support relate to one another? The degree of relationship will not be great because the

Table 4.29

Relationship of Sex to Various Types of System Support

Sex	Service experience*		Trust in local political leaders		General attitudes toward bureaucracy		Public vs. private preference		Government helpful		Rejection of bureaucratic stereotypes		Confidence in national leadership		Symbolic nationalism		Inter-personal trust	
	Unfav	Fav	Unfav	Fav	Unfav	Fav	Unfav	Fav	Unfav	Fav	No	Yes	Unfav	Fav	Unfav	Fav	Unfav	Fav
Male	18.0%	24.1%	17.5%	27.5%	25.1%	19.5%	33.7%	22.7%	25.0%	37.0%	24.5%	13.8%	20.8%	25.5%	16.9%	18.6%	29.3%	34.7%
Female	13.4	23.0	15.0	27.0	20.5	23.0	23.0	28.3	16.2	42.2	17.0	19.2	22.0	28.6	18.0	18.7	27.8	35.9

*Percentages combine two extreme positions at favorable or unfavorable ends of the scale. Total N's for each column vary from 220 for service experience (unfavorable) to 574 for government helpful (favorable).

measures for these dimensions appeared as relatively independent factors in factor analysis. Nevertheless, one or two may prove more central in a consistent pattern of relationships with the others.

The interrelationships of the dimensions of system support (Table 4.30) show that confidence in national leadership (I) is positively related to the three measures of agency attitudes (.54, .47, and .47) and also correlates with interpersonal trust, but at a lower level (.30). It is only slightly related, however, to evaluation of service experiences (.14), or constraint experience (.14). Interpersonal trust, in addition to a positive relationship with confidence in national leadership, is associated to a minor extent with favorable attitudes toward agencies (.23, .31, and .21), but not significantly with agency experience. Attitudes toward agencies, as measured by the three indices (C, G, K), are related to confidence in political leadership and are also associated with agency experience (.29, .28, .21, .16, .25, and .21). These correlations, though not high, are higher than any of the other coefficients with service or constraint experience. Agency attitudes are thus the most central of all our indicators of system support, in that they relate in both directions to other indices, to the more general level of confidence in national leadership, and to the more specific level of experience with agencies.

Table 4.30

Interrelationship of Dimensions of System Support

	(A)	(B)	(C)	(D)	(E)	(F)	(G)	(H)	(I)	(J)	(K)	(L)
(A) Service experiences	X											
(B) Constraint encounters	.02	X										
(C) General attitudes toward bureaucracy	.29	.28	X									
(D) Public vs. private preference	.12	.03	.37	X								
(E) Symbolic nationalism	-.01	.04	-.03	-.13	X							
(F) Trust in community leadership	.00	-.02	.15	.05	.03	X						
(G) Rejection of negative bureaucratic stereotypes	.21	.16	.52	.25	-.06	.14	X					
(H) Interpersonal trust	.09	-.01	.23	-.08	.00	.09	.31	X				
(I) Confidence in national leadership	.14	.14	.54	.22	.00	.11	.47	.30	X			
(J) Trust in local political leaders	.15	.01	.29	.11	-.03	.55	.25	.13	.22	X		
(K) Government helpful	.25	.21	.53	.30	-.01	.15	.50	.21	.47	.28	X	
(L) Favorable to government intervention	-.07	-.02	-.03	.01	-.15	.00	.02	-.03	-.04	.02	.04	X

Note: Pearson product-moment correlations are used.

Types of System Support Related to Attitudes Toward
Specific Problems

How well do the various dimensions of system support predict to beliefs about handling of specific problems? Data on five such specific questions are available which can be considered dependent variables with respect to our indices of system support:

1) Whether local people can be helpful in getting a government office to do something;

2) Whether congressmen or public officials are helpful in getting action from an agency;

3) Whether cooperating with a government office is the most useful method of getting results;

4) Whether government services should be extended or cut back;

5) Whether various types of problems should be handled by the government or by business.

We would expect that people who show high levels of system support would have favorable attitudes toward government on all these problems. We would also anticipate that differences exist among the measures of support in predicting to these attitudes toward the problems listed above.

Specifically, we would expect the level of correlations of our four measures of system support with attitudes toward specific problems would decrease in the following order:*

1) Satisfaction with personal experience with service agency.

2) Favorable attitudes toward government offices.

3) Confidence in national leadership.

4) Interpersonal trust.

The rationale for these expectations is that the experiential level and agency-attitude level are closer to actual problems which people face, that confidence in national leadership is more remote from pragmatic issues, and that interpersonal trust is diffuse and lacks specific targets. Some support for this rationale is provided by the findings that our measure of relative deprivation, with either income or education controlled (but not relative deprivation alone), is related to interpersonal trust and confidence in democratic mechanisms, whereas other measures of system support are not so related. There is also a relationship between high status, among status congruent respondents, and both interpersonal trust and confidence in democratic mechanisms. Both relative deprivation and status congruence, as

---

*Our measure of nationalism is too restricted to be included in this list.

concepts, lack specificity and are, therefore, removed from pragmatic issues.

Our prediction that interpersonal trust would show little relationship to specific issues was supported by the findings (Tables 4.30 and 4.31). People high in trusting others were no more likely than the distrustful to be positive in their attitudes about particular problems. The trustful had no more confidence than the distrustful in the helpfulness of local leaders in getting action from public agencies, but they were slightly more positive about political leaders (.13). There was no relationship between interpersonal trust and opinions about extending or cutting back governmental services (L). Both the trustful and distrustful prefer the government to private enterprise for handling types of service in the public domain (D). Only when it comes to ways of getting things done by public agencies is there some relation to interpersonal trust (Table 4.31). The trusting people are much more likely to say that cooperation with the agency is the way to get results (79 percent) than are the people low in trust (55 percent). Interpersonal trust as a general predisposition does not readily engage or gear into instrumental activities related to government. This may be because it is not a matter of a deep and pervasive distrust. To color other attitudes, it may have to reach some critical degree of intensity and extensity. But it does gear into more generalized attitudes, such as political cynicism and general evaluations of public agencies. People alienated with respect to general trust in others may still be positive in their relationships with the personnel they encounter in a given agency.

Table 4.31

Percent of Respondents Who Believe that Giving
Information to Agency Personnel and Cooperating with
Them Is Sufficient for Obtaining Service by Level of
Personal Trust

1 Low personal trust	55.0%
2	63.2
3	56.4
4	76.5
5	65.6
6	69.2
7 High personal trust	79.2

Confidence in national political leadership, and political cynicism resemble general attitudes toward administrative agencies in their slight positive correlations with more pragmatically oriented responses. In general, there is some support for our expectation that the agency attitude would be more predictive of specifics, but it is only *slight* support, and the two types of system support are more alike than different. They do show one difference in the questions concerning the kind of agency which should handle various types of problems. The index measuring confidence in leadership correlates with giving government rather than private business responsibility for handling crime, safety standards, environment pollution, and unemployment compensation, but shows no correlation with handling retirement, health and medical problems, aid to the needy, and job retraining. On the other hand, the indices of favorable attitude toward government offices relate positively to preferring government to business when it comes to handling the latter set of problems of job retraining, health and medical problems, retirement, and aid to the needy. In addition, these favorable attitudes correlate with unemployment compensation as a problem for government handling, but not with car safety, preventing environmental pollution, or crime control (for two of the three attitudinal indices).

We have previously viewed these attitudinal indices as reflecting two levels of system support—the index measuring confidence in national leadership as the *more abstract* level, and the indices reflecting evaluation of administrative agencies as the *intermediate* level (the one more likely to engage instrumental activity). It is interesting, then, to find that the more abstract level of confidence in national leadership is associated with preference for government handling of personal problems. This would accord with the more pragmatic approach shown at the level of administrative agency support as compared with the higher level of support shown in the political leadership scale. Overall, there is more linking of preference for government over private industry to the intermediate level of attitudinal support than to the abstract level of confidence in national political leadership.

INTERPRETIVE SUMMARY

The interpretation of our data is complicated by two considerations: one theoretical, the other methodological. The first concerns levels of perceptual and cognitive organization. Do people have separate belief levels such that their specific experiences and memories of those experiences comprise one system, and their more generalized attitudes comprise another? Or is there a simple unified cognitive structure embracing generalized beliefs, memories of old experiences, and perceptions of more recent happenings? We would favor the theory that people do have complex organizations of memories and beliefs, and that they do have levels and systems reflecting specific experiences which differ from their more general belief systems. The boundaries between the two are not always clearly defined. The functional approach in perception has demonstrated that values do affect perceptual responses. But the outcome of numerous experiments has been to show how minor a role such functional determinants play and to· show the special conditions necessary for their effective operation. People do discriminate between what they see, what they have experienced, what they want to happen, and what they believe. They may sometimes discriminate poorly between perception and belief, but they do discriminate.

The second consideration is methodological. Even though one grants the possibility that people know the difference between their own experiences and their value orientation, they may not preserve these differences in an interview about past experiences. Since there are no objective controls which force a person to be accurate in recounting his experience, the respondent may not be talking about the episode at the agency, but about his own beliefs. Thus, *one general interpretation* of our findings would be that the report the individual gives us of an encounter with a public agency is highly colored by his own general attitudinal orientation. If he is opposed to public bureaucracy and believes it inferior to private enterprise, he will report his own experiences with a negative bias—namely, he has been treated inconsiderately, unfairly, etc. A *second general interpretation* would be that the interaction with the people at the agency and the particular experiences are primary in determining the specific reactions about the office. The interview, by asking about the details of the episode at the agency, sets a reality framework for response. It may be influenced by global attitudes, but such influence is minor compared to the facts of the experience itself.

The major difference of consequence between the two interpretations is that the first approach would not have to explain relationships between general attitudes and specific beliefs. The two are seen as a unified system. Hence, the first interpretation would have the task of explaining away the apparent differences in the data between the two levels. The second approach would have the task of accounting for the relationships that do appear between the two levels.

The data support the second interpretation more than the first. In the first place, there is consistent and strong evidence that many people do respond differently when they talk about their specific experiences with public offices than when they talk about government offices in general. This is all the more striking in that the questions directed at the two levels were fairly similar and occurred within a few minutes of one another in the interview. The easy response would have been to give the same answer to both types of questions. Moreover, the differences across the board were highly consistent—a much more favorable response in dealing with the specifics of experience than with general evaluative attitudes. This discrepancy is readily explained if one accepts the notion that the global attitudes reflect the general stereotypes of the culture about public bureaucracy.

In the second place, there is a supporting line of evidence which concerns the reactions elicited when questions dealt with personal attributes of agency personnel rather than agency functioning. People in public offices were perceived as similar to the client, as workers doing a job, and as people who are helpful and considerate. Even for those respondents who saw some groups getting preferential treatment, there was no agreement about target groups. Our findings here are in agreement with those of Janowitz, Wright, and Delany (1958). In their investigation people reported favorably about their personal contacts with individual civil servants but, at the same time, were critical of the way the agency functioned.

Another difficulty for the first interpretation would be the relationship between types of experiences and evaluative attitudes. Bad experiences reduce the appraisal of public agencies, but good experiences do not improve the appraisal. This could be readily explained within the second interpretation—namely, the understandable relationship between experience and attitude familiar in psychological literature. Good experiences are readily assimilated to rising expectations. If one follows the first interpretation, one would have to assume that the negative attitudes (e.g., bureaucracy is bad) are held so much more strongly than positive attitudes that people are more consistent in overall negative reactions than positive reactions.

A second even more serious problem for the first interpretation is that the nature of the experience is related in a meaningful way to more general attitudes. Where people have had difficulty with a constraint agency, considerate treatment by agency people does not completely erase the negative consequences of the unpleasant experience, although inconsiderate treatment intensifies the negative effect. On the other hand, where the experience is with a service agency and hence not as negative to begin with, there is no negative effect when the agency personnel have been considerate. In short, the variations in response in evaluating offices follows some variations in experience in a consistent fashion, if one accepts the respondent's report as an account of his encounter. If, however, these reports are viewed as accounts of experiences heavily biased by general attitudes, it is difficult to explain the differences. It is more convincing, then, to accept the respondent's account of his encounter with a public office as reflecting more of his immediate personal experience than the general stereotypes he held when he entered the office. If, in fact, the global orientation were the determining factor, it would be difficult to account for the high level of positive responses to specific agency functioning. Since people usually acquire these general attitudes before specific experiences with an agency, they should on this theory show the same level of response whether the question is general or specific.

It can be argued further that people actually organize their cognitions both at a pragmatic empirical level, and at a more general ideological level. Ideologically, they may be against large public bureaucracies; pragmatically, they are all for them, as our findings indicate. The cognitive structures representative of pragmatic empirical orientations do interact with more general values systems under special conditions. The basic weakness in theories of cognitive consistency is to assume that such special conditions are common conditions, with resulting congruity in the psychological field. One type of compelling circumstance is a negatively toned experience in relation to a neutral or positive belief. The effect is to move the attitude in the direction of the experience. Positive experiences do not have the same effect in changing attitudes in a more positive direction. Thus, people will still speak of the inefficiency of bureaucracy and will handle the discrepancy between this belief and their own experiences with a public agency by saying that the agency people are efficient and helpful, but the bureaucrats in Washington waste time and money.

CHAPTER 5

SUMMARY AND CONCLUSIONS

This research has been primarily an attempt to understand the experiences of people when they try to get help with a number of common but serious problems: finding a job when out of work, getting training for a better job, getting compensation for accidents or injuries, getting unemployment compensation, getting relief or public assistance, getting medical and hospital care, getting retirement benefits. In addition to these questions of service, we were interested secondarily in the citizen's experience with agencies of constraint—licensing, taxing, police agencies. In both functions—service and constraint—we concentrated our attention on agencies of government, asking in the first instance what the government was doing for the individual and in the second some of the things it required of him.

PURPOSE AND DESIGN

We undertook this research out of a conviction that evaluation of government agencies is both important and neglected. Its importance stems from the fundamental structure of American society; it is, as is often said, an organizational society. This means that the satisfactions and frustrations that an individual experiences, the quality of individual and social life, are mediated to a large extent by formal organizations, many of them agencies of government. Goods and services are delivered, or access to them is denied, by such organizations. Redress of grievances is provided or prevented by them. In recent years the idea of social indicators, measures of the quality of life, has become something of a slogan. Few social indicators are more important than the functioning of government agencies.

In spite of the popularity of the term *evaluation research*, there has been a conspicuous neglect of systematic assessment of the op-

179

erations of public agencies and programs. The small fraction of evaluated programs is by no means representative; the research is sporadic, and the results not geared to the improvement of agency functioning. These facts would be less important if the usual mechanisms of consumer choice, available alternatives, and significant, if imperfect, competition were operative. For most government agencies none of these conditions exists; rather, they operate services subject only to remote and complex kinds of control. The feedback loop between consumers and producers of government services needs to be closed, and this research is an attempt to show how that can be made to happen.

There are many ways of going at such research, and the present effort must be considered a pilot study. It is an unusual pilot study, however, in that it is based on a national probability sample of the population of the United States. It is unusual also in the unit of analysis with which we chose to work—the episode. The episode can be thought of as a brief encounter between an individual and an agency of government. Imagine, for example, a person who finds himself in need of a job, or assistance with any of the other problems included in our inquiry. He goes to the appropriate government office and thus initiates an episode that has many characteristics in common with similar encounters in the lives of other people who seek help from the same or other agencies.

On one side of the desk sits the applicant for service, with all the needs, experiences, and idiosyncratic characteristics that combined to bring him there. On the other side of the desk sits a person whose function it is to determine the validity of the presenting request, the goodness of fit between it and the franchise of the agency, and thus the entitlement of the person. It is likely to be a brief conversation, although the preliminaries may be long. It ends with a decision, or a referral, either of which may satisfy or frustrate the client. It may also end the person's contact with the agency, or it may initiate additional contacts.

The universe of such episodes, through time, can be thought of as the sum of services rendered or refused, the output of all government agencies of service and constraint. If the episodes are summed across individuals who share similar presenting problems, we have the basis for evaluating particular agencies, the quality of particular services. If the episodes are summed across agencies for particular individuals, we have the basis for determining how well different persons and sub-groups are served. Indeed, the life of the individual can be looked at in terms of the unique set of such episodes in which he has been the principal actor. That set sums the services rendered by the government and received by that individual, and says much about the quality of his life.

As a concept, the episode can be thought of as an intervening element in a causal sequence. It is an interactive product of the properties of the client and those of the agency, including its representative. The episode in turn predicts to the client's evaluation of the agency and makes some incremental or decremental contribution to his support or opposition toward the larger political system of which the agency is a part. This is the rudimentary model that guided the present research, and it is illustrated in Figure 1:

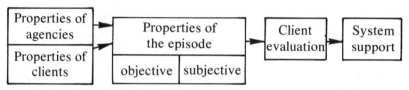

Figure 1.   The Client Episode and Its Causal Sequence

If the model were thought of in dynamic terms, several feedback loops would be specified. For example, the initial level of system support that characterizes a particular individual in part reflects his previous experiences or episodes, and his evaluation of a particular experience is also likely to be moderated by previous encounters and by his level of system support at the initiation of the present episode. These hypothetical connections are not shown in Figure 1. Moreover, all the relationships that are shown are not equally substantiated by the present research. For example, almost no data were collected on the properties of the agencies themselves (size, number of echelons, location, and the like).

The present study deals with four main categories of variables: client characteristics, mostly demographic; utilization of or experience with different agencies; evaluation of the agency experience; and degree of support for the larger governmental and social system.

In this report, we first examined the background characteristics of those individuals who had used various service agencies and those who had encountered problems with constraint agencies. Conversely, we were interested in those groups of people who had underutilized services. Secondly, the satisfaction or dissatisfaction of clients was studied along a number of dimensions characterizing a particular episode of contact with an agency. Finally, we were interested in the more general or ideological attitudes toward government and the relationship of general attitudes to specific experiences. Specific experiences and general attitudes are conceived as two possible levels at which people are tied into the political system. Other levels, which were studied in less detail, include confidence in democratic mechanisms, confidence in national leadership, commitment to national symbols, and trust in one's fellows.

UTILIZATION

Government services are widely utilized. It is not just small segments of the population with special problems who make use of government agencies; a majority do. Approximately 58 percent of our respondents reported contact with at least one of seven service areas: employment service, job training, workmen's compensation, unemployment compensation, public assistance, hospital and medical care, and retirement benefits. Over 25 percent of our sample reported having received unemployment compensation at some time, and almost 24 percent had utilized job-finding services. Only about 8 percent reported having received workmen's compensation and some 6 percent having used government hospital and medical services. Low utilization does not necessarily imply low need. For example, some 30 percent of respondents report that they need job training, whereas less than 9 percent have in fact received job training, and there is a nine point discrepancy (33 percent to 24 percent) between need and utilization of employment services. Many more people report a need for job finding or job training services than for public assistance.

Only 15 percent of all respondents reported difficulty in one or more of the four constraint areas studied: driver licensing, traffic violations, income tax, and police interference with individual's rights. Some 6 percent reported problems with their income taxes, the constraint problem encountered most frequently of the four.

It is, of course, a statistical possibility to describe the "typical" utilizer of government services, but it would be misleading; different service agencies cater to different clientele. In general, more men than women use service agencies, although twice as many women as men receive public assistance. On the other hand, men are about twice as likely as women to receive the four work-related services. The discrepancy is less, but still marked, among employed men and women.

Blacks are only one-third as likely as whites to receive retirement benefits but are twice as likely to utilize job-finding and job-training services. Job-finding and job-training services are principally utilized by those under age 40 while social security recipients are generally 65 or older. Public assistance and government hospital and medical services are utilized predominantly by people low in income, education, and occupational status. Other services, such as unemployment compensation and job training, are used by broader groups. A working status code involving four categories—working, unemployed, retired or permanently disabled, and other (e.g., housewives, students)—indicates that the unemployed are particularly likely to have received services for job finding, job training, public assistance, and hospital and medical care.

Demographic variables explained about 21 percent of the variance in utilization (Multiple R = .45). The same characteristics explained only some 12 percent of the variance in encounters with control agencies (Multiple R = .34). In the case of the constraint experiences, age is the best predictor, with those under age 30 more likely to experience difficulty in all four areas. There are no significant racial differences; blacks are not likely to report more problems than are whites. Similarly, the less educated do not report more constraint encounters than the more educated; blue collar workers are more likely than white collar workers to report constraint problems, except in the area of income tax. More expected are the findings that the unemployed report more problems with constraint agencies than do people in other work-status categories, and males report more encounters than do females.

Knowledge of the existence of government agencies is an important determinant of utilization; it is, of course, a necessary but not sufficient condition. Among people who reported they had a problem, the percentage who had not utilized the appropriate agency varies from 2 percent for public assistance to 70 percent for job training. The proportion of non-users who reported problems, but who did not know of the existence of the relevant agency, is also variable. Of the non-users who reported a problem finding a job, 28 percent did not know that the government provided a job-finding service. In other areas of service, lack of knowledge is even more prevalent; 55 percent of those non-users with a medical or a hospital problem and 49 percent of those non-users who were injured or disabled on the job lacked knowledge of the existence of an appropriate service agency. The need for dissemination of information about government services is considerably more acute in some service areas than others. Moreover, people with problems are frequently among the uninformed.

In general, non-users who knew of a relevant agency did not avoid it because of specific negative feelings toward the agency. Other means of solving the problem, such as the person's own efforts, the help of relatives and friends, or even waiting for the problem to go away, were the reasons cited for not seeking governmental assistance.

EVALUATION

People do have opinions about their encounters with public bureaucracy, both in terms of their overall satisfaction with services and in terms of their reactions to specific aspects of the experience. The major finding was the relatively high degree of satisfaction with the various agencies. There were, however, significant differences among the specific agencies. Retirement services were the most favorably rated, with more than 90 percent of their clientele pleased with their experiences. The four work-related agencies had about 75 percent of their clients satisfied. Welfare and the medical/hospital care agencies received the poorest ratings, with less than 60 percent expressing satisfaction.* This breakdown was rather consistent throughout the evaluations of specific attributes of the agencies as well. Retirement service clients typically gave the most favorable appraisal of their treatment in relation to particular aspects of the encounter, such as ease of finding the right person to deal with, fairness of treatment, efficiency, etc. Welfare and health services were generally rated lowest on almost all attributes.

In addition to the finding that most people were relatively satisfied with public services, the data were also not supportive of certain negative stereotypes about bureaucracy. Respondents did not perceive the service bureaucracies as inefficient, unfair, and error-ridden in their own encounters with them. Nor did they find the personnel in these offices elusive, irresponsible, or authoritarian. Overall, approximately three out of five clients stated that their problem had been resolved. Only one in five thought the agency personnel had not exerted enough effort to be helpful. Only one in ten felt that the appropriate bureaucrat had been hard to find, and only one in five thought that the agency had been inefficient. A particularly significant finding was that most respondents (three out of four) felt that they had been treated fairly. Furthermore, 47 percent said they had the right to appeal decisions which were not to their liking. But only 14 percent of those who were aware of the appellate process actually exercised that privilege.

A major finding related to the evaluation of services was the fact that the demographic characteristics of clients were rather weak predictors of satisfaction. While satisfied clients were more likely to be

---

*On January 1, 1974, the administration and disbursement of benefits of three public assistance programs—Old Age Assistance, Aid to the Disabled, and Aid to the Blind—were transferred from the state department of social services to the Social Security Office. Present data were collected in the spring of 1973; thus our data and interpretation do not reflect the effects of the transfer.

older, white, female, rich or poor rather than middle income, and better educated, none of these relationships was particularly strong. Age was the best indicator, with the young being consistently less satisfied than the older. However, if we take all the major demographic characteristics of the client together with the type of agency utilized, we can account for only 14 percent of the variance in satisfaction.

Since the survey also examined bureaucratic encounters with four types of agencies which exercise some kind of control over people, certain comparisons with service agencies can be made. As might be expected, control agencies were evaluated less favorably than service agencies, which is to be expected because of the negative type of function performed. In addition, however, the questions dealing with control agencies made their negative function salient by asking people about their difficulties with such agencies. For service offices, however, the contact rather than the problem aspect was emphasized in the interview.

Constraint agency procedures drew heavier fire than those of service agencies with almost one-fourth of the constraint group reporting threats and pressures from governmental personnel. In contrast to service agencies, the control offices were not generally seen as efficient. About 35 percent felt that their operations had been efficient.

The more negative evaluation was also found in opinions of equitable treatment. Slightly less than half of the respondents with control agency experiences felt that they had been treated fairly or with consideration. In addition, relatively more people with control than with service experiences believed that favored treatment was given to certain people, such as the rich or those who had connections.

SYSTEM SUPPORT

Attitudes toward the political system are complex. While some 61 percent of respondents agree that by and large most government offices do a good job, they are less enthusiastic about such general characteristics as promptness, fairness, considerate treatment, and the like.

Yet when specific experiences are compared with such general evaluations, one finds that people's specific experiences are more positive than their general attitudes. For example, 80 percent of respondents felt they received fair treatment in their contact with government agencies, but only 42 percent rated government offices in general as being fair. There seems to be a clear separation of generalized attitudes from the specific attitudes derived from an individual's direct experiences.

A closer examination of the data reveals that general evaluation is related to specific experience if the experience was negative, but not if it was positive. A negative experience with an agency lowers one's general evaluation of government, but a positive experience does not raise it. Individuals with no experiences and individuals who have had positive experiences with government agencies give essentially the same general evaluation of government services; individuals who have had a negative experience give substantially lower general evaluations. The same trend is found for service agencies and for control agencies in such areas as promptness of service, fair treatment, and considerate treatment. Evaluation of specific experiences transfers to the general level when the evaluation is negative, but not when it is positive.

The general low rating of characteristics of governmental services may be a function of stereotypes of public bureaucracy held by Americans. This interpretation is consistent with findings which compare public bureaucracy with private enterprise. While the modal response was to say the two organizational forms were about the same, the minority, those who expressed a preference, generally favored private enterprise over public agencies on all six criteria: taking care of problems, giving considerate treatment, giving fair treatment, being careful and avoiding mistakes, correcting mistakes, and giving prompt service. Such responses seem inconsistent with the responses of positive evaluation that most individuals gave to their specific agency experiences.

The negative evaluations of government in general are inconsistent as well, it seems, with the preferences expressed by respondents for the allocation of major social tasks. Respondents were asked about a list of such tasks, including the prevention of pollution, the control of crime, the provision of job retraining, and the delivery of hospital and medical benefits. Not only did respondents prefer that government rather than private enterprise handle all listed problems, but within the government, the preference was given to state and federal agencies rather than to local units. Only 21 percent of respondents felt business should handle job retraining; 9 percent felt that business should take care of safety standards for autos, and only 1 percent felt it was within the province of business to control crime.

These seeming inconsistencies can be reconciled if we assume that people are characterized by cognitive complexity rather than cognitive consistency and that we have tapped two modes of response: the ideological and the pragmatic. Thus general evaluations of bureaucracy may tap the ideological level, and the specifc evaluations of experiences may tap the pragmatic level. Furthermore, when ideology and pragmatism compete, as in the case of whether government or business should handle various problems, pragmatism prevails over ideology. Apparently we are dealing with an ideology of stereotypes rather than strong personal values and convictions. Although the public evaluates government less favorably than it does private enterprise in most respects, government bureaucracy is preferred over business for handling many of the country's problems.

Attitudes toward government, both at the specific level of agency functioning and the more general level of the evaluation of public bureaucracy, are indications of the support for the national political system. Based on the theoretical work of Easton (1965) and the empirical work of Miller and his colleagues (1972, 1973), we propose six levels of system support: (1) trust in one's fellows; (2) confidence in specific administrative agencies which one has encountered; (3) support for administrative agencies as a system; (4) confidence in representative democracy; (5) confidence in political leadership; and (6) commitment to national symbols. Not all six levels could be adequately represented in a 35-minute interview. No attempt was made to ask questions on confidence in representative democracy, but questions on the other five levels were included. A factor analysis of the data revealed nine factors, two separate factors for service and constraint experiences, four factors on support for administrative agencies, as well as separate factors of confidence in national leadership, nationalism, and interpersonal trust (see Table 4.16 and 4.17).

Our findings combined with those of Miller show that confidence in government leadership has consistently declined since 1958 with further erosion occurring between 1972, the post-election period, and the date the sample was taken, April and May 1973. Trend data on interpersonal trust likewise show a decline in recent years. For example, responses to the statement that most people can be trusted have declined from 53 percent in 1964 to 45 percent in 1973. For the most part, however, the decline in general trust is not as dramatic as the decline in confidence in national leadership.

It seems, however, that at other levels system support is strong. Many people express distrust of national political leaders and speak almost in cliches about the relative inefficiency of government, but they expect to find the local offices open and functioning when they need unemployment compensation or reach the age of retirement. Moreover, there is support for the nation and its symbols at the most general level. The problems of erosion seem to involve the intermediate levels of system support.

Our model of levels of system support (and our data) suggests that individuals may be tied into the system in differing degrees at the various levels, and that grave problems of alienation arise only when all or most levels of support break down for a particular group. We therefore examined in greater detail four particular groups which might be considered vulnerable to alienation: (1) the socially and economically deprived, (2) the young, (3) blacks, and (4) women. In general, we found little evidence for a serious condition of alienation in any of these groups, although they do not show a high degree of support for the system either. The most disaffected are the young and blacks.

IMPLICATIONS FOR PUBLIC POLICY

The discontinuity between people's pragmatic evaluations of the specifics of agency functioning and their ideological orientation toward a public bureaucracy raises serious questions about the development of public policy. The formulation of public policy calls for generalized statements of program objectives and should furnish a rationale for many specifics of program operation. Ideally, the statement of policy should determine many of the specifics of implementation, and in turn, the policy should be modified by particular experiences in the attempt to operationalize it. Practice and theory should mean continuing interaction of the specific and the general. What is assumed is a connection between the two levels. But for the rank-and-file, the connection is lacking. People do not tie their particular experiences with governmental offices to their ideals of public bureaucracy and public programs. Without this linkage, then, they can be supportive at one level and destructive at another. People do not relate the agencies which they know about through direct experience with symbols of government. The connection could be made through an appreciation of the objectives of a given policy or through knowledge of what the program is trying to do. But for the majority of people, the policy makers are remote and their basic goals are not understood.

In place of a conception of public programs and policies, people turn to a personal image of politicians in Washington. The political actors in the national scene are often perceived as rascals, and events of the last two years have strongly reinforced these perceptions. People's frustrations about daily problems such as employment, inflation, and shortages can be channeled in two directions. The one would be demagogic and populist, directed against incumbent scoundrels and utilizing slogans and stereotypes. The other could be system directed and aimed at structural reform and policy change.

Our findings suggest that people respond realistically to factors in the framework of their own experience, but that they do not carry the same realism to more general issues. At the more remote and general levels they can embrace doctrines at variance with their specific beliefs. They do not connect the two. Hence they may be more ready to accept populist doctrines than logically conceived programs. Reason and logic are primary considerations at the level of direct contact with reality, but they are less reliable when problems transcend direct experience.

Somehow people need to become more involved in policy formulation if they are to have an understanding of program objectives and their implementations. How to encourage such involvement has long been recognized as a problem critical to the survival of political democracy. Various mechanisms have been suggested, and even put into practice, to bridge the gap between people's limited specific experiences with government and their knowledge of public policies. We have witnessed such attempts as the Town Meeting of the Air, local forums for the discussion of issues, more systematic communication between elected representatives and their electorates, some granting of local autonomy in the administration of national programs, and special organizations to involve citizens in common problems. John Gardner's Common Cause and Ralph Nader's several organizations are current examples. The increased use of such involvement mechanisms and their creative multiplication along new lines may be strengthened by the younger generation with its higher levels of expectation and aspiration. Future studies of public bureaucracy should explore progress toward citizen involvement, the efficacy of different mechanisms of involvement, and the conditions which facilitate their development.

DILEMMAS IN THE DELIVERY OF GOVERNMENT SERVICE

It is the function of a pilot study to explore issues in an area of potential research, and to develop or try out ways of working in that area. These have been the focus of our efforts, but a not unexpected by-product has been an increased sensitivity to some of the persisting problems of delivering government services efficiently, appropriately, and on the grand scale required by a population of a quarter-billion people. Some of these problems are briefly sketched in the remaining pages of this monograph.

The Criterion Problem

One of the chief difficulties, both methodological and conceptual, in evaluating public services might be called the criterion problem. What are the criteria by which a social agency should be judged successful? Those criteria which are easiest to calculate and have been utilized most frequently involve "body counts"—the number of cases opened, the number of cases closed, number of clients handled, cost per client, recidivism rate, and so forth. There are many limitations to this approach, including an emphasis on quantity and a disregard for quality of service.

A second approach, which gained popularity during the "War on Poverty," is evaluation of the ratio of costs to benefits. But there are severe limitations to cost-benefit analysis when ultimate costs and benefits are difficult to assess. In such circumstances those costs and benefits which can be easily calculated are the ones which *are* calculated. Emphasis is thus given to short-range economic factors while long term and psychological factors tend to be neglected. An example is Borus, Brennan and Rosen's (1974) cost-benefit analysis of the Neighborhood Youth Corps. In their study, the money earned in subsequent jobs was one criterion of success. On this basis, training men rather than women would give the program a better rating.

There are attempts to solve this problem by stating the value of social-psychological factors in economic terms—Human Resources Accounting is an example—but it is difficult to get agreement on the monetary value of factors such as increased self-esteem or decreased misery. Furthermore, cost-benefit analysis often tends to favor the status quo in evaluating social programs, and even to encourage some restriction of function. For example, a cost-benefit analysis may well reveal that a program is most cost-beneficial when it handles those people who have the fewest problems. Such people may need less training, counseling, money, or whatever service the agency dispenses. The truly needy may be rejected on the basis that helping them is not cost-beneficial.

A third approach at specifying criteria for service evaluation is the value-added approach. Such evaluations would assess the amount of "value" which is added to the individual as a result of his encounter with a particular agency. This approach is a variant of cost-benefit analysis and raises the same basic problem—specification of the proper value of the service. Furthermore, "repair" programs such as those which offer public assistance and hospital and medical benefits usually cannot utilize the value-added concept since in fact value may not be added. The value-added approach does have the advantage, however, of eliminating the conservatizing trend of cost-benefit analysis; those individuals who show the most value added are likely to be those with little of the relevant value—job skills, for example—in the first place.

The approach taken in the present study is to assess agency functioning in terms of client reaction and satisfaction. It is easy to dismiss this criterion as being subjective and inadequate. But people's knowledge of whether agencies exist for given problems, of where to go to get help, and of how to obtain help are all relevant to agency effectiveness, despite their subjective character. Moreover, client reactions with respect to their treatment cannot be dismissed lightly because they are psychological judgments. They relate to many particular aspects of agency functioning. For example, if a large majority complain about the favoritism of one agency but are happy about the considerate and equitable treatment in another agency, then there are some specifics to work on in the improvement of service. Even at the global level of overall satisfaction with an agency, the subjective character of the evaluation does not rule it out as a criterion. Indeed, it can even be argued that it is the ultimate criterion. If people are satisfied, what more can or should be added? And if they are not satisfied, does not something remain to be done? Such an approach has the added advantage of looking to consumers of services for a criterion. Because of the monopolistic nature of most human service agencies, consumers cannot express their dissatisfactions with one agency by turning to another. In Hirschman's (1970) terms, clients can not employ an exit option. Their satisfactions and dissatisfactions, however, can be recorded and utilized by the agency in efforts to improve organizational functioning and to justify the agency's entitlement to scarce resources.

The possibility of using satisfaction as a criterion brings up the question: Should recipients of public services be satisfied? The idea of satisfied recipients of welfare or unemployment compensation may raise the spectre of overdependency for many Americans. Our data would indicate that satisfaction with services is hardly to be equated with preferring dependency as a way of life. We would argue that, as part of the right to government services, each individual should be satisfied with such aspects of the service as promptness and courtesy, right of appeal, etc. It is these more concrete aspects of agency functioning which should be used for feedback in efforts to improve organizational effectiveness.

The Problem of Coverage

Closely related to the criterion problem is the problem of coverage. What clientele should be served and with what range of services? For some services these questions are given explicit answers by government in the enabling legislation or in the appropriation of funds. If one looks at the entire spectrum of needs and services, however, such specificity of service and entitlement is exceptional. Specificity with respect to the intended goal of service programs is also uncommon.

In the present research, the problem of coverage emerged in terms of utilization and underutilization. Some 58 percent of our sample reported some past contact with one or more of the seven selected sectors of governmental service. We also found that services are provided for a variety of interest groups, that there is no one recipient group to whom government services are directed, but that many people who encounter problems neither get nor seek help. Whether these facts indicate too much service or too little must be decided partly in terms of intentions and goals.

What is the goal of government service programs? Is it primarily one of income redistribution? Is it primarily a means of providing security to all Americans? Is it designed to provide aid in those areas that private enterprise does not cover? Government programs have largely been enacted in time of need with little thought given to how the particular program fits into the overall scheme of social welfare. This point has been noted in particular about the various programs of the Veterans' Administration (Steiner, 1971). Thus it is difficult to evaluate a figure which shows that 58 percent of Americans have had contact with service agencies of the government. Is the figure too high, too low, just right?

At the pragmatic level, there is indication of underutilization, but at the ideological level it is hard to say whether utilization is too high or too low. Our data show that people prefer that government rather than business handle major problem areas, which include dispensing various social services. However, there is evidence that many Americans, while they hold the government responsible for providing services to needy groups, question how many recipients of public services are truly needy. There is concern among citizens, administrators and policymakers about the amount of "cheating" by clients of service agencies. The mass media probably foster the image of numerous ineligibles receiving public assistance, unemployment compensation, workmen's compensation, and the like. Thus, while the government has received a mandate to provide necessary social services (Harris, 1973), it is not at all clear whether the popular mandate intends service to 10 percent or 90 percent of the population.

On a pragmatic level, more respondents indicate that they have problems than use agencies. For example, about one-third of respondents indicated a problem with finding a job or getting job training. However, whether the general public would approve of government funded job training facilities for up to one-third of the adult population is open to question.

A more vital and pressing concern is with the characteristics of underutilizers. Who are the people who indicate need for services and yet do not receive those services? Some of the neediest individuals, those who have low levels of education and income and who are not employed, also lack knowledge of relevant agencies. Perhaps more extensive efforts should be expended to provide information to these individuals. The lowest groups on the socio-economic ladder do not always show the greatest gap between perceived need and utilization, however. It is possible that low expectations of some of the neediest groups prevent them from expressing higher need levels. In short, the problem of coverage is large—intended versus delivered, needed versus sought, ideal versus actual.

The Problem of Socialization

The criterion of client reaction is limited in that there are other factors productive of favorable evaluation of an agency besides its possible effectiveness in rendering a service. People in a bureaucratic society may be socialized into low expectations of organizational functioning and may have developed a great deal of frustration tolerance. The high levels of satisfaction for service agencies in our data raise the question of how much of this reflects efficient problem solution and how much well-learned lessons about the ways of bureaucracy.

Socialization into organizations in American society begins when one enters kindergarten or sooner. High school graduates already have experienced 12 years of dealing with bureaucracy. The process of obtaining passes, excuses, and permission slips to be granted entrance or exit serves a useful apprenticeship for dealing with bureaucracies later in life. It can be argued that the more successfully clients are socialized in advance of their encounters with service agencies, the less critical and the more satisfied they are likely to be. Satisfaction, then, may tell as much about the clients as about the agency.

If an examination of socialization processes is made more carefully, however, it cannot be concluded that there is one general process that makes all people agreeable to all aspects of bureaucratic routine. Socialization into organizational society can mean ready acceptance of procedures, provided they meet standards of equity. The most thoroughly socialized Englishman, who cheerfully queues up in the long line before the office window, is not going to be happy if the official behind the window disrupts the order of the line by personal preferential treament. Socialization, then, can mean both acceptance of conventional practices and acquisition of standards which make people sensitive to new criteria and actually raise their expectations. In semi-feudal countries, people may accept authoritarian, personalized discrimination which even a U. S. Army sergeant could not get away with.

The fact that different socialization practices produce different standards can be seen in the American educational system. The amount of socialized acceptance of organizational procedures does not increase with the amount of schooling. In fact the reverse is the case, with more critical standards for organizational performance expressed by people who have moved higher in the educational system.

It should not be concluded, then, that socialization as a general process tells us very much about client satisfaction. We need to break down the problem into the types of expectancies created by various socialization practices for different groups of people. We thus may want to discount some of the satisfaction expressed by the poorly educated and be cautious about accepting at face value all the criticisms of the well educated. What is needed here is an exploration into the expectations and standards of groups of clients about the goals and practices of the agency. Knowledge is needed about whether there is something of a generalized acceptance of bureaucratic practice, and if so, whether this acceptance is predicated upon standards of fairness, equity, or considerate treatment of the individual or some other criteria.

In short, people may have some standards on the basis of which they evaluate agencies. Their priorities with respect to such standards need to be ascertained. The socialization issue thus provides no simple explanation of the behavior and feelings of people in their bureaucratic encounters, but it is helpful in suggesting specific lines for future research.

The Problem of Agency Objectives

We have discussed the problems of criteria, coverage, and socialization thus far without reference to the basic goals or functions of the agency. Within the context of government directives, the agency can operate to meet its obligations fully; it can define its task in selective terms to achieve success; or it can be concerned primarily with the ease of its own internal operations. These three orientations include varying amounts of social space. In the first instance the frame of reference is societal, in the second instance governmental, and in the third internal, i.e., concerned only with the administration of the agency.

To achieve the optimization implied in the first approach requires more than the good intentions of agency administrators. It calls for feedback cycles to furnish information about the specifics of agency functioning and to provide penalties and rewards for different types of performance. The feedback can be from the clientele to higher levels in government who can then exert pressure to improve matters.

In the absence of adequate feedback about basic objectives, lower level administrators are inclined to be motivated by two considerations: (1) How can the operation be run smoothly with as few embarrassing and difficult problems as possible for agency officials? (2) How can the agency achieve some limited objective which will ensure some palpable success? The first orientation of bureaucrats, namely to paper over problems and to attempt a push-button kind of administration, is countered by the dynamics of present day society with a changing turbulent environment, by competition among lower level officers to move up in the structure, and by the internalization of goals of service by some public employees. The second tendency, to redefine the major goal in terms of a limited objective, is in some ways a more serious problem for public agencies.

Within limits, organizations attempt to minimize risk-taking, maximize successes, and thus increase the probability of survival. Service bureaucracies are not exceptions to this principle, and it can be seen as operating on two levels. On the policy level, the agency may be organized to deal only with relatively easy, or low-risk problems. At this level, an agency is low risk if its objectives are simple and sanctioned, its access to resources ensured, and if it takes only minimal risks in capital outlay and effort in helping individual clients.

On the more pragmatic level of day-to-day decisions, agencies minimize their risks by tending to select those clients who represent the best chance of benefitting from the service, a problem to which reference has already been made in connection with cost-benefit criteria of agency performance. The type of individual who stands to benefit the most, or whose eligibility is not in question, may be considered as low risk. Thus, for instance, job training programs may tend to choose low-risk, able-bodied young males as representing a greater possibility of substantially increasing their earnings than women or high-risk older people unless, of course, the latter groups are protected by statute or by the formal objectives of the organization.

The same question can be formulated in terms of where higher-risk individuals can go for help. Conceivably an individual may be passed from agency to agency, down some hierarchy that reaches from executive placement to custodial care, until he finds an agency willing to help him. Such a hierarchy of services may develop also within each problem area, reflecting the riskiness or difficulty in the client's situation. At best, other services are then created to fill the needs of the residual group; at worst, they remain unserved.

Applications of the Criterion of Clientele Evaluation

In discussing the criterion problem we called attention to some of the advantages of utilizing the evaluation of the people served by the agency. We would like to apply this criterion in an attempt to specify some aspects of agency policy and functioning associated with satisfactory performance in meeting client needs.

In general, there is less dissatisfaction when governmental services meet two criteria: (1) a clear set of eligibility requirements, and (2) a uniform application of services to clearly specified entitlements. Social security meets both criteria and heads the list of services in client satisfaction. Public assistance and medical and hospital care, on the other hand, fall short of meeting these two requirements and are found at the bottom of the list. Other factors besides clear criteria of eligibility and uniform treatment are involved in the differential satisfaction rankings, but these two requirements are not without their importance.

Where there are clear specifications by an agency for eligibility, people are more likely to avail themselves of its service. The retiree or the surviving spouse, because of the objective nature of his status, can readily turn to the social security office for his benefits. The human in need of support from welfare programs lacks this ready entrance into the system. Confusion about eligibility leads to feelings of unfairness among some potential clients.

The same type of logic may be applied to the job-training programs. While those individuals who utilized job-training services were relatively satisfied, many respondents who felt the need for such services indicated that they did not receive agency help. Among the reasons given for not utilizing an agency's services were the beliefs by respondents that they were not eligible for services. Instead of the present system of multiple job-training agencies, many with the rather vague imperative of helping "underprivileged minorities," there might be a system of specific criteria set up for applicants.

No doubt one of the reasons for the present muddled social policy is a lack of clear commitment on the part of policy makers. For example, most of the present job-training programs are set up to teach manual skills to disadvantaged minority groups. Yet the data indicate that respondents with relatively high levels of education (at least a high school diploma) express a need for job training. If, however, a job-training program existed only for individuals with a family income under a specified amount, people in middle income brackets would not expect the government to provide them with job training. People under age 62 do not complain about the social security agency because they cannot get retirement benefits. Although age limits for social security are arbitrary, they are clearly understood and accepted by Americans. Questions of coverage are recognizable as public problems separate from agency performance.

The second requirement is the uniform treatment of all those falling into a clearly defined category. It is not enough to have objective criteria of eligibility, it is also important to treat all of the people in the same category in the same fashion. The two criteria tend to go together in that it is easier to provide uniform service once the people who are entitled to it are specified. Social security is characterized by a set of rules detailing both eligibility and level of benefits for all elderly people. Clients cannot be treated differently. The present welfare system, on the other hand, is a categorical system of aid to various interest groups. Different criteria exist for the aged, the blind, the disabled, and families with dependent children. In addition to differences in category, there are also individual differences in service based on amount of savings, cost of renting an apartment, expense of transportation, etc. The welfare system then becomes open to complaints of preferential treatment. A more satisfactory system (from the point of view of the client), would be to have a standard set of requirements for the receipt of welfare, based, for example, on total income and number of persons in the household. If social policy is such that, for example, the blind are entitled to added compensation, there might be a special agency for the blind to which people could apply for aid over and above welfare monies.

This approach argues for a standardization of service, which in turn implies federal guidelines, well publicized eligibility criteria, and separate agencies for various services. Though standardization has sometimes made government agencies the target of criticism as impersonal bureaucracies, the facts are that in dealing with the distribution of services or benefits, fairness and equity call for the same treatment for people with the same entitlement. Equal pay for equal work has become the rallying cry to combat discrimination whether on the basis of race, sex, or personal preference. Standardization may not be desirable in other areas of social life, but it is the means for achieving equity in the distribution of rewards and returns.

The old cry of the social worker against bureaucracy still echoes in the doctrine of individualized treatment—"Organized charity, crimped and iced; in the name of a cautious, statistical Christ." But if the social worker has to make decisions on benefits and services as he evaluates the merits of each case, we open the way to all kinds of preferential and prejudiced treatment. The worker is, moreover, likely to impose his own values on the recipient's utilization of benefits, e.g., in choosing alcohol vs. food. An alternative policy is that benefits be given on the basis of objective criteria of entitlement and that individuals utilize these benefits as they will. If objective criteria are lacking for some of the present complex ways of distributing services, then there should be a move to a simplification of standards as in the proposal for a guaranteed annual income. National programs, to be fairly administered, require well-defined and recognizable criteria of entitlement which are independent of the uses to be made of the benefits. In this way government may preserve equity on the one hand and avoid undue interference in the life of the individual on the other.

It has been argued, moreover, that the move toward universalism is critical for the survival of service programs. Franklin Roosevelt saw this as essential for the preservation of a social security program. Robert Lekachman (1974) sums up the matter as follows:

> Social programs that are generally perceived as universal in coverage tend to flourish in public favor and grow in financial outlay. By grim contrast, efforts to help minorities, unless they aid wounded war veterans, the blind, or the victims of tornadoes and earthquakes, arouse fierce opposition; survive, if survive they do, in perpetually desperate financial straits, and afford standing temptation for exploitation as succulent political issues by conservative demagogues. A striking illustration of the usual fate of the selective program is the

trials of welfare. Aid for Dependent Children (AFDC), like old-age benefits, began in 1935. The contrast in their popularity is instructive. (p.590)

This does not mean that people's individual problems should be ignored by a heartless, bureaucratic society. There should be counselling services of various types under both public and private auspices to help people on a variety of problems from vocational rehabilitation to marital difficulties. Such services should be separate, however, from the distribution of benefits.

Another advantage of agencies based on clear criteria of eligibility is an improved referral system. One of the largest problems among practitioners in the field of social welfare is keeping track of all other agencies to which an individual might apply. A system of standardized services with clear eligibility criteria would simplify the task of steering needy persons to relevant agencies. While social security rules are very complex, most human service workers could probably tell a client whether or not he would be eligible for benefits. On the other hand, how many people know the criteria of eligibility for JOBS-NAM, Job Corps, Concentrated Employment Program, WIN, etc.? The Model Cities Program has spawned numerous projects, most of which fold after one or two years—just when the community becomes aware of their existence.

In the 1960's, the buzz words of new service agencies were para-professionals, relevance, rapport, team approach, and non-directive leadership. The lack of these elements in social security and unemployment compensation offices has not had a negative effect on the satisfaction of clients. Our data suggest that these factors may be less important for client satisfaction than clear eligibility criteria.

Standardization of service does create something of a derivative organizational dilemma in that it can lead to job standardization for people in the agency. As jobs become standardized, the autonomy of the job incumbent declines, and he finds little in his work to challenge his abilities. Standardization of service, however, does not necessarily mean a fully routinized role for the agency member. The critical issue is one of job fractionation, and jobs do not have to be broken down along the lines of standardization of service.

The social security administration can be used to illustrate the difference between standardization of service and standardization of job. In the social security administration, services are relatively standard. There are criteria of age and number of quarterly credits of work accumulated. The jobs, however, are not as standardized as they might be. The social security claims representative spends 12 weeks in training, learning the intricacies of the social security laws and other pertinent information. That person is then able to handle all aspects of the claims process.

A PROGRAM OF RESEARCH

This monograph reports the results of a pilot study and looks toward the development of a program of research on the functioning of public agencies. Like most programs, it will, if it progresses, develop the types of research that meet its objectives. Three such types can be easily envisioned, each with its own strengths and weaknesses.

Type I   Special Organizational Studies

This first type requires samples of the personnel of given agencies and samples of their clients. Its objective is the discovery of relationships between organizational characteristics and the functioning of the agency. For example, such characteristics as size, number of hierarchical levels, relationship of technical and social subsystems, use of feedback, and philosophy of management may be related to the efficiency, adequacy, and fairness of agency operations as determined by the experiences of the clientele or potential clientele. To get at the specifics of how and why an agency functions as it does, and how effective it is, requires detailed study of particular agencies, including both members of their staffs at various hierarchical levels and members of the particular publics they service. A national sample cannot match agency personnel with agency clientele. Nor can it readily accumulate enough cases for given agencies to provide adequate samples of their specific publics. Nor can public responses be related to the realities of the programs being administered, since this would require detailed knowledge of such programs.

Type II   National Samples of Reactions to Public Agencies

The depth studies of specific agencies need to be complemented by national surveys which deal with the extent to which the public avails itself of public services and the extent of favorable and unfavorable experiences with public agencies in the nation as a whole.

It is important, moreover, to know the climate of opinion in which agencies function, to ascertain the support they receive from various segments of the public, to discover the general directions in which people want governmental agencies to move, and to see how these reactions to public agencies are related to general orientations of support for the political system at different system levels. For these purposes national surveys are the best strategy; moreover, many of these measures for the nation as a whole comprise important social indicators which should be repeated to show trends in the larger society.

Attempts to combine both of these objectives in a single type of research study will not accomplish either purpose. Utilizing both the field approach to the study of specific organizations and the national survey approach to the social environment of public agencies can play to the strength of each of the two methodological strategies. Moreover, the findings from the two types of studies can be related to provide meaningful generalizations about agency functioning. A basic linkage between the two can be provided by including a section in the national survey on the respondent's experiences with some public services, a section which would parallel the questions asked in the organizational study.

The dynamics of relationships which appear more clearly in the depth study can be extended to explain some of the relationships found in a broader range of agencies in the nationwide study. For example, we will know from the depth study the seriousness of given types of grievances and so researchers will be in a better position to evaluate complaints as they appear in the national sample. In turn, there should be a section in the specific organizational study utilizing a few of the same questions of general attitudes toward agencies. The purpose, then, is to combine the two strategies, not in a single all-purpose study of unmanageable proportions, but through linkages between field studies and national surveys, provided by overlapping questions and similar objectives in the research design.

Type III   Experiments and Quasi-experiments

Many proposals for new programs, new services, or new modes of delivery present the possibility but not the certainty of success. This is a common state of affairs in any new enterprise, and in order to deal with it, industry is accustomed to think in terms of pilot plants, agronomists in terms of test plots, and research workers in terms of experiments. Donald Campbell (1969) has argued that we must become *an experimenting society,* a society that improves itself by testing its proposed solutions on a scale at which failure can be afforded. The delivery of government service is well-suited to such efforts, and offers the possibility of public benefit and scientific gain.

Appendix A

General Sampling Procedure

Description of the General Sampling Procedure of Survey Research
Center's National Sample of Dwellings

The Survey Research Center's sample is designed to represent dwellings in conterminous United States exclusive of those on military reservations. The 74 sample points, currently located in 37 states and the District of Columbia, include 12 major metropolitan areas, 32 other Standard Metropolitan Statistical Areas (SMSA's), and 30 counties or county-groups representing the non-metropolitan or rural portions of the country.

Over all regions, the SMSA's and counties are assigned to 74 relatively homogeneous groups or strata. Twelve of these strata contain only one primary area each; these are the two Standard Consolidated Areas and the 10 largest SMSA's, outside the Consolidated Areas, which are included with certainty. The remaining 62 strata average a little over two million population and may contain from two to 200 or more primary areas (SMSA's or county groups). From each stratum one primary area is selected with probability proportionate to population. This sampling process leads to approximately equal sample sizes from the 62 sample areas.

Instead of independent selections within each of the 62 strata, controlled probability selection is introduced for a more efficient sample. Within each of the four geographic regions, the selections of primary areas are linked by a procedure that controls the distribution of sample areas by states and degree of urbanization beyond the controls effected through the formation of the 62 strata. This controlled selection yields a more balanced sample and increases the precision of sample estimates.

As the multistage area sampling continues within the 74 primary units, the area is divided and subdivided, in two to five stages, into successively smaller sampling units. By definition and procedure, each dwelling belongs uniquely to one sampling unit at each stage. Within the primary areas, cities, towns and rural areas are the secondary selections. Blocks or clusters of addresses in cities and towns, and chunks of rural areas are the third-stage units. In a fourth stage, there is a selection of small segments or clusters of housing units where interviews are taken for a study. In a last stage of sampling, one or more respondents may be selected from among household members.

Probability selection is enforced at all stages of the sample selection; the interviewer has no freedom of choice among housing units or among household members within a sample dwelling.

Appendix B

Interview Schedule

The questionnaire used in the survey on bureaucratic encounters in April and May of 1973 is reproduced here.

SECTION C:

We are also interested in what people think and feel about government offices and agencies and in their experiences with these offices and agencies. We are interested in all levels of government--local, state and federal and all types of government agencies and programs. For example, Social Security, Medicare, Medicaid, Veterans Administration, Internal Revenue Service, State Unemployment Commission, County Social Services Bureau, City Welfare Department, Vehicle Licensing Bureau, etc.

C1. By and large do you think most government offices do a good job?

| 1. YES | 5. NO | 8. DON'T KNOW |

C2. Would you like to see the people of this community have more control of government offices?

| 1. MORE CONTROL | 2. LESS CONTROL | 8. DON'T KNOW |

C3. Do you think that people in the government waste a lot of money we pay in taxes, waste some of it, or don't waste very much of it?

| 1. A LOT | 2. SOME | 3. DON'T WASTE VERY MUCH | 8. DON'T KNOW |

C4. How much of the time do you think you can trust the government in Washington to do what is right--just about always, most of the time, or only some of the time?

| 1. JUST ABOUT ALWAYS | 2. MOST OF THE TIME | 3. SOME OF THE TIME | 8. DON'T KNOW |

C5. Would you say the government is pretty much run by a few big interests looking out for themselves or that it is run for the benefit of all the people?

| 1. FEW BIG INTERESTS | 2. BENEFIT OF ALL | 8. DON'T KNOW |

C6. Do you feel that almost all of the people running the government are smart people who usually know what they are doing or do you think that quite a few of them don't seem to know what they are doing?

1. KNOW WHAT THEY ARE DOING	2. DON'T KNOW WHAT THEY ARE DOING	8. DON'T KNOW

C7. Do you think that <u>quite a few</u> of the people running the government are dishonest, <u>not very many</u> are, or do you think <u>hardly any</u> of them are dishonest?

1. QUITE A FEW	2. NOT MANY	3. HARDLY ANY	8. DON'T KNOW

C8. And how much do you feel that having elections makes the government pay attention to what the people think--<u>a good deal</u>, <u>some</u>, or <u>not much</u>?

1. A GOOD DEAL	2. SOME	3. NOT MUCH	8. DON'T KNOW

C9. (CARD C9, GREEN) We want to know how <u>good</u> or how <u>bad</u> you think government offices are on the following things. If they are excellent, give them a 7, the highest point on the scale. If they are very bad, give them a 1, the lowest point on the scale. You can give them any number from 1 to 7 depending upon how good or bad you think they are.

First let's take prompt service. How good or how bad do you think most government offices are in giving prompt service?

a. GIVING PROMPT SERVICE   _____

b. Really taking care of problems   _____

c. Giving considerate treatment to the people they deal with   _____

d. Giving fair treatment   _____

e. Being careful and avoiding mistakes   _____

f. Correcting mistakes   _____

C10.   How do you think most government offices compare with most business organizations, I mean private enterprise, on these same points?

First, let's take prompt service. Would you say government offices are better than business organizations in giving prompt service, business organizations are better than government offices, or both are about the same?

	1. GOVERN-MENT OFFICES BETTER	2. BUSINESS ORGANI-ZATIONS BETTER	3. BOTH THE SAME
a. GIVING PROMPT SERVICE			
b. How about really taking care of problems. (Would you say government offices are better, business organizations are better or both are about the same?)			
c. Giving considerate treatment of the people they deal with...			
d. Giving fair treatment...			
e. Being careful and avoiding mistakes...			
f. Correcting mistakes...			

C11. (CARD C11, BEIGE) Now I'm going to read you a list of things that are sometimes handled by government agencies. For each one, please tell me what <u>kind</u> of office or agency would handle it <u>best</u>. (IF NO CLEAR PREFERENCE, LET R MAKE TWO CHOICES.)

	A. TOWN OR CITY GOVT (1)	B. COUNTY GOVT (2)	C. STATE GOVT (3)	D. FEDERAL GOVT (4)	E. PRIVATE OR BUSINESS RATHER THAN GOVT OFFICE (5)	8. DON'T KNOW (8)
a. Unemployment compensation						
b. Payment for health and medical services						
c. Retraining people for new or better jobs						
d. Retirement benefits						
e. Relief for the needy and aid to dependent children						
f. Controlling crime						
g. Preventing the pollution of the environment; keeping the water we drink and the air we breathe safe						
h. Safety standards for automobiles						

C12. (CARD C12, YELLOW) I'm going to read you some statements about the
government and government agencies. Please tell me how strongly you
agree or disagree with each statement.

	A. STRONGLY AGREE (1)	B. AGREE (2)	C. DIS- AGREE (4)	D. STRONGLY DISAGREE (5)
a. The government should do less for people if it means lower taxes.				
b. The government should do more for people if it can do so without increasing taxes.				
c. The government should do more for people even if it means higher taxes.				
d. It is only fair that the more fortunate people with money should pay high taxes to help the needy.				
e. Many of the people who are getting welfare payments are really cheating the government.				
f. A good deal of the money for public assistance never gets to the people who really need it.				
g. Most of the people who work for governmental offices work hard and try to do a good job.				
h. The people who gain the most from government offices are the officials who run the agencies.				
i. There are too many government offices doing the same thing.				
j. The people in government offices are usually very helpful.				
k. The people in government offices like to use their authority to push you around.				

	A. STRONGLY AGREE	B. AGREE	C. DIS- AGREE	D. STRONGLY DISAGREE
	(1)	(2)	(4)	(5)
l. We are really much better off with government services as they are than we would be without them.				
m. The trouble with government offices is that no official is really willing to take responsibility for anything.				
n. The trouble with government offices is that no one person really takes an interest in your problems.				
o. It is becoming difficult for an individual to have any private life because government pries and interferes in his personal affairs.				

C13. Now I am going to ask you about a number of things which happen to people from time to time. We would like to know if any of these things has ever happened to you and whether you have gotten any help from government offices or agencies.

First of all, how about <u>finding a job</u> when you are out of work? Have you ever done this?

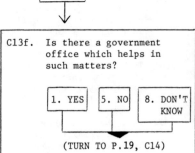

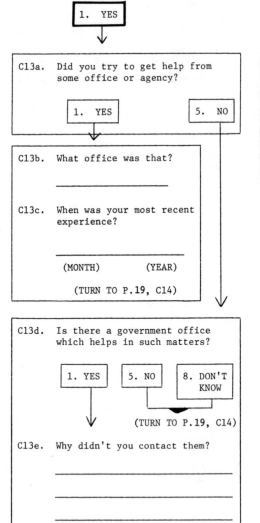

C14. How about getting <u>training for a better job</u>? Have you ever wanted to do this?

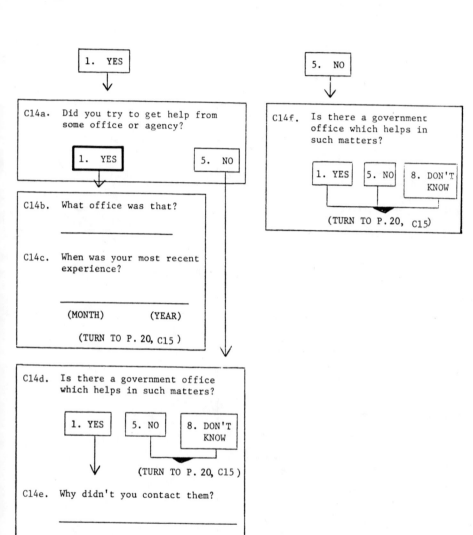

C14a. Did you try to get help from some office or agency?

1. YES

5. NO

C14b. What office was that?

_____

C14c. When was your most recent experience?

_____

(MONTH)   (YEAR)

(TURN TO P. 20, C15)

C14d. Is there a government office which helps in such matters?

1. YES   5. NO   8. DON'T KNOW

(TURN TO P. 20, C15)

C14e. Why didn't you contact them?

_____

_____

_____

C14f. Is there a government office which helps in such matters?

1. YES   5. NO   8. DON'T KNOW

(TURN TO P. 20, C15)

C15.   How about getting <u>compensation for accidents or injuries</u> on the job? Have you ever had to do this?

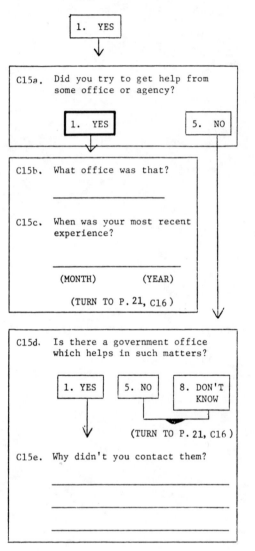

1. YES

C15a. Did you try to get help from some office or agency?

1. YES   5. NO

C15b. What office was that?

_____

C15c. When was your most recent experience?

_____

(MONTH)   (YEAR)

(TURN TO P. 21, C16)

C15d. Is there a government office which helps in such matters?

1. YES   5. NO   8. DON'T KNOW

(TURN TO P. 21, C16)

C15e. Why didn't you contact them?

_____

_____

_____

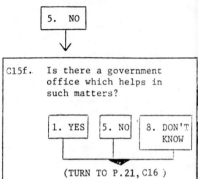

5. NO

C15f. Is there a government office which helps in such matters?

1. YES   5. NO   8. DON'T KNOW

(TURN TO P. 21, C16)

C16. How about getting <u>unemployment compensation</u>? Have you ever done this?

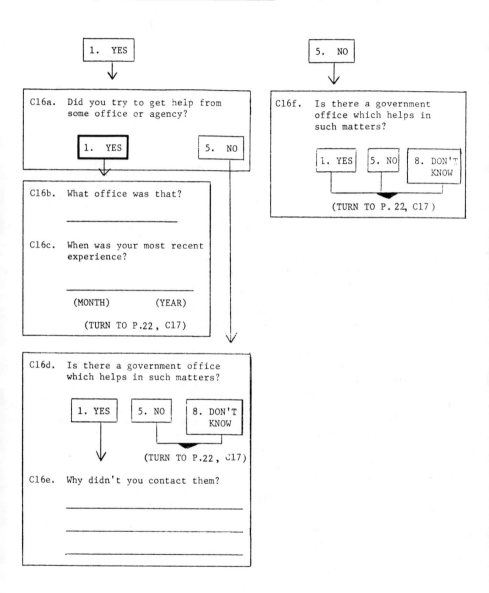

C16a. Did you try to get help from some office or agency?

    1. YES   5. NO

C16b. What office was that?

_____

C16c. When was your most recent experience?

_____

(MONTH)   (YEAR)

(TURN TO P.22, C17)

C16d. Is there a government office which helps in such matters?

    1. YES   5. NO   8. DON'T KNOW

(TURN TO P.22, C17)

C16e. Why didn't you contact them?

_____

_____

_____

C16f. Is there a government office which helps in such matters?

    1. YES   5. NO   8. DON'T KNOW

(TURN TO P. 22, C17)

C17. How about getting <u>help for dependent children</u> or other forms of <u>relief and public assistance</u>? Have you ever had to do this?

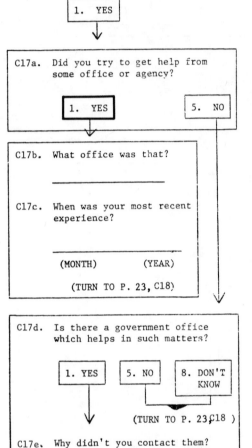

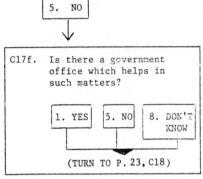

C18. How about <u>medical and hospital care</u> for illness, accidents and operations (for yourself or any children)? Have you ever had any problems getting proper care?

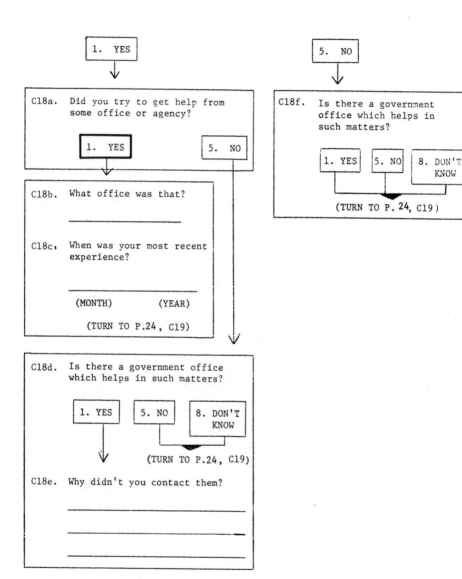

1. YES

5. NO

C18a. Did you try to get help from some office or agency?

1. YES
5. NO

C18b. What office was that?

_____

C18c. When was your most recent experience?

_____

(MONTH) (YEAR)

(TURN TO P.24, C19)

C18d. Is there a government office which helps in such matters?

1. YES
5. NO
8. DON'T KNOW

(TURN TO P.24, C19)

C18e. Why didn't you contact them?

_____

_____

_____

C18f. Is there a government office which helps in such matters?

1. YES
5. NO
8. DON'T KNOW

(TURN TO P. 24, C19)

C19. Are you <u>retired</u>, or getting <u>retirement benefits</u>?

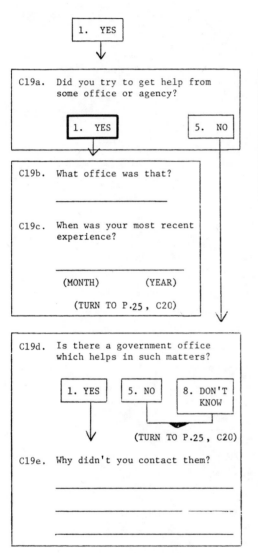

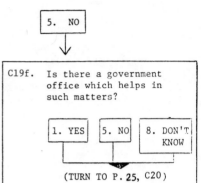

C19a. Did you try to get help from some office or agency?

   1. YES   5. NO

C19b. What office was that?

_____

C19c. When was your most recent experience?

_____

(MONTH)   (YEAR)

(TURN TO P.25 , C20)

C19d. Is there a government office which helps in such matters?

1. YES   5. NO   8. DON'T KNOW

(TURN TO P.25 , C20)

C19e. Why didn't you contact them?

_____

_____

_____

C19f. Is there a government office which helps in such matters?

1. YES   5. NO   8. DON'T KNOW

(TURN TO P. 25, C20)

C20. Besides the things I have mentioned, have you ever had any other problems where you feel the government might have been of help?

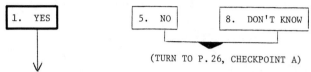

| 1. YES | | 5. NO | 8. DON'T KNOW |

(TURN TO P. 26, CHECKPOINT A)

C20a. What was that? (IF MORE THAN ONE, UNDERLINE THE PROBLEM MOST IMPORTANT TO RESPONDENT.)

_____

_____

_____

C20b. Did you try to get help from some office or agency (<u>MOST IMPORTANT PROBLEM</u>)?

| 1. YES | | 5. NO |

C20c. What office was that?

_____

C20d. When was your most recent experience?

_____

(MONTH)   (YEAR)

(TURN TO P. 26, C21)

C20e. Is there a government office which helps in such matters?

| 1. YES | 5. NO | 8. DON'T KNOW |

(TURN TO P. 26, CHECKPOINT A)

C20f. Why don't you contact them?

_____

_____

_____

INTERVIEWER CHECKPOINT A

```
┌──────────────────────────────────────────────────────────────────┐
│  ☐ 1.  R DID NOT CONTACT ANY GOVERNMENT AGENCY OR OFFICE IN ANY OF │
│        Q's C13-C20 ──────────→ TURN TO P.29, C36.                 │
│                                                                    │
│  ☐ 2.  R CONTACTED A GOVERNMENT AGENCY OR OFFICE ON ANY OF Q's     │
│        C13-C20.                                                     │
└──────────────────────────────────────────────────────────────────┘
```

C21. Of the experiences with government agencies you have mentioned, which was the most important to you?

_____

C21a. What office did you go to?

_____

C22. Was that a local, county, state or federal agency or program?

| 1. LOCAL | 2. COUNTY | 3. STATE | 4. FEDERAL | 8. DON'T KNOW |

C23. Tell me about what you went to the office for and what happened there?

_____

_____

_____

_____

_____

C24. Was it hard to find an office or official who could handle your problem?

| 1. YES | | 5. NO |

C25. How much effort did the people at the office make to help you? Would you say it was more than they had to, about right, less than they should have or no effort at all?

| 1. MORE THAN THEY HAD TO | 3. ABOUT RIGHT | 5. LESS THAN THEY SHOULD HAVE | 6. NO EFFORT AT ALL |

C26. Do they give you any choice about things at that office or do you have to take what they decide?

| 1. HAVE CHOICE | 5. TAKE WHAT THEY DECIDE |

C27. How satisfied were you with the way the office handled your problem? Would you say you were...

| 1. very satisfied | 2. fairly well satisfied | 4. somewhat dissatisfied | 5. very dis- satisfied |

C28. How efficient did you think the office was in handling your problem? Was it...

| 1. very efficient | 2. fairly efficient | 4. rather inefficient | 5. very in- efficient |

C29. Do you feel you were treated fairly, or unfairly by the office?

| 1. FAIRLY | 5. UNFAIRLY | 3. MIXED | 8. DON'T KNOW |

(TURN TO P.28, C30)   (TURN TO P. 28, C30)

C29a. In what ways were they not fair?

_____

_____

_____

C30. Was there someone at a higher level in the office to whom you could appeal for help if things were not working out all right?

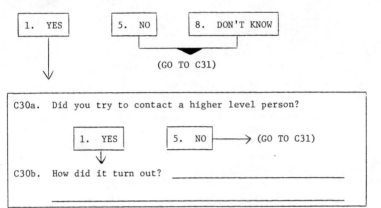

| 1. YES | 5. NO | 8. DON'T KNOW |

(GO TO C31)

C30a. Did you try to contact a higher level person?

| 1. YES | 5. NO | → (GO TO C31) |

C30b. How did it turn out? _____

_____

C31. Do some kinds of people get better treatment than others from this office?

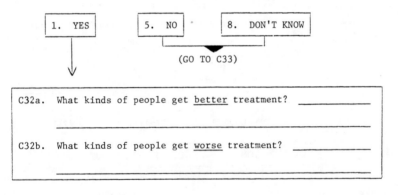

| 1. YES | 5. NO | 8. DON'T KNOW |

(GO TO C33)

C32a. What kinds of people get <u>better</u> treatment? _____

_____

C32b. What kinds of people get <u>worse</u> treatment? _____

_____

C33. Are the people working in the office pretty much people like you?

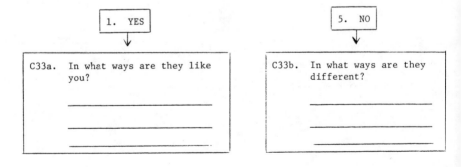

| 1. YES | 5. NO |

C33a. In what ways are they like you?

_____

_____

_____

C33b. In what ways are they different?

_____

_____

_____

C34. Besides the experience we have been discussing, how many times have you been in contact with (NAME OF OFFICE) within the past two years?

_____TIMES | 0. NO OTHER CONTACTS | ⟶ (GO TO C36)

C35. In general, how satisfactory have these experiences been?

_____

_____

C36. We have been talking about getting help from government offices on different kinds of problems. People also have experiences with government offices because <u>the government wants them to do things</u> like getting their driver's licenses renewed or paying their taxes. Have you had or are you having any <u>difficulties</u> or <u>problems</u> with government offices or officials about any of the following matters?

		YES (1)	NO (5)
a.	Problems getting a driver's license or a car license or getting them renewed?	☐	☐
b.	Problems about settling traffic violations	☐	☐
c.	Problems about taxes or filling out forms for any tax office?	☐	☐
d.	Problems with the police or other officials interfering with your rights? (SPECIFY IF "YES")	☐	☐

_____

_____

e.	Have you had other problems about things the government wants you to do? (SPECIFY IF "YES")	☐	☐

_____

_____

_____

INTERVIEWER CHECKPOINT B

☐ 1. R ANSWERED "YES" TO ONE ITEM IN C36

   ☐ 2. R ANSWERED "YES" TO <u>MORE</u> THAN ONE ITEM IN C36

      ☐ 3. R ANSWERED "NO" TO ALL ITEMS IN C36 ⟶ TURN TO P. 34, C50

C37. Of the problems we have just been talking about, which was the most
      important to you?

_____

C37a. Would you tell me more about your experience with (ITEM NAMED
       IN C36 OR C37)?

       _____

       _____

       _____

       _____

       _____

C38. About when was that? _____ YEAR

C39. How much difficulty did this make for you? Would you say a great
      deal of difficulty, some difficulty, or only a little difficulty?

| 1. A GREAT DEAL OF DIFFICULTY | 3. SOME DIFFICULTY | 5. A LITTLE DIFFICULTY |

C40. Did the government office or official make the problem worse by their way of handling it?

| 1. YES | 5. NO |

C41. Did the government office or official treat you fairly?

| 5. NO | | 1. YES | 8. DK |

(GO TO C42)

C41a. In what ways were they not fair?_____

_____

_____

_____

_____

C42. Was the matter settled quickly or as soon as one would expect, or did it take much longer than was really necessary?

_____

_____

C43. Did the government officials treat you with consideration?

| 5. NO | | 1. YES | → (TURN TO P. 32, C44)

C43a. Would you tell me about it? _____

_____

_____

_____

C44.   Did they make mistakes in handling your case?

| 1. YES | | 5. NO | → (GO TO C45) |

C44a.   Were they willing to correct their mistakes?

| 1. YES | 5. NO |

C45.   Was there someone at a higher level in government to whom one could appeal if things were not working out all right?

| 1. YES | 5. NO | 8. DK |

(GO TO C46)

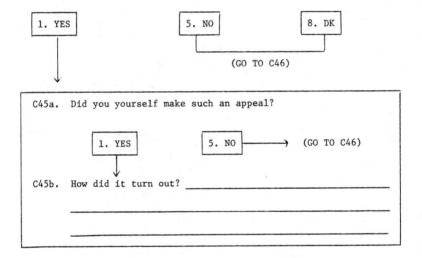

C45a.   Did you yourself make such an appeal?

| 1. YES | 5. NO | → (GO TO C46) |

C45b.   How did it turn out? _____

_____

_____

C46.   Looking at the whole experience, would you say the government officials handled it very poorly, poorly, farily well or very well?

| 1. VERY POORLY | 2. POORLY | 4. FAIRLY WELL | 5. VERY WELL |

C47.   How efficient was the office in handling your problem? Would you say very efficient, fairly efficient, rather inefficient or very inefficient?

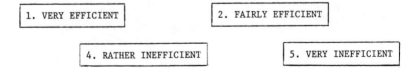

| 1. VERY EFFICIENT | 2. FAIRLY EFFICIENT |

| 4. RATHER INEFFICIENT | 5. VERY INEFFICIENT |

C48. Do some kinds of people get better treatment from this office?

| 1. YES | 5. NO | 8. DK |

(GO TO C49)

C48a. What kinds of people get <u>better</u> treatment? _____

_____

C48b. What kinds of people get <u>worse</u> treatment? _____

_____

C49. Are the people who work at the office pretty much people like you?

| 1. YES | 5. NO |

C49a. In what ways are they like you?

_____

_____

_____

_____

C49b. In what ways are they different?

_____

_____

_____

_____

C50. (CARD C50 - ORANGE) How helpful are the following people in getting a government office to do something? First let's take your Congressman or other person in public office. Would you say this person is very helpful, somewhat helpful, or not helpful at all?

		A VERY HELPFUL (1)	B SOMEWHAT HELPFUL (3)	C NOT HELPFUL (5)	DON'T KNOW (8)
a.	Your Congressman or other person in public office				
b.	The political boss in your community				
c.	A community leader				
d.	A person who has friends in the agency				
e.	An expert about the rules and procedures of the agency				
f.	The right person in the agency				

C51. (CARD 51 - WHITE) Have you ever used any of these people in getting help from a government agency?

1. YES   5. NO ——→ (TURN TO P. 35, C52)

C51a. Which ones? _____

C52. (CARD C52 - GREEN) Which of the following do you think is the most useful method for getting a government office or agency to do something you want? (INTERVIEWER CHECK ONE)

☐ A. Doing favors for some person in the office or agency?

☐ B. Just giving all necessary information to the people in the agency and cooperating with them

☐ C. Taking the time to become friends with someone in the office or agency

☐ D. Bringing pressure through publicity

☐ E. Demonstrating and picketing

☐ F. Writing to the editor or an action column in your local newspaper

C52a. What is the least useful method? _____
                                                    (LETTER OF ITEM)

C53. (CARD C52 - GREEN) Have you ever tried any of these methods?

| 1. YES | | 5. NO | ⟶ (GO TO C54) |

C53a. Which ones? _____

_____

C54. What do you think the government should do about young men who evaded the draft? Should they be sent to prison, should they be made to serve their country in some way or should they be given amnesty; that is, no punishment?

| 1. SENT TO PRISON | 2. GIVEN AMNESTY | 3. MADE TO SERVE THE COUNTRY IN SOME WAY |

C55.   If a foreigner visiting this country were to criticize many things
       about America, what would your reaction be? Would you feel that he is
       being insulting; that he is just showing bad manners; or would you
       feel that he has every right to express his own opinion?

| 1. INSULTING | 3. SHOWING BAD MANNERS | 5. EXPRESS OPINION |

C56.   Do you think that our schools are putting enough emphasis on teaching
       children to be partiotic Americans?

| 1. YES | 5. NO |

C57.   How do you feel about Americans who won't rise when the Star Spangled
       Banner is being played? Do you strongly approve, approve, don't care,
       disapprove, or strongly disapprove?

| 1. STRONGLY APPROVE | 2. APPROVE | 3. DON'T CARE | 4. DISAPPROVE | 5. STRONGLY DISAPPROVE |

C58.   Generally speaking, would you say that most people can be trusted, or
       that you can't be too careful in dealing with people?

| 1. MOST PEOPLE CAN BE TRUSTED | 5. CAN'T BE TOO CAREFUL |

C59.   Would you say that most of the time people try to be helpful, or that
       they are mostly just looking out for themselves?

| 1. TRY TO BE HELPFUL | 5. JUST LOOKING OUT | 8. DK |

C60.   Do you think most people would try to take advantage of you if they
       had the chance, or would they try to be fair?

| 1. TRY TO TAKE ADVANTAGE | 5. TRY TO BE FAIR | 8. DK |

TIME TO NEAREST MINUTE _____

WAS THIS SECTION INTERRUPTED   ☐ 1. YES   ☐ 2. NO

SECTION H:

H. In this last section we would like to get a little background information about you and your family.

H1. Are there any children or young people under 18 years of age living here? I don't need their names, just their relationship to the head of the household and their ages.

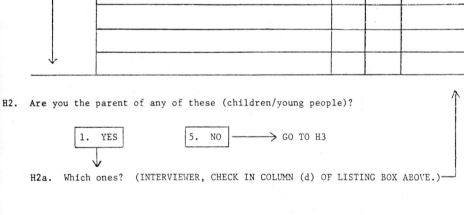

☐ NO CHILDREN IN HU ⟶ (GO TO H3)

	(a) Relationship to Head of HU	(b) Sex	(c) Age	(d) ✓ Children of R
Persons Under 18 Years				

H2. Are you the parent of any of these (children/young people)?

☐ 1. YES ☐ 5. NO ⟶ GO TO H3

H2a. Which ones? (INTERVIEWER, CHECK IN COLUMN (d) OF LISTING BOX ABOVE.)

H3. What is the month and year of your birth? _____   _____

(MONTH)   (YEAR)

RESPONDENT'S EDUCATION

H4. What was the highest grade of school or year of college you completed?

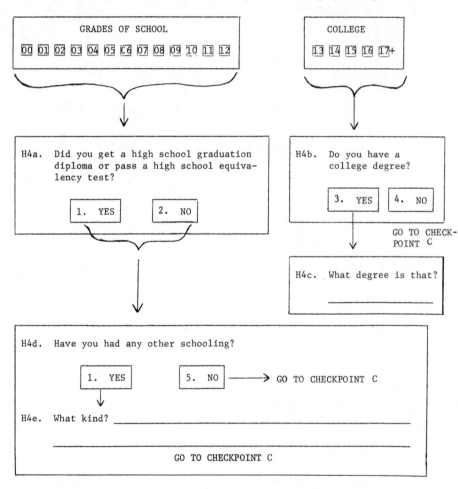

GRADES OF SCHOOL

00 01 02 03 04 05 06 07 08 09 10 11 12

COLLEGE

13 14 15 16 17+

H4a. Did you get a high school graduation diploma or pass a high school equivalency test?

1. YES   2. NO

H4b. Do you have a college degree?

3. YES   4. NO

GO TO CHECKPOINT C

H4c. What degree is that?

_____

H4d. Have you had any other schooling?

1. YES   5. NO ⟶ GO TO CHECKPOINT C

H4e. What kind? _____

_____

GO TO CHECKPOINT C

INTERVIEWER CHECKPOINT C

☐ 1. R IS HEAD OF FAMILY ⟶ (TURN TO P. 48, H6)

☐ 2. R IS NOT HEAD OF FAMILY ⟶ (TURN TO P. 47, H5)

EDUCATION OF HEAD OF FAMILY (IF R IS NOT HEAD)

H5. What was the highest grade of school or year of college (HEAD) completed?

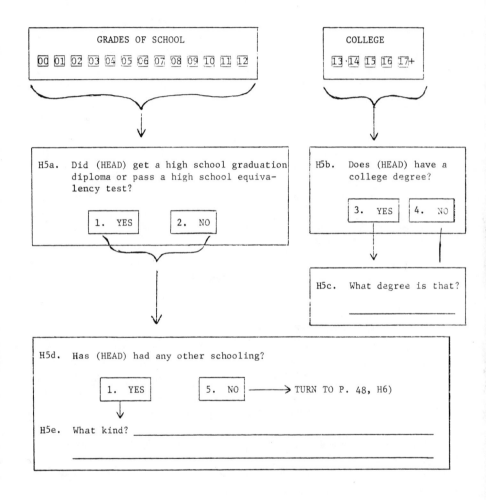

GRADES OF SCHOOL

00 01 02 03 04 05 06 07 08 09 10 11 12

COLLEGE

13 14 15 16 17+

H5a. Did (HEAD) get a high school graduation diploma or pass a high school equivalency test?

1. YES   2. NO

H5b. Does (HEAD) have a college degree?

3. YES   4. NO

H5c. What degree is that?

_____

H5d. Has (HEAD) had any other schooling?

1. YES   5. NO ———→ TURN TO P. 48, H6)

H5e. What kind? _____

_____

TWO-PAGE RESPONDENT

H6. Are you presently employed, or are you

| 1. WORKING NOW | 2. TEMPORARILY LAID OFF; ON STRIKE; SICK LEAVE | 3. LOOKING FOR WORK | 4. UNEMPLOYED |

H7. What is your main occupation? (What sort of work do you do?)

_____

_____

H7a. Tell me a little more about what you do.

_____

_____

H7b. What kind of (business/industry) is that in?

_____

H7c. Are you employed by someone else, are you self-employed or what?

| 1. SOMEONE ELSE | 2. SELF-EMPLOYED | (GO TO H7f) |

> H7d. (CARD H7d - BLUE) Which of the terms on this card best describes your employer? Just tell me the letter?
>
> _____(LETTER FROM CARD)
>
> IF R ANSWERED "A" OR "C" PUBLIC SCHOOL, PUBLIC HOSPITAL ASK....
>
> H7e. Do you think of yourself as a government employee?
>
> | 1. YES | 5. NO | 8. DK |

H7f. About how many hours do you work on your job in an average week?

_____(HOURS A WEEK)

H8. Have you ever done any work for pay?

| 1. YES | 5. NO | → (TURN TO P. 50 CHECKPOINT D) |

H8a. What sort of work did you do on your last regular job? (What was your occupation?)

_____

H8b. Tell me a little more about what you did?

_____

H8c. What kind of (business/industry) was that in?

_____

H8d. Were you employed by someone else, were you self-employed or what?

| 1. SOMEONE ELSE | 2. SELF-EMPLOYED |

(TURN TO P. 50, CHECKPOINT D)

> H8e. (CARD H7d-BLUE) Which of the terms on this card best describes your employer? Just tell me the letter?
>
> _____(LETTER FROM CARD)
>
> IF R ANSWERED "A" OR "C" PUBLIC SCHOOL, PUBLIC HOSPITAL ASK...
>
> H8f. Did you think of yourself as a government employee?
>
> | 1. YES | 5. NO | 8. DK |

EMPLOYMENT SECTION

unemployed, retired, or what?

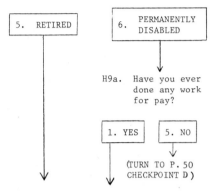

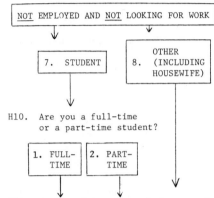

5. RETIRED

6. PERMANENTLY DISABLED

NOT EMPLOYED AND NOT LOOKING FOR WORK

7. STUDENT

8. OTHER (INCLUDING HOUSEWIFE)

H9a. Have you ever done any work for pay?

1. YES   5. NO

(TURN TO P. 50 CHECKPOINT D)

H10. Are you a full-time or a part-time student?

1. FULL-TIME   2. PART-TIME

H9b. What kind of work did you do when you worked? (What was your occupation?)

_____

_____

H11. Are you doing any work for pay at the present time?

1. YES   5. NO

(GO BACK TO H7 "WORKING NOW")

H9c. Tell me a little more about what you did?

_____

H9d. What kind of (business/industry) was that?

_____

H9e. Were you employed by someone else, were you self-employed or what?

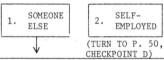

1. SOMEONE ELSE   2. SELF-EMPLOYED

(TURN TO P. 50, CHECKPOINT D)

H9f. (CARD H7d-BLUE) **Which of the terms** on this card best describes your employer? Just tell me the letter?

_____(LETTER FROM CARD)

IF R ANSWERED "A" OR "C" PUBLIC SCHOOL, PUBLIC HOSPITAL ASK....

H9g. Did you think of yourself as a government employee?

1. YES   5. NO   8. DK

CARD H7d

A. Public school, college or university

B. Private school, college or university

C. Public hospital or clinic

D. Private hospital or clinic

E. Local government: city or town

F. County government

G. State government

H. Federal government

I. Private company or individual

H18.   (CARD H18, GREEN) To get an accurate picture of people's financial situation, we need to know the income of all the families we interview. Would you please tell me the letter on this card that indicates how much income <u>you and your family</u> received from all sources during last year, 1972; I mean before taxes or any deductions?

A.	Under $2000	(01.)		J.	$11,000 - $12,499	(10.)
B.	$2000 - $2999	(02.)		K.	$12,500 - $14,999	(11.)
C.	$3000 - $3999	(03.)		L.	$15,000 - $17,499	(12.)
D.	$4000 - $4999	(04.)		M.	$17,500 - $19,999	(13.)
E.	$5000 - $5999	(05.)		N.	$20,000 - $22,499	(14.)
F.	$6000 - $7499	(06.)		O.	$22,500 - $24,999	(15.)
G.	$7500 - $8999	(07.)		P.	$25,000 - $29,999	(16.)
H.	$9000 - $9999	(08.)		O.	$30,000 - $34,999	(17.)
I.	$10,000 - $10,999	(09.)		R.	$35,000 and over	(18.)

H18a.   Does that include everyone in your family who lives here?

| 1.   YES | 5.   NO |

(GO TO H19)

H18b.   What should the letter be if you include everyone?

_____

EXPLANATION OF DISCREPANCIES: _____

_____

H19.   (Do you/does your family) own or are you buying this (home/apartment), or do you pay rent or what?

| 1. OWNS OR IS BUYING | 2. PAYS RENT | 3. NEITHER OWNS NOR RENTS |

IF R WONDERS WHY H20 - H22 ARE INCLUDED YOU MAY USE THIS EXPLANATION

Because more and more people these days have vacation and second homes, we need to know how many addresses a person has so we can see what difference it makes in our sample.

H20.   Do you (and the other person(s) living here) consider this to be your usual place of residence?

1. YES ⊢→ (GO TO H21)   5. NO

H20a.   (IF NO) What are the usual living arrangements?

PERSON (RELATION TO HEAD)   LIVING ARRANGEMENTS

_____   _____

_____   _____

H21.   Is there someone, 18 or older, who has a <u>usual</u> place of residence here, but hasn't been listed because he is temporarily living elsewhere -- in the army or navy, for example, or working out of town?

1. YES   5. NO ⊢→ (TURN TO P. 54, H22)

H21a.   (IF YES) How is that?

PERSON (RELATION TO HEAD)   LIVING ARRANGEMENTS

_____   _____

_____   _____

H22. (Aside from what you've already told me) are you (or any other person here) keeping another place of residence for use part of the year, such as for weekends, vacations, going to school, or working?

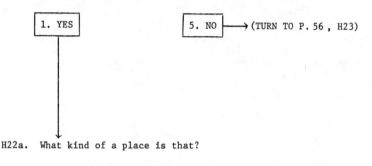

1. YES

5. NO ⟶ (TURN TO P. 56 , H23)

H22a. What kind of a place is that?

(IF MORE THAN ONE, INDICATE EACH)

☐ 1. CAMPER, VAN, OR BUS EQUIPPED
     FOR EATING AND SLEEPING

☐ 2. TENT

☐ 3. TRAILER PULLED BY A CAR OR A
     PICKUP

☐ 4. YACHT OR SELF-PROPELLED
     HOUSEBOAT

DO NOT ASK
H22b - H22g
ABOUT THESE
PLACES

☐ 7. OTHER _____
     _____
     _____

	OTHER RESIDENCES MENTIONED IN H22a	
	FIRST PLACE	SECOND PLACE

DESCRIPTION: _____ _____

_____ _____

(IF "OTHER" [CODE 7] RESIDENCES MENTIONED IN H22a)

H22b. In what state or country is it located?   _____ _____

(IF LOCATED IN CONTINENTAL USA)

H22c. About how many days a year is it
occupied by (you/someone from this
household)?   _____ _____

H22d. Is that (TYPE OF PLACE) wholly
owned by someone here in this
household? Are you buying it,
paying rent, or what?

R OR OTHERS LIVING IN SAMPLE HU:

    1. SOLE OWNERS OR ARE BUYING   ☐ 1.   ☐ 1.

    2. RENT   ☐ 2.   ☐ 2.

    OTHER (DESCRIBE)   _____ _____

                                        _____ _____

ASK THE FOLLOWING PROBES AS APPLICABLE;
IF ANSWER IS SELF-EVIDENT, CHECK BOXES
WITHOUT ASKING

H22e. Is it located in a facility which   ☐ 1. YES   ☐ 1. YES
is mostly for short term use --
such as a hotel, or a trailer park   ☐ 5. NO   ☐ 5. NO
which usually rents by the day?

H22f. Are residents required to pay a fee   ☐ 1. YES   ☐ 1. YES
for meals from a common dining hall
even if they don't eat there?   ☐ 5. NO   ☐ 5. NO

H22g. Is it one of five or more similar   ☐ 1. YES   ☐ 1. YES
units owned by the same person and
closed during certain seasons of the   ☐ 5. NO   ☐ 5. NO
year?

H23. Are you married, separated, divorced, widowed, or have you never been
      married?

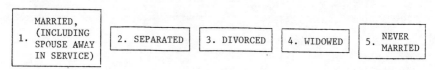

1. MARRIED, (INCLUDING SPOUSE AWAY IN SERVICE)   2. SEPARATED   3. DIVORCED   4. WIDOWED   5. NEVER MARRIED

H24. Generally speaking, do you usually think of yourself as a Republican, a
      Democrat, an Independent, or what?

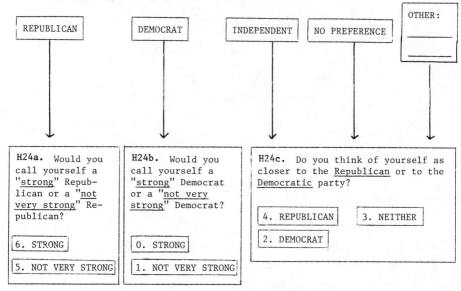

REPUBLICAN   DEMOCRAT   INDEPENDENT   NO PREFERENCE   OTHER:

H24a. Would you call yourself a "strong" Republican or a "not very strong" Republican?

6. STRONG

5. NOT VERY STRONG

H24b. Would you call yourself a "strong" Democrat or a "not very strong" Democrat?

0. STRONG

1. NOT VERY STRONG

H24c. Do you think of yourself as closer to the Republican or to the Democratic party?

4. REPUBLICAN   3. NEITHER

2. DEMOCRAT

H25. Do you have a telephone here at home?

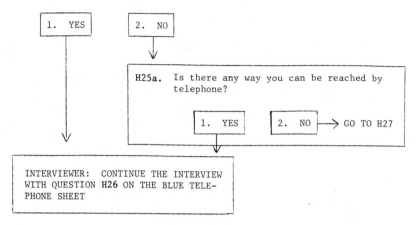

H27. These are all the questions I have. Thank you very much for your help. When we are finished with this survey we can send you some of our findings as our way of thanking you. Just put your name and mailing address on this card, and send it in, the postage is prepaid. (INTERVIEWER: PUT PROJECT NUMBER ON REPORT REQUEST CARD.)

TIME TO NEAREST MINUTE _____

WAS THIS SECTION INTERRUPTED   ☐ 1. YES ☐ 2. NO

REMEMBER TO FINISH OBSERVATION SHEET AND THUMBNAIL SKETCH

COMPLETE THE FOLLOWING QUESTIONS BY OBSERVATION

J1. ETHNIC GROUP:

| 2. BLACK | 3. CHICANO; PUERTO-RICAN; MEXICAN- OR SPANISH-AMERICAN | 4. AMERICAN INDIAN |

| 5. ORIENTAL | 1. CAUCASIAN | 7. OTHER (SPECIFY) _____ |

J2. NUMBER OF PERSONAL CALLS MADE TO OBTAIN INTERVIEW

(EXCLUDE PHONE CALLS): # _____

J3: TYPE OF STRUCTURE IN WHICH FAMILY LIVES:

01. TRAILER	07. APARTMENT HOUSE (5 OR MORE UNITS, 3 STORIES OR LESS)
02. DETACHED SINGLE FAMILY HOUSE	08. APARTMENT HOUSE (5 OR MORE UNITS, 4 STORIES OR MORE)
03. 2-FAMILY HOUSE, 2 UNITS SIDE BY SIDE	09. APARTMENT IN A PARTLY COMMERCIAL STRUCTURE
04. 2-FAMILY HOUSE, 2 UNITS ONE ABOVE THE OTHER	10. OTHER (SPECIFY): _____
05. DETACHED 3-4 FAMILY HOUSE	
06. ROW HOUSE (3 OR MORE UNITS IN AN ATTACHED ROW)	

J4. (FROM TELEPHONE SHEET) WAS A TELEPHONE NUMBER OBTAINED FOR R?

☐ 1. YES   ☐ 5. NO

J5. TO BE RATED BY THE INTERVIEWER: CONSIDERING ALL THE THINGS YOU HAVE
HEARD FROM THIS RESPONDENT AND THE THINGS THAT YOU HAVE BEEN ABLE TO
OBSERVE, WE WOULD LIKE YOU TO RATE HOW YOU THINK THE RESPONDENT REALLY
FEELS ABOUT HIS LIFE AS A WHOLE. CHECK ONE.

| 7. DELIGHTED | 6. PLEASED | 5. MOSTLY SATIS-FIED | 4. MIXED (ABOUT EQUALLY SAT-ISFIED AND DISSATISFIED) |

| 3. MOSTLY DISSATISFIED | 2. UNHAPPY | 1. TERRIBLE |

J6. INTERVIEWER: COPY INFORMATION FOR <u>ALL</u> PERSONS 18 AND OLDER FROM COVER SHEET.

(a) List by Relationship to Head	(b) Sex	(c) Age	(d) Enter "R" to Identify Respondent
HEAD OF HOUSEHOLD			

J7. <u>THUMBNAIL SKETCH</u>

Appendix C

Background Information on Legislation and Programs

To aid in the understanding of the government services included in this investigation, a number of relevant programs are described here including Social Security, Employment Service functions, Unemployment Compensation, public assistance programs and the Veteran's Administration.

The Social Security Act of 1935 marked the beginning of many government services. The term social security usually refers to four types of benefits—old age, survivors, disability and health insurance (OASDHI). These four programs are regarded as insurance programs because beneficiaries have contributed to the fund. OASDHI may thus be distinguished from welfare payments. Steiner (1971) reports that social security helps more poor persons than do welfare programs.

Today about nine out of every 10 American workers are covered by social security compared with six out of 10 at the program's inception. Since 1935 over 173 million social security account numbers have been issued. In 1967 about 87 million persons had earnings credited to their accounts. The largest group of employees excluded from social security are state and local government employees, most of whom have their own retirement funds.

In general, retirement benefits are payable at age 62 at a reduced rate or at age 65 at the full rate. Widows and widowers are also eligible for social security if the spouse was eligible for benefits. Elderly persons may still work and receive Social Security up to a certain amount. Persons at age 72 may receive Social Security regardless of income level.

Survivor benefits are payable to dependent widows at age 60 and dependent widowers at age 62. Dependent parents and children are also eligible for benefits.

Disability benefits are payable to a disabled worker after a six month waiting period. Disabled workers are transferred to the retirement benefit program at age 65. Disabled persons may also be eligible for workmen's compensation but the combined benefit must not exceed 80 percent of the person's average monthly earning before becoming disabled.

Medicare is the health insurance part of social security. It was added with the 1965 amendments to the Social Security Act and consists of two parts: compulsory hospital insurance and voluntary medical insurance. An individual is automatically eligible for Medicare at age 65 whether or not he is retired. People who have been getting disability benefits for more than two years are also eligible for Medicare as of July 1973.

There are two branches to state employment service offices. One branch takes care of unemployment compensation and the other serves as a state employment agency. Generally both functions are housed in the same building, but in some metropolitan areas, there are separate facilities for each function. The state employment service generally retains counselors who help people find jobs. In addition there are a number of job-training programs available through the employment service. Programs come and go with alarming rapidity; however, some of the recent programs include the following:

● The Manpower Development and Training Act of 1962 provides money for those persons who are unable to get jobs without training. Training may be on-the-job, in a classroom, or a combination of the two.

● Job Corps is for those 16 to 19 year olds whose family incomes are below the poverty level. Recipients receive remedial education as well as job training, usually in an away-from-home residential center.

● JOBS-NAM is a program sponsored by the National Association of Manufacturers to hire hard-core unemployed. The employment service is responsible for recruiting and referring hard-core unemployed and following up to ensure job retention.

● The Work Incentive Program (WIN) was established to train AFDC recipients for gainful employment. The department of social services is the recruiting and referral agency. The ultimate goal of WIN is job placement although job-training is an integral part.

There are other programs administered by the employment service, but the foregoing examples serve to demonstrate the variety of job-training programs affiliated with employment service offices.

Unemployment compensation is intended to protect workers who are covered under the law when they are unemployed through no fault of their own, and when they are able and willing to work. It is distinguishable from welfare in that a means test is not required for the receipt of unemployment compensation. Each state has its own unemployment insurance law, and the program is state-administered although there are federal guidelines in the Social Security Act to ensure some measure of uniformity among the states. The employer pays the total cost of unemployment insurance as unemployment is considered a cost of doing business. The United States is unusual in this respect; most other countries with some form of unemployment insurance also tax employees and/or use government funds.

Recipients of unemployment compensation today as compared to recipients in 1939 receive a smaller proportion of benefits to gross wages, but on the average receive benefits sooner for a longer time, and are able to buy more real goods with their money.

Workmen's compensation laws for accident and illness imply liability without fault; i.e., employers assume liability for industrial accidents and diseases whether or not there is any fault on the part of the employee. Like unemployment, accidents and industrial diseases are considered a cost of doing business. Each state has its own workmen's compensation law which is state-administered. Under workmen's compensation, employers are generally exempt from damage suits.

The U. S. Department of Labor estimates that two million persons each year suffer occupational injury or death. About 80 percent of them are covered by workmen's compensation. All workmen's compensation laws cover injury and death. The laws of 40 states now cover all occupational diseases; the laws of the others cover enumerated diseases. There is considerable variation by state in provisions and contingencies of workmen's compensation laws. The U. S. Department of Labor has recommended standards in a number of areas such as whether the injured worker or the state selects a physician, the length of the waiting period before receiving benefits, etc.; but the states may or may not elect to adopt those standards. Benefits do vary considerably by state, but benefits in each state include one or more of the following categories: medical and hospital benefits, disability benefits, death benefits (funeral expenses), benefits to survivors, and rehabilitation services for those injured workers who may be retrained for gainful employment.

The present system of public assistance was initiated with the Social Security Act of 1935. Public assistance, however, was designed as a stop-gap measure until social security was fully operational. It was theorized that the need for the public relief section of social security would wither away. Instead, however, welfare rolls have continued to grow. Thus in addition to the social insurance part of social security, there is provision for federal financial participation in assistance to specified types of needy persons—the aged, the blind, the disabled, and dependent children. These federal funds are available to the states on a matching basis. The individual's income and other resources must be considered in determining need, but each state specifies the acceptable standard of living. Based on the determined standard of living, each state provides worksheets which the caseworker uses to establish the level of need of individuals. The state then specifies the amount of money allotted to individuals given a particular level of need.

An old age assistance (OAA) client could receive a maximum of $250/month in Alaska or a maximum of $75/month in Mississippi as of 1972. Couples receive less than twice the individual allotment. The amount of money which a disabled (APTD) or blind (AB) person may receive is the same as the amount received by an elderly person in 30 states. The difference in the other states is generally small.

The monthly amount defined as meeting the basic needs of a family of four on AFDC (Aid to Families with Dependent Children) varies from $400/month in Alaska to $184/month in North Carolina. It is interesting, however, that 37 states do not provide as much money as their own standard of need determines. For example, a state may determine that an AFDC family of four would need $350/month in order to live according to the standard of living specified as minimal by the state, and yet only provide monthly allotments of $300/month. This is in marked contrast to the other three categorical areas (blindness, old age and disability), where allotted monthly payments generally equal the determined need.

In January of 1973, approximately 15.1 million people received payments under the four above-mentioned public assistance categories or a fifth general assistance category (for those needy not fitting into the other four categories).

The five categories of people on public welfare are also eligible for food stamps or surplus food depending upon which form of aid states offer. In addition these people may be eligible for enrollment in the Work Incentive Program which is a joint program with the Department of Labor. A relief worker at a local level may counsel the client about these various benefits, but whether this occurs will vary from state to state and even from locality to locality.

The newest addition to the public assistance program is Medicaid, medical care for the poor which was introduced as part of the 1965 amendment to the Social Security Act. The largest group of recipients receiving Medicaid are AFDC clients, but the largest expenditure of money is for old age assistance clients. People receiving public assistance are automatically eligible for Medicaid. Other individuals who are needy, but not sufficiently poor to receive welfare, may still be eligible for some Medicaid benefits. Medicaid, medical aid for the poor, should not be confused with Medicare, medical care for the aged.

The Veteran's Administration provides a variety of benefits for veterans. Benefits have been added in a piecemeal fashion over the years and have not been coordinated with service benefits available to the general public. Veteran's benefits may be categorized under health care compensation and pension, and educational and other readjustment benefits including unemployment compensation, housing assistance and life insurance. Veterans may receive job counselling, or training and pensions, for example, from the Veteran's Administration, whereas non-veterans would receive such services from other agencies. The Veteran's Administration then duplicates services provided by other agencies. Generally there are higher levels of benefits and less red tape in the services provided by the Veteran's Administration in comparison to relevant non-veteran agencies.

Appendix D

Additional Tables

Table D.1

Relationship of Sex to Contact with Government
Service and Constraint Agencies

	Sex		
Contact	Male	Female	Total
No contact	30%	43%	37%
Service contact only	49	47	48
Service and constraint contact	15	6	10
Constraint contact only	6	4	5
Total	100%	100%	100%
N	(611)	(820)	(1,431)

Table D.2

Relationship of Race to Contact with Government
Service and Constraint Agencies

	Race			
Contact	White	Black	Other	Total
No contact	39%	24%	30%	37%
Service contact only	46	65	44	48
Service and constraint contact	10	7	17	10
Constraint contact only	5	4	9	5
Total	100%	100%	100%	100%
N	(1,246)	(126)	(57)	(1,431)

251

Table D.3

Relationship of Occupation to Contact with Government Service and Constraint Agencies

| | Occupation | | | | | | | |
	Professional & Technical	Managerial	Clerical & Sales	Skilled	Semi-skilled	Laborers	Farmers	Total
Contact								
No contact	41%	47%	40%	23%	27%	28%	32%	34%
Service contact only	39	28	45	58	59	61	64	50
Service and constraint contact	13	14	10	14	12	8	4	11
Constraint contact only	7	11	5	5	2	3	0	5
Total	100%	100%	100%	100%	100%	100%	100%	100%
N	(158)	(74)	(284)	(149)	(193)	(183)	(28)	(1,072)

Table D.4

Relationship of Education to Contact with Government Service and Constraint Agencies

| | Years of Education | | | | | | |
	8 or fewer	9-11	12	12+ non-academic training	1-3 college	BA and over	Total
Contact							
No contact	24%	36%	45%	36%	34%	46%	37%
Service contact only	64	52	45	47	43	31	48
Service and constraint contact	6	8	7	14	13	14	10
Constraint contact only	1	4	3	3	10	9	5
Total	100%	100%	100%	100%	100%	100%	100%
N	(277)	(234)	(291)	(198)	(261)	(163)	(1,431)

Table D.5

Relationship of Income to Contact with Government Service and Constraint Agencies

Contact	0-$2,999	$3,000-4,999	$5,000-7,499	$7,500-9,999	$10,000-12,499	$12,500-14,499	$15,000-19,999	$20,000+	Total
No contact	20%	19%	35%	36%	43%	46%	42%	57%	37%
Service contact only	71	64	54	47	43	37	44	19	48
Service and constraint contact	7	13	9	13	11	10	7	12	10
Constraint contact only	2	4	2	4	3	6	7	12	5
Total	100%	100%	100%	100%	100%	100%	100%	100%	100%
N	(172)	(155)	(179)	(185)	(203)	(155)	(157)	(166)	(1,372)

Table D.6

Relationship of Age to Contact with Government Service and Constraint Agencies

Contact	18-20	21-24	25-29	30-39	40-49	50-59	60-69	70+	Total
No contact	51%	36%	38%	36%	41%	50%	29%	20%	37%
Service contact only	20	48	35	49	47	39	62	74	48
Service and constraint contact	18	14	18	10	7	7	4	6	10
Constraint contact only	11	12	9	5	5	4	5	0	5
Total	100%	100%	100%	100%	100%	100%	100%	100%	100%
N	(71)	(132)	(180)	(268)	(230)	(214)	(199)	(135)	(1,431)

Table D.7

Relationship of Work Status to Contact with
Government Service and Constraint Agencies

| | Work Status | | | | |
Contact	Working	Unem-ployed	Retired/permanent disability	Other	Total
No contact	39%	20%	13%	49%	37%
Service contact only	44	53	79	40	48
Service and constraint contact	12	25	6	5	10
Constraint contact only	5	2	2	6	5
Total	100%	100%	100%	100%	100%
N	(839)	(64)	(185)	(344)	(1,431)

Table D.8

Relationship of Geographic Region to Contact with
Government Service and Constraint Agencies

| | Geographic Region | | | | |
Contact	West	North Central	North-east	South	Total
No contact	30%	38%	36%	42%	37%
Service contact only	47	48	50	47	48
Service and constraint contact	14	10	9	8	10
Constraint contact only	9	4	5	3	5
Total	100%	100%	100%	100%	100%
N	(255)	(423)	(315)	(430)	(1,431)

Bibliography

Adams, L. P. *Public attitudes toward unemployment insurance: a historical account with special reference to alleged abuses.* Kalamazoo, Mich.: W. E. Upjohn Institute for Employment Research, 1971.

Allport, G. W. The composition of political attitudes. *American Journal of Sociology,* 1929, *35,* 220-238.

Alston, J. P. and Dean K. I. Socioeconomic factors associated with attitudes toward welfare recipients and the causes of poverty. *Social Service Review,* 1972, *46,* 13-23.

Bakke, E. W. *Citizens without work.* New Haven, Conn.: Yale University Press, 1940.

Becker, J. M. *Twenty-five years of unemployment insurance: an experiment in competitive collectivism.* Kalamazoo, Mich.: W. E. Upjohn Institute for Employment Research, 1961.

Bengtson, V. L. and Lovejoy, M. C. Values, personality, and social structure: an intergenerational analysis. *American Behavioral Scientist,* 1973, *16,* 880-912.

Blackwell, K. and Ferguson, K. Pensions: are there holes in your security blanket? *Ms.,* 1973, *2,* 14-18.

Blumenthal, M., Kahn, R. L., Andrews, F., and Head, K. *Justifying violence: attitudes of American men.* Ann Arbor: Institute for Social Research, 1972.

Borus, M. E., Brennan, J. P., Rosen, S. A benefit-cost analysis of the neighborhood youth corps. In Y. Hasenfeld and R. English (Eds.), *Human service organizations,* Ann Arbor, Mich.: University of Michigan Press, 1974.

Briar, S. Welfare from below: recipients' view of the public welfare system. In J. TenBroek (Ed.), *The law of the poor,* San Francisco, Calif.: Chandler, 1966.

Campbell, D. T. Reforms as experiments. *American Psychologist,* 1969, *24,* 409-429.

Chamber of Commerce of the United States. *Analysis of workmen's compensation laws.* Washington, D. C.: Chamber of Commerce of the United States, 1964.

Cicirelli, V. *The impact of Headstart: an evaluation of the effects of Headstart on children's cognitive and affective style.* Vol. 1, Bladensburg, Md.: Westinghouse Learning Corp., 1969.

Council of State Governments. *Workmen's compensation: a challenge to the states.* Lexington, Kentucky: Council of State Governments, 1973.

Easton, D. *A systems analysis of political life.* N. Y.: Wiley, 1965.

Eldersveld, S. J. Citizen and government: a comparative analysis. *Economic and Political Weekly,* 1967, Feb., 1-29.

Eldersveld, S. J., Jagannadhom, V., and Barnabas, A. P. *The citizen and the administrator in a developing democracy,* New Delhi, India: Indian Institute of Public Administration, 1968.

Feagin, J. R. America's welfare stereotypes. *Social Science Quarterly,* 1972, *52,* 921-933.

_____. *Federal employees compensation act amendments of 1960.* Report No. 1743, 86th Congress, 2nd Session, House of Representatives. Washington, D. C.: United States Government Printing Office, 1960.

Goodwin, L. *Do the poor want to work? A social-psychological study of work orientations.* Washington, D. C.: Brookings Institution, 1972.

Haber, W., Fauri, F., and Cohen, W. Significant findings on the impact of the 1957-1958 recession in relation to unemployment insurance. Unpublished manuscript, 1959.

Harris, L. and Associates. *Confidence and concern: citizens view American government.* Washington, D. C.: United States Government Printing Office, 1973. Report to the Sub-committee on Intergovernmental Relations of the Committee on Government Operations, U. S. Senate, Parts 1, 2, 3.

Hartmann, G. W. The contradiction between the feeling-tone of political party names and public response to their platforms. *Journal of Social Psychology,* 1936, *7,* 336-356.

Hirschman, A. O. *Exit voice, and loyalty.* Cambridge, Mass.: Harvard University Press, 1970.

Holden, M. *The politics of poor relief: a study in ambiguities.* Madison, Wisc.: Institute for Research on Poverty, 1973.

Huber, J. and Form, W. *Income and ideology.* N. Y.: Free Press, 1973.

Hyman, H. H. and Wright, C. R. Evaluating social action programs. In P. Lazarsfeld, W. Sewell, and H. Wilensky (Eds.) *The uses of sociology,* N. Y.: Basic Books, 1967.

Janowitz, M., Wright, D., and Delany, W. *Public administration and the public—perspectives toward government in a metropolitan community,* Ann Arbor, Mich.: Bureau of Government, Institute of Public Administration, University of Michigan, 1958.

Johnson, F. C. Workmen's compensation enactments in 1967. *Monthly Labor Review,* 1967, *90,* 6-16.

Kallen, D. J. and Miller, D. Public attitudes toward welfare. *Social Work,* 1971, *16,* 83-90.

Lansdale, R. T. *State social welfare board report on welfare fraud.* Department of Social Welfare, State of California, 1965.

Lansdale, R. T. *Inadequacies of statewide programs of public assistance in urban areas: a statement of the problem and an exploratory examination of one segment.* Baltimore, Md.: University of Maryland School of Social Work, 1965.

Lekachman, R. What works, what doesn't. *The Nation,* 1974, *19,* 589-591.

Levens, H. Organizational affiliation and powerlessness; a case study of the welfare poor. *Social Problems,* 1968, *16,* 18-32.

Levitan, S. A. *Programs in aid of the poor for the 1970s.* Baltimore, Md.: Johns Hopkins Press, 1969.

Meyers, S. M. and McIntyre, J. *Welfare policy and its consequences for the recipient population: a study of the AFDC program.* Washington, D. C.: United States Government Printing Office, 1969.

Miller, A. H. *Political issues and trust in government: 1964-1970.* Paper delivered at 1972 Annual meeting of the American Political Science Association. Washington, D. C., 1972.

Miller, A. H., Brown, T. A., and Raine, S. *Social Conflict and political estrangement, 1958-1972.* Paper delivered at 1973 Midwest Political Science Association Convention, 1973.

Mondale, W. F. Social accounting, evaluation and the future of the human services. *Evaluation,* 1972, *1,* 29-34.

Moynihan, D. P. The crises in welfare. *The Public Interest,* 1968, *10,* 3-29.

Myers, R. J. Summary of provisions of the old-age, survivors, and disability insurance system, the hospital insurance system and the supplementary medical insurance system. Unpublished manuscript. 1965.

Ogren, E. H. Public opinion about public welfare. *Social Work,* 1973, *18,* 101-107.

Papier, R. L. *Unemployment compensation experience of beneficiaries in Columbus, Ohio: 1930-1940.* Columbus, Ohio: Bureau of Business Research, The Ohio State University, 1943.

Parsons, T. *Structure and process in modern societies.* New York: Free Press, 1960.

——————. The public employment program: an evaluation. The National Urban Coalition, 1972.

Rein, M. Determinants of the work-welfare choice in AFDC. *Social Service Review,* 1972, *46,* 539-566.

Runciman, W. G. *Relative deprivation and social justice.* Berkeley: University of California Press, 1966.

Schiller, B. R. Empirical studies of welfare dependency: a survey. *The Journal of Human Resources,* 1973, *8,* (supplement), 19-32.

Schiltz, M. E. *Public attitudes toward social security, 1935-1965.* Wash., D. C.: United States Government Printing Office, 1970.

Stagner, R. Fascist attitudes: their determining conditions. *Journal of Social Psychology,* 1936, *1,* 438-453.

Steiner, G. *The state of welfare.* Washington, D. C.: Brookings Institution, 1971.

_____. Summary of social security amendments of 1972, public law 92-603. Washington, D. C.: United States Government Printing Office, 1972.

Trattner, W. I. *From poor law to welfare state.* New York: Free Press, 1974.

United States Department of Agriculture. *Impact of the food stamp program on three local economies: an input-output analysis.* Washington, D. C.: United States Government Printing Office, 1972.

United States Department of Commerce. *1970 census of population: general population characteristics.* Washington, D. C.: United States Government Printing Office, 1972.

United States Department of Health, Education and Welfare. *Changes in AFDC.* Washington, D.C.: United States Government Printing Office, 1973.

United States Department of Health, Education and Welfare. *Medical assistance financed under the public assistance titles of the Social Security Act.* Washington, D. C.: United States Government Printing Office, 1969.

United States Department of Health, Education and Welfare, Office of Research and Statistics. *The evolution of Medicare.* Washington, D. C.: United States Government Printing Office, 1969.

United States Department of Health, Education and Welfare, Social and Rehabilitation Service. *Findings of the 1971 AFDC study.* Department of Health, Education and Welfare Publications No. (SRS) 73-03759, April, 1973.

United States Department of Health, Education and Welfare, Social and Rehabilitation Service. *Number of recipients and amount of payments under Medicaid.* Department of Health, Education and Welfare Publications No. (SRS) 73-03153, October, 1972.

United States Department of Health, Education and Welfare, Social Security Administration. *A brief explanation of Medicare.* Washington, D. C.: United States Government Printing Office, 1973.

United States Department of Health, Education and Welfare, Social Security Administration. *Disabled? Find out about social security disability benefits.* Washington, D. C.: United States Government Printing Office, 1973.

United States Department of Health, Education and Welfare, Social Security Administration. *If you become disabled.* United States Government Printing Office, 1971.

United States Department of Health, Education and Welfare, Social Security Administration. *Social security handbook.* Washington, D. C.: United States Government Printing Office, 1966.

United States Department of Health, Education and Welfare, Social Security Administration. *Social security programs in the United States.* Washington, D. C.: United States Government Printing Office, 1968.

United States Department of Health, Education and Welfare, Social Security Administration. *Your 1973 social security deduction.* Washington, D. C.: United States Government Printing Office, 1973.

United States Department of Health, Education and Welfare, Social Security Administration. *Your social security.* Washington, D. C.: United States Government Printing Office, 1972.

United States Department of Labor. *State workmen's compensation laws: a comparison of major provisions with recommended standards.* Washington, D. C.: United States Government Printing Office, 1971.

United States Department of Labor. *Summary of state workmen's compensation laws.* Washington, D. C.: United States Government Printing Office, 1970.

United States Department of Labor, Manpower Administration. *Evaluation of coverage and benefit provisions of state unemployment insurance laws.* Washington, D. C.: United States Government Printing Office, 1966.

United States Department of Labor, Manpower Administration. *Interviewers' handbook for selection and referral to training and placement.* Washington, D. C.: United States Government Printing Office, 1969.

United States Office of Management and Budget. *Catalog of federal domestic assistance.* Washington, D. C.: United States Government Printing Office, 1972.

Williams, C. A. *Insurance arrangement under workmen's compensation.* Washington, D. C.: United States Department of Labor, Wage and Labor Standards Administration, 1969.

Williams, W. and Evans, J. The politics of evaluation: the case of Head Start. In P. Rossi and W. Williams (Eds.) *Evaluating social programs.* New York: Seminar Press, 1972.

Index